New Adventures in Wine Cookery

By California Winemakers

THE WINE APPRECIATION GUILD

Other books published by The Wine Appreciation Guild:
THE CHAMPAGNE COOKBOOK
EPICUREAN RECIPES OF CALIFORNIA WINEMAKERS
GOURMET WINE COOKING THE EASY WAY
FAVORITE RECIPES OF CALIFORNIA WINEMAKERS
WINE COOKBOOK OF DINNER MENUS
EASY RECIPES OF CALIFORNIA WINEMAKERS
THE POCKET ENCYCLOPEDIA OF CALIFORNIA WINE
IN CELEBRATION OF WINE AND LIFE
WINE CELLAR RECORD BOOK
WINE COOKING FOR EVERYDAY
CORKSCREWS: An Introduction to Their Appreciation
THE CALIFORNIA WINE DRINK BOOK

Published by:
The Wine Appreciation Guild
1377 Ninth Avenue
San Francisco, CA 94122
(415) 566 - 3532
(415) 957 - 1377

ISBN 0-932664-10-5
Library of Congress Catalog Number
Printed in The United States of America

Designed by: Colonna, Caldewey, Farrell; Designers
Cover Photo: Bill Miller
Illustrations: Susann Ortega

Contents

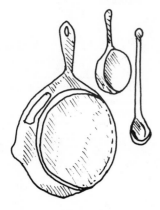

Winemakers, their wives, families and colleagues are among the most food and flavor conscious people in the world.

Part of the life work of the winemaker is to guide nature in the development in wine of beauty, aroma, bouquet and subtle flavors, so that the final nectar delights the eye, offers perfume to the nose and unique pleasure to the sense of taste.

In the production of the wine type called Vermouth, winemakers work with many of the herbs and spices used in cooking, such as marjoram, rosemary, sage, saffron, coriander, clove, cinnamon, thyme and nutmeg. Many Vermouths contain the flavors extracted from more than 50 herbs and spices. Some of the winemaker's skills are passed on to those who prepare and share his meals.

Wine families think of wine when they think of food. They think of it both as a table beverage and as an ingredient in the recipes they cook.

Wine is part of their daily diet, leading to more flavorful dishes, comfortable living, merriment and goodfellowship at meal times. This is why we asked California's winemakers and their families to share with you the exciting adventures they have had in wine cooking. They are continually adding wine to new combinations of foods, to the delight of their guests.

The same is true for professors and other staff members of the Department of Viticulture (grape growing) and Enology (winemaking) and the Department of Food Science and Technology of the University of California, who contributed their favorite recipes. Grape and wine research and teaching at the University have converted the ancient art of winemaking in California into a modern science which makes possible consistent production of high quality wines. The experimental winery and the extensive experimental vineyards at the University's Davis campus have been a vital force in helping California winemakers attain new peaks of quality.

For similar reasons, we requested recipes from members of the Department of Viticulture and Enology at Fresno State College, which likewise trains scientifically skilled winemakers and other technologists who help produce the wines of California.

To all our contributors, we give our heartfelt thanks for sending in to us for publication their favorite recipes—some originating in their families and some obtained from outside sources—but all so good that they warrant serving over and over again.

The joys of the table are indeed an adventure for all of us who savor good food, good wine. We look forward to some dishes as to old friends, always delightful and pleasing. Then there is the avenue of new eating experiences—an untried dish, yet to be tasted. For many persons, the enjoyment of food is anticipated throughout its preparation, the table being only the final step in the adventure of good eating.

To those of us for whom good food starts in the kitchen, there is always the challenge to lift a good dish out of the ordinary to the superior. The methods need not be complicated or difficult. Often only one new ingredient, or a different blend of flavorings, will add the desired distinction. Cooks throughout history have discovered that wine can be the element to arouse such flavor magic when it is added to the dish.

Used as a seasoning in cooking, wine serves to blend and point up all the food flavors. If a stronger wine flavor is desired, some seasonings may be cut down, and the amount of wine increased according to individual taste. No alcohol will remain in the dish, because the heat of cooking quickly evaporates it. Wine also acts as a tenderizer, helping to soften tougher cuts of meat as well as flavor them.

What kind of wine should be used? Most experts agree that wines used in cooking need not be expensive, but that they must be of sound quality and palatable, a term which applies dependably and unfailingly to all California wines. One easy practice to follow is to cook with some of the same California wine you plan to serve with a meal.

The recipes presented here will be truly an adventure for the cook in the preparation of any dish. And remember—adventure in cooking does not have to be time-consuming or difficult. It means only that every dish is prepared with an interesting combination of ingredients, reliably measured, using the exciting seasoning and taste-blender . . . wine.

BOTTLE SIZE	FLUID OUNCES	APPROXIMATE MEASUREMENT FOR RECIPE USE
Fifth (common size)	25.4 or 750 ml.	3 ⅛ cups
Tenth (a half bottle)	12.8	1 ½ cups
Half-gallon jug or bottle	64	8 cups
Gallon jug	128	16 cups

A 4/5-quart bottle of table wine will pour 6 servings, averaging 4 ounces or more. Dessert and appetizer wines are usually poured in 2½ to 4 ounce servings.

Wine "bottle" when mentioned in this book means 25.4 fluid ounces or 750 ml. This size is also referred to as a "fifth," meaning 1/5 gallon, or 4/5 quart, or simply "large bottle."

Towns mentioned in most cases indicate location of winery referred to.

This book is designed to let you look while you cook. You can fold it back and lay it flat. Or, you can fold it back and stand it up. Slip a rubber band around each side to keep pages upright when book is standing.

Drink no longer water but use a little wine for thy stomach's sake.
                                                        -I Timothy 5:23

Thousands of years before Omar Khayyam poetically coupled a jug of wine with a loaf of bread (and thou), the fermented juice of the grape was intimately, irrevocably—and very wisely—linked to food.

Wine itself was looked upon as a food. It was consumed as a food. It was used with other foods, at mealtimes.

True, wine was also regarded as a sacred fluid to be used in religious rites—perhaps because of its blood-red color. It was regarded, too, as a medicine, and today wine ranks as one of the oldest medical agents known to physicians. But above all it was prized as a foodstuff.

No one knows how wine first won this place in the ancient cookbooks. What is known is that, after many years of work and the expenditure of millions of dollars in intensive research, scientists have now come to realize that this combination of wine and food was one of the luckiest, healthiest, and safest discoveries of mankind.

Consider how wine appears to these scientists—

First, it is a mixture of chemicals.

There are hundreds, perhaps thousands, of different chemicals in a single bottle of wine, some known and others still unidentified, some simple and others infernally complex, some deriving from the grape and others created during the complicated processes of fermentation and aging.

There are whole families of alcohols, aldehydes, organic acids and tannins.

There are nutritious sugars, minerals, pigments, which appear to act as antibiotics, and half a dozen members of the Vitamin-B complex.

Second, wine is a medical agent.

Since the beginning of written history, wine has been listed as one of the most widely-applicable agents in the prevention and treatment of disease. Long before the invention of new synthetic tranquilizers, it was prescribed and used effectively for the treatment of emotional tension. Long before the discovery of insulin, it was used in the control of diabetes. Long before the development of the barbiturates, it was used as a valuable sedative.

Now recent investigations—beginning in the laboratory and then expanding to the clinic and the hospital—are showing that wine can be prescribed to stimulate appetite, to improve digestive processes, to aid in convalescence after surgery, to help in the care of the elderly, and to play a role in control of high blood pressure and heart disease.

Third, wine is a food.

After decades of polemic and debate (but not much laboratory work until recent years), investigators have finally been able to establish that wine is a source of useful food energy. Its alcohol and its sugars provide calories, and its minerals and vitamins help fill the body's needs for these substances.

Certainly wine is not a perfect food (neither is milk, nor eggs, nor meat, nor bread). Some people cannot and should not drink wine (just as some people can't take milk, or strawberries, or eggs, or chocolate). And when wine is used, it should be used as part of a well-balanced diet (as is true for all other foods).

And finally, wine has certain built-in safety factors of vital importance.

Until recently, many experts were content to regard wine as merely a bottle of alcohol plus some delightful flavors and some red coloring matter. Now it has become apparent that this isn't the whole story.

For example, there are all those other chemicals in wine. In the body, they slow the absorption of alcohol into the bloodstream, they keep the amount of alcohol in the blood at relatively low and safe levels, and they prevent dangerous high peaks in blood-alcohol concentrations.

Equally important, there is the ancient tradition of using wine with solid food. This tradition is undoubtedly historical, charming, delightful and perhaps romantic; it is also of paramount physiological and medical importance. For when wine—or any other alcoholic beverage—is taken with food, the absorption of alcohol into the blood is even more effectively controlled, and dangerous concentrations are avoided.

Here, scientists believe, may be the major explanations for one of the most important socio-medical observations of modern times: in practically every cultural group which uses wine with meals, views wine as a food, considers the use of wine calmly and dispassionately as neither a virtue nor a vice, and holds over-indulgence as gluttonous and socially unacceptable, there the excessive use of alcohol is a problem of relatively little significance.

To the housewife (unless she has her Ph.D. in biochemistry or physiology), such scientific facts should not be allowed to outshadow the gastronomic value of wine. But when she cooks with wine, or serves wine at dinner, she might well keep in mind that she is following one of the safest rules in modern nutrition—

Eat when you drink, and drink only when you eat.

Bon appetit!

ALCOHOL EVAPORATES

What happens to the alcohol in wine used in cooking? The alcohol evaporates (beginning at 172 degrees, well below the 212 degrees at which water boils). Heat leaves only the delicious wine flavors in foods. When the alcohol disappears, so do most of the calories in the wine.

VINTAGE YEAR

California is blessed with dry sunny weather during the grape growing season. This means you need not worry about the "vintage year" of a California wine—every year is a good wine year. Adequate sunshine and absence of rainy, cloudy summers means that grapes ripen fully each and every year so that, regardless of brand and price, you will get a sound high quality wine.

WINE FOR COOKING

Spoilage of left over wine for cooking may be prevented by adding a few drops of olive oil to the partially filled bottle to keep the air away from the wine. A thin film of the oil will float on the wine's surface.

NATURAL GRAPE SUGAR

The sweetness of the sweet California wines is the natural sugar of the grape. California State law prohibits addition of cane or other sugars, in the traditional table or dessert wines. California's long, gentle, sunlit seasons ripen the grapes fully, developing their sugar to the optimum point for winemaking. Thus, California is able to produce nearly 85% of all wines consumed in the United States.

MARINATING DISHES

Meats may be tenderized and improved in flavor by marinating one or two hours before cooking. Marinate foods in glass, porcelain or enamel or stainless steel rather than in aluminum, as the latter, while not harmful, might affect taste. Foods may be cooked with wine in aluminum pans without affecting flavor.

STAINS

Wine stains may be removed from tablecloths by stretching the stained portion over a bowl, securing with a rubber band, sprinkling with salt, and pouring boiling water from a height of two to three feet. It is also a good idea to sprinkle salt on wine stains at the time of any spillage.

CORKING WINE

Save screw cap bottles ("fifth" and "tenth" sizes) for re-bottling wines left over from large containers. Fill to the brim to eliminate as much air space as possible. If corked bottles are used, corks too large to fit a bottle may be softened by soaking in boiling water for a few minutes so they fit easily.

BLENDS AND VARIETALS

Most of the world's wines are blends of two or more wines. Among notable exceptions are some of California's varietal wines, each named for and made primarily of a single grape variety. By law, these must be at least 51 percent of the grape for which they are named. Often producers use the juice of the named variety exclusively.

WINE ACIDITY

In wine, acidity is the word normally used to indicate the quality of tartness or sharpness to the taste, the presence of agreeable fruit acids, an important favorable element in wine quality.

TO "FLAME" A DESSERT

The easiest way to "flame" a dessert or a drink with brandy is to soak a sugar cube first and light that. It acts like a wick. Slightly warm brandy ignites more easily than cold brandy.

Punches

"What, my good friend, if you gave us a glass of punch in the meantime; it would help us to carry on the siege with vigor."

Oliver Goldsmith

How easily, gracefully, *completely* you can entertain, when you've discovered the wonderful taste and color range of California wines! From a quick Sherry "on the rocks" to the frosty foam of Champagne to toast a bride or a birthday . . . from a fragrant "Mint-Wine Cooler" to refresh you on a summer's day, to a homey mug of hot "Winter Punch before the fireplace . . . wine offers you such infinite variety of use and flavor, to suit both season and setting. Here California's winemakers tell their own most successful wine drinks—cocktails, coolers, punches and others. Try them for more adventurous entertaining, and you'll discover new favorites of your own.

SIERRA SUNRISE

William Perelli-Minetti, A. Perelli-Minetti & Sons, Delano

As an appetizer before breakfast, this prepares one for a day of horseback riding in the mountains.

> *2 parts orange juice*
> *1 part California Dry Vermouth*
> *1 part California Brandy*
> *1 squeeze lemon*

Fill a 10-ounce glass with ice. Add all ingredients. Mix and serve. Serves 1.

CHAMPAGNE CONTINENTAL

Paul R. Heck, Korbel Champagne Cellars, Guerneville

I recommend this highly and think it is going to replace the spirits drink·known as "Screwdriver". It does not cost any more than the Screwdriver and it tastes wonderful.

> *⅓ fresh orange juice*
> *2 ice cubes*
> *⅔ California ''Nature'' Champagne*

Pour orange juice over ice in glass. Add Champagne and serve. Serves 1.

V.G.B.

Michael Biane, Brookside Vineyard Company, Guasti

V.G.B.'s, to my own knowledge, are my own invention. For an easy and delicious cocktail right after you get home from work, and while the wife is trying to feed the kids, cook dinner, and maintain her sanity, it's terrific.

Place 3 or 4 ice cubes in an all-purpose wine glass. Fill halfway with California Sweet Vermouth; fill the rest of the way with ginger beer.

VALLEY OF THE MOON COCKTAIL

Mrs. August Sebastiani, Sebastiani Vineyards, Sonoma

> *2 eggs*
> *2 tsp. powdered sugar*
> *1 cup California Port*
> *½ cup California Brandy*
> *Cracked ice*

Break eggs into a shaker glass. Add sugar, Port, Brandy and cracked ice. Shake well. Strain and serve. Serves 4-6.

SHERRY DAIQUIRI

Michael Baine, Brookside Vineyard Company, Guasti

Sherry Daiquiris have been around for some time under various other names, none of which I can recall.

> 8 to 10 ice cubes, crushed
> 1 (6-oz.) can frozen lime juice
> 1½ (6-oz.) cans California Dry Sherry

Combine crushed ice, lime juice and Sherry in electric blender. Blend and serve immediately. Serves 9.

SHERRY COOLER

Tony Kahmann, Wine Public Relations Consultant

> 1 part California Dry Sherry
> 2 parts sparkling water
> Twist of lemon peel
> Slice of orange

Combine Sherry and sparkling water and pour over ice in a tall glass. Place lemon peel on edge of glass, dropping into drink. Drop orange slice into glass. Serves 1.

FREMONT FRUIT BOWL

Richard Elwood, Llords & Elwood Winery, Fremont

> 1 quart sliced fresh fruit (peaches,
>   apricots, strawberries, raspberries
>   or cherries)
> 1 (4/5-qt.) bottle California Brandy
> 1 (4/5-qt.) bottle fruit liqueur
>   (same flavor as fresh fruit)
> 4 (4/5-qt.) bottles California Riesling
> 4 (4/5-qt.) bottles California
>   Champagne

Cover fruit with Brandy; allow to stand one hour or longer. Chill remaining ingredients. Drain liquid from fruit, pressing lightly in sieve to get all the juice. Pour into punch bowl over block of ice along with liqueur and Riesling. Add Champagne just before serving. Decorate with sliced fresh fruit and two or three sprigs of mint. Serves 80.

FROZEN BRANDY SOUR

Mrs. Norbert C. Mirassou, Mirassou Vineyards, San Jose

> 1 (6-oz.) can frozen lemonade
>   concentrate
> 3 (6-oz.) cans water
> 1 Tbs. frozen orange juice
>   concentrate (optional)
> 1½ cups California Brandy

Combine all ingredients; freeze. When ready to serve, spoon some of the mixture into blender and give it a quick whirl (or beat with rotary beater). Serve with garnish of maraschino cherry and slice of orange. **Serves 8.**

KEY TO THE CELLAR

James L. Riddell, Vie-Del Company, Fresno

This cocktail has pleasing complexity, and maintains its aperitif character even though sweet enough to satisfy the less sophisticated drinker.

> 2 Tbs. California Sherry
> 2 tsp. triple sec
> 2 tsp. California Brandy
> 2 tsp. California Dry Vermouth
> 1 tsp. lemon juice
> 1 twist orange peel

Shake all liquid ingredients with ice in cocktail shaker and strain into cocktail glass. Garnish with orange peel. Serves 1.

MODESTO COCKTAIL

Lyman M. Cash, E. & J. Gallo Winery, Modesto

>1 Tbs. California Brandy
>1 Tbs. California Dry Vermouth
>1 Tbs. California Sauterne
>1 cocktail onion

Combine all ingredients. Serve chilled or over ice. Serves 1.

PINK TREAT

Brother Gregory, The Christian Brothers, Napa

Here's a festive bowl for the holiday season.

>3 (4/5-qt.) bottles California Rosé,
> chilled
>1 (6-oz.) can frozen lemonade
> concentrate
>2 quarts raspberry sherbet
>1 (4/5-qt.) bottle California Pink
>Champagne or Sparkling Burgundy
>Ice

Pour into a punch bowl the Rosé and lemonade concentrate. Stir in raspberry sherbet. Mix thoroughly. Pour in sparkling wine, add ice and serve immediately. Makes about 30 servings.

CHAMPAGNE PUNCH NO. 1

*Mrs. J. H. "Mike" Elwood, Llords & Elwood Winery,
Fremont*

Get the punch cold *before* adding ice, so as not to dilute the mixture.

>2 Tbs. sugar
>1 quart fresh strawberries, quartered
>1 cup black cherries, quartered
>8 ounces (1 cup) California Brandy
>4 ounces (½ cup) kirsch
>4 ounces (½ cup) triple sec
>2 (4/5-qt.) bottles California
> Champagne
>2 (4/5-qt.) bottles California Sauterne
> or other white table wine

Combine sugar, fruit, Brandy, kirsch and triple sec; chill several hours. When ready to serve, place block of ice in punch bowl; pour fruit-liqueur mixture over ice. Add Champagne and Sauterne. Stir quickly and serve. Serves about 60.

CHAMPAGNE A LA SAN FRANCISCO

Mrs. Russel Overby, United Vintners, Inc., San Francisco

>1 hollow-stemmed Champagne glass
>Gin
>California Pink Champagne

Chill glass and ingredients. Fill stem of glass with gin. Pour in Champagne until glass is three-fourths full. Serve. Serves 1.

BRANDY MANHATTAN

Mrs. Greg Goorigian, Vie-Del Company, Fresno

>4 parts California Brandy
>1 part California Sweet Vermouth
>1 tsp. maraschino cherry juice
>Dash of bitters

Combine all ingredients with ice. Shake well. Serve in chilled glasses. Garnish with maraschino cherries.

APRICOT-PINEAPPLE COOLER

*Vincent E. Petrucci, Fresno State College,
  Department of Viticulture & Enology*

>¾ cup California Muscatel
>⅓ cup apricot nectar
>⅓ cup unsweetened pineapple juice
>1 sprig of mint

Half fill a tall (12-oz.) glass with cracked ice. Add Muscatel, apricot nectar and pineapple juice. Stir well to blend and chill ingredients. Garnish with a sprig of mint. Serves 1.

OLD FASHIONED CHAMPAGNE BOWL

Hanns J. Kornell, Hanns Kornell Cellars, St. Helena

> 1 (4/5-qt.) bottle California
>   Champagne
> 2 large oranges
> ½ cup sugar or to taste
> 3 Tbs. fresh lemon juice
> 1 cup California white table wine

Chill Champagne thoroughly. Halve oranges lengthwise and cut into thin slices. Place in punch bowl, and sprinkle with sugar, lemon juice and table wine. Chill 1 hour or longer. Stir to be sure all sugar is dissolved, then pour in chilled Champagne. Serve at once. Makes about 1½ quarts.

RUBY PUNCH BOWL

John A. Parducci, Parducci Wine Cellars, Inc., Ukiah

> 1½ cups water
> 2 cups sugar
> 2 sticks cinnamon
> 2 tsp. whole cloves
> ⅛ tsp. salt
> 2 (4/5-qt.) bottles California
>   Burgundy or other red table wine
> 1 pint chilled cranberry juice
>   cocktail
> 1 quart chilled apple cider
> Ice cubes
> Thin lemon or lime slices

Bring water, sugar, spices and salt to a boil. Lower heat and simmer for 10 minutes; strain out and discard spices; cool syrup. Combine spiced syrup with wine, cranberry juice cocktail and cider. Turn into punch bowl; add ice cubes and lemon slices. Makes about 1 gallon.

PACIFIC PUNCH

Mrs. Theodore Cadlolo, Cadlolo Winery, Escalon

> 2 (½-oz.) packages cherry-
>   flavored soft drink powder
> 1½ cups sugar
> 1 (6-oz.) can frozen lemonade
> 1 (12-oz.) can pineapple juice
> ½ cup tropical fruit concentrate
>   (or to taste)
> 1 (4/5-qt.) bottle California Burgundy
> 4 quarts water

Combine all ingredients; mix well. Pour into large punch bowl over block of ice. Garnish with fruit, if desired. Makes about 75 servings, 3-oz. size.

VINEYARD PUNCH

Mrs. Norbert C. Mirassou, Mirassou Vineyards, San Jose

> 1 cup water
> 3 sticks cinnamon
> 2 (6-oz.) cans frozen grape juice
>   concentrate
> 2 (6-oz.) cans frozen grapefruit juice
>   concentrate
> ½ cup lemon juice
> 2 cups California Port
> 2 (1-qt.) bottles ginger ale, chilled

Simmer water and cinnamon together for 5 minutes; cool and strain. Combine spiced water with fruit juice concentrates, lemon juice and Port. Chill several hours. When ready to serve, pour chilled mixture into punch bowl and add ginger ale. Makes about 35 servings, 3-oz. size.

HURRICANE PUNCH

Robert S. McKnight, Di Giorgio Wine Company, Di Giorgio

> Juice of 20 lemons
> 2 pounds sugar
> 4 oz. (½-cup) maraschino
>   (optional)
> 3 (4/5-qt.) bottles California Brandy
> 12 oz. (1½-cups) curacao
> 8 oz. (1 cup) rum
> 3 (4/5-qt.) bottles California
>   Champagne

Mix lemon juice, sugar and maraschino. Add Brandy, curacao and rum; chill thoroughly. When ready to serve, pour over block of ice in punch bowl. Add Champagne just before serving. This is good with various hors d'oeuvres, and especially with caviar canape. Make 60 to 70 servings.

GOLDEN PUNCH

Mrs. Greg Goorigian, Vie-Del Company, Fresno

> *1 (4/5-qt.) bottle California Sauterne*
> *   or other white table wine*
> *3 cups canned pineapple juice,*
> *   chilled*
> *1 cup orange juice*
> *½ cup lemon juice*
> *Juice of 1 fresh grapefruit*
> *1 cup strong tea*
> *1¼ cups sugar*
> *¼ tsp. powdered ginger*
> *Ice*
> *Fresh or canned grapes for*
> *   bottom of bowl*
> *1 (4/5-qt.) bottle California Sec*
> *   Champagne or 1 quart bottle*
> *   sparkling water*

In a punch bowl, combine Sauterne, pineapple, orange, lemon and grapefruit juices and tea. Mix sugar and ginger; add to punch bowl, stirring until dissolved. Add ice cubes, ice block or orange juice frozen with lemon slices. Just before serving, add grapes and Champagne. Makes about 35 servings, 4-oz. size.

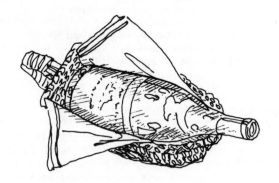

DELANO EGG NOG

Fred Perelli-Minetti, A. Perelli-Minetti & Sons, Delano

> *12 eggs, separated*
> *1½ cups sugar*
> *1 quart whipping cream, beaten*
> *1 quart cold milk*
> *1 (4/5-qt.) bottle California Brandy,*
> *   chilled*
> *Grated nutmeg*

Beat egg yolks with 1 cup of sugar until very light yellow and stiff. Beat egg whites with remaining ½ cup sugar until stiff; combine with beaten yolks. Fold in beaten cream; add milk slowly. Add Brandy very slowly, stirring constantly. Pour into chilled serving bowl; serve in mugs. Sprinkle with grated nutmeg. Serves 24-30.

MINT COOLER

Mrs. Massud S. Nury, Vie-Del Company, Fresno

> *1 quart boiling water*
> *2 Tbs. black tea leaves*
> *2 Tbs. chopped fresh*
> *   mint leaves*
> *2 (4/5-qt.) bottles California*
> *   red table wine*
> *½ cup lemon juice*
> *1 cup honey*
> *1 quart bottle sparkling water*
> *Lemon slices*
> *Sprigs of fresh mint*

Pour boiling water over tea and mint leaves; steep 5 minutes and strain liquid into a punch bowl. Cool. Add wine, lemon juice, honey, sparkling water and ice. If a sweeter punch is desired, mix in additional sugar or honey to taste. Garnish with slices of fresh lemon pierced with a sprig of fresh mint. Makes about 1 gallon.

COUNTRY SYLLABUB

Country Syllabub: Mix half a pound of white sugar with a pint of sweet white wine; and grate in nutmeg. Prepare them in a large bowl, just before milking time. Then let it be taken to the cow, and have about 3 pints milked into it; stirring occasionally with a spoon. Let it be eaten before the froth subsides.
> —MISS LESLIE'S COMPLETE COOKERY
>   Published 1863, Philadephia

Try this old-time reciept as an afternoon refreshment, or as a brunch beverage; you don't have to wait for milking time these days. Merely mix 1 cup sugar with ¼ teaspoon nutmeg and 2 cups California White Wine Port or Sweet Sauterne. Add 1½ quarts rich milk or light cream, beat until frothy and serve in cups with a sprinkling of nutmeg.

SOPHISTICATED STRAWBERRY SHAKE

> *1 cup sliced strawberries*
> *⅓ cup sugar*
> *Few grains salt*
> *1 egg*
> *1 cup milk*
> *1 tbs. lemon juice*
> *⅔ cup California Burgundy or*
> *   other red table wine*

Have all ingredients well chilled. Combine strawberries, sugar, salt, egg and milk, and blend in electric blender. Stir in lemon juice and wine, and serve at once. If blender is not available, force strawberries through a sieve, and combine with sugar, salt and egg. Beat until well blended with rotary beater. Stir in milk, then add lemon juice and wine and mix. Serves about 4.

ORANGE BLOSSOM FLIP

John A. Pedroncelli, J. Pedroncelli Winery, Geyserville

1 (6-oz.) can frozen orange juice
    concentrate
1 cup cream
¾ cup California Sherry
1 egg
Few grains salt
2 ice cubes

Put all ingredients into an electric blender (or beverage mixer or covered quart jar). Mix at high speed (or shake vigorously and thoroughly) until frothy and well blended. Beverage will about double in quantity. Makes about 1 quart.

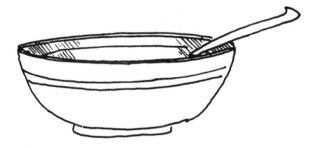

HOLIDAY SPECIAL

Mrs. Don Rudolph, Cresta Blanca Wine Company,
Livermore

1 (6-oz.) can frozen tropical fruit
    punch concentrate
1 (6-oz.) can frozen lemonade
    concentrate
1 quart water
1 (4/5-qt.) bottle California Sauterne
1 cup California Brandy
1 cup vodka
1 (6-oz.) can frozen pineapple
    juice concentrate
1 (4/5-qt.) bottle California
    Champagne
1 (1-qt.) bottle lemon-flavored
    sparkling water
1 (1-qt.) bottle sparkling water

Combine tropical fruit and lemonade concentrates with water, freeze. Chill punch bowl. Combine Sauterne, Brandy, vodka and pineapple juice concentrate; chill. When ready to serve, pour Sauterne mixture into punch bowl, add Champagne and sparkling waters. Use the frozen tropical fruit punch-lemonade mixture as the ice. Makes about 45 servings, 3 oz. size.

WINE PUNCH, LIVERMORE

Mrs. Ernest A. Wente, Wente Bros., Livermore

10 lbs. granulated sugar water
⅔ cup green tea leaves
4 (46-oz.) cans pineapple juice
4 (46-oz.) cans grapefruit juice
1 gallon orange juice
2 quarts lemon juice
8 large bottles California Sauterne,
    Chablis, or other white
    table wine
4 quart bottles sparkling water or
    4 large bottles California
    Champagne

Prepare a simple syrup by dissolving sugar in enough hot water to make 2 gallons. Make two gallons tea. Chill all ingredients. Combine ingredients except sparkling water or Champagne and wine and store for several hours or a day. Just before serving, add wine, and sparkling water or Champagne. Serves 400.

RASPBERRY SPARKLE

Add 3 tablespoons fresh lemon juice to a 10-oz. package of frozen raspberries which have been thawed and pressed through a sieve. Just before serving, gently mix in one 4/5 quart bottle of California Sparkling Burgundy.

BRANDINI

Brandini made by Mrs. Greg Goorigan of Vie-Del Company, Fresno, combines 4 parts California Brandy to 1 part California Dry Vermouth for a refreshing cocktail. Combine Brandy and Vermouth with ice, and shake until ice begins to melt. Serve in chilled glasses, garnish as desired.

DELANO EXPORT
Mrs. Fred Perelli-Minetti, A. Perelli-Minetti & Sons, Delano

1 part grapefruit juice
1 part California Brandy
1 part California Sweet Vermouth

Combine all ingredients. Serve chilled. Serves 1.

WINTER PUNCH
Mrs. Richard Elwood, Llords & Elwood Winery, Fremont

12 whole cloves
1 large orange, unpeeled
1 tablespoon sugar
1 (4/5-qt.) bottle California white
    table wine or Champagne
3 ounces California Brandy

Stick cloves into orange. Roast orange over an open fire until light brown. Cut orange into slices; place in saucepan. Add sugar; warm for an instant. Add wine and Brandy. Serve in preheated cups. Serves 8.

GLOG
J. H. "Mike" Elwood, Llords & Elwood Winery, Fremont

2 (4/5-qt.) bottles California Brandy
1 (4/5-qt.) bottle California Sherry,
    Port or red table wine
1 cup sugar
24 whole cloves
12 cardamom seeds
2 or 3 sticks cinnamon
1 cup raisins
1 cup blanched, unsalted almonds

Combine all ingredients in saucepan. Heat to just below boiling. Serve in preheated mugs or glasses. Makes about 25 servings, 3-oz. size.

APPLE CIDER ROSÉ

For a spicy hot fruit drink, heat apple juice with whole cinnamon sticks and cloves. Remove spices, pour in California Muscatel to taste and heat to a simmer. Serve in heavy mugs topped with a thin slice of lemon.

ORANGE BRUNCH SAUTERNE
Rose Marie Pangborn, University of California, Department of Viticulture & Enology, Davis

I enjoy many types of California table and dessert wines. But, have you ever tried reconstituting frozen orange juice with California Dry Sauterne? An invigorating eye-opener!

MULLED SAUTERNE CUP
Mrs. Frank Franzia, Franzia Brothers Winery, Ripon

1 (6-oz.) can frozen pineapple
    juice concentrate
¾ cup California Sauterne or
    other white table wine
2½ cups water
⅛ tsp. ground cloves
⅛ tsp. ground all spice
Dash of salt
1 Tbs. sugar

Combine all ingredients. Heat slowly to just below boiling. Serve hot in preheated cups. Makes about 10 servings, 3-oz. size.

CALIFORNIA CAUDLE
Mrs. E. F. Handel, East-Side Winery, Lodi

This makes a good drink for the holidays.

> 6 egg yolks
> 4 cups California Muscatel or
>   other dessert wine
> 6 cups strong black tea
> 1 cup sugar
> Grated nutmeg

Beat egg yolks until light and lemon colored. Add wine and tea; beat with rotary beater. Add sugar. Heat in double boiler. Serve in heated mugs topped with a sprinkling of grated nutmeg. Serves 12 to 20.

HOT BUTTERED SHERRY
Jake Rheingans, Sanger Winery Association, Sanger

> 1 (6-oz.) can frozen tangerine
>   juice concentrate
> ¾ cup California Dry Sherry
> 2½ cups water
> 1 Tbs. sugar
> ¼ tsp. powdered cinnamon
> Dash salt
> Soft butter
> Cinnamon sticks for stirrers

Combine tangerine juice concentrate, Sherry, water, powdered cinnamon and salt. Heat slowly to just below boiling. Pour into mugs and top each serving with a tiny bit of butter. With each mug serve a whole cinnamon stick for a stirrer. Makes 6 servings, 5-oz. size.

Hors d'Oeuvres

"A glass of sherry before dinner will revive a tired man and whet his appetite."

—Old English Proverb

From cocktail hour entertaining to late TV snacks, the hors d'oeuvre and its many relative have become a persistent part of the daily American diet. Whether hot or cold, simple or elaborate, food served before dinner or between meals should be stimulating to the palate, rather than filling. At its simplest, just wine served alone will be appetizing and festive. And adding a little California wine when preparing even the easiest of cocktail spreads and dips will liven them up—giving your favorite snacks a real party note, yet keeping them light and refreshing.

CANAPES SAN JOSE

Mr. E.A. Mirassou, Mirassou Vineyards, San Jose

2 (3-oz.) packages cream cheese
1 cup ground boiled ham
¼ cup California Sherry
½ tsp. Worcestershire sauce
Salt
50 (1½-inch) squares or rounds of
  bread (approximately)
50 pecan halves (approximately)
Paprika or minced parsley for
  garnishing

Place cream cheese in bowl and mash with fork; add ham and mix well; add Sherry, Worcestershire sauce and salt. Spread mixture on bread squares or rounds; top each canape with pecan half; sprinkle with paprika, parsley. Makes about 50 canapes.

SHERRIED CHEESE CANAPES

Mrs. Alfred Fromm, The Christian Brothers, Napa

1½ cups grated sharp Cheddar cheese
¼ tsp. dry mustard
¼ tsp. onion salt
Dash of pepper
4 to 5 Tbs. California Dry
  Sherry
24 melba toast crackers
Fresh or dried parsley

Combine cheese, mustard, onion salt, pepper and Sherry. Spread on crackers. Place under broiler for about 1 minute, or until cheese is brown and melted. Garnish with parsley. Serves 24.

RANCHER'S APPLE CANAPES
Mrs. E. Jeff Barnette, Martini & Prati Wines, Inc.,
Santa Rosa

We live on a small ranch near the Martini & Prati Winery and have several apple trees. I am always trying to originate recipes using apples as well as wine. For this I usually use Roman Beauties or Golden Delicious apples.

> *4 medium-sized apples*
> *California Sherry or*
> *white table wine*
> *5 slices bacon*
> *1 (3-oz.) package cream cheese, at*
> *room temperature*
> *2 Tbs. heavy cream or*
> *evaporated milk*

Pare apples; cut out apple balls with melon ball cutter. Place balls in quart jar; cover with wine. Cover jar; let stand at least 2 to 3 hours. Slowly fry bacon until brown and crisp; drain on paper toweling and crumble. Mix softened cream cheese and cream to right consistency to coat apple balls easily. Drain apple balls; roll in paper toweling to dry. Coat balls with creamed cheese mixture. Place a pick in each ball; dip one end in the crumbled bacon. (Finely chopped nut meats may be used instead of crumbled bacon.) Serves 8 to 10.

QUICK ANTIPASTO
Mrs. John M. Filice, San Martin Vineyards Company,
San Martin

I serve this antipasto in a small dish in the center of a chop-plate, surrounded with small round slices of French bread. I might as well warn you if you serve this dish, be prepared to give the recipe to your guests—everyone begs for it, especially when they hear how easy it is to prepare.

> *1 (1-pt.) jar giardiniera, well drained*
> *1 (12-oz.) jar artichoke hearts in oil,*
> *undrained*
> *1 (8-oz.) can whole button mushrooms,*
> *well drained*
> *1 (7 or 8-oz.) can large ripe olives,*
> *well drained*
> *2 (8-oz.) cans tomato sauce*
> *1 (7½-oz.) can water-packed tuna,*
> *well drained*
> *4 Tbs. California white wine*
> *vinegar*

Combine all ingredients, mixing well. Place in covered casserole; refrigerate at least 24 hours. Mix well once or twice while mixture marinates. This dish is especially good when served at an informal meal, such as a barbecue. Serves 10-12.

SHERRIED OLIVES
W.V. Cruess, University of California, Department
of Food Science & Technology, Berkeley

> *1 (8-oz.) can pitted ripe olives*

Drain liquid from olives and discard. Place olives in pint jar or other container with cover. Add enough Sherry to cover completely. Cover and let stand overnight. Drain olives and serve with salad or as an appetizer. (Remaining Sherry can be used to flavor meat or fish.)

VARIATIONS: If desired, add one of the following to the olives and Sherry: 1 clove garlic, sliced; a few fennel seeds; a little oregano and basil; ½ tsp. hickory liquid smoke; or dash of Tabasco sauce.

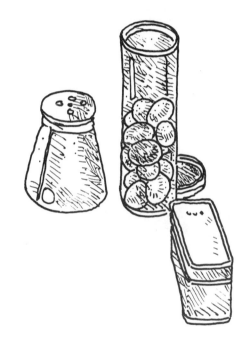

CHEESE PUFFS
Anne Vercelli, Souverain Winery, Healdsburg

> *½ cup butter*
> *1 lb. unsliced bread (white)*
> *2 egg whites, beaten*
> *¼ cup White Wine*
> *1-3 oz. package cream cheese*

Melt butter and cheeses over hot water. Meanwhile cut bread into cubes, about one inch square. When cheese is melted, stir in wine and fold in beaten egg whites. Dip bread cubes in cheese mixture. Place on oiled sheet pan and place in freezer. When frozen remove to plastic bag and set in freezer. To serve place on a baking sheet and bake in a 400 degree oven for 8-10 minutes or place under a broiler for a few minutes until cheese puffs begin to brown. Makes 3 dozen puffs.

NAPA CELERY

Mrs. J. F. M. Taylor, Mayacamas Vineyards, Napa

> *Reserved wine stock from Tripe*
> *Hors d'oeuvre (see page 25)*
> *or any California white table wine*
> *3 to 4 dozen (3-inch) lengths of*
> *celery*
> *¾ cup oil*
> *½ tsp. curry powder*
> *1 tsp. herb mix*
> *1 tsp. savory salt*
> *2 Tbs. tarragon vinegar*
> *3 to 4 dozen anchovy fillets*
> *3 to 4 dozen narrow strips pimiento*

Heat wine stock to simmering. Remove strings from celery with vegetable peeler. Gently simmer celery pieces in enough stock or wine to cover (no more than a dozen at a time). As they are cooked, remove from stock and drain well; place in a flat casserole. Combine oil, curry powder, herb mix, savory salt and vinegar; pour over celery, coating each piece. Marinate at least 1 day. Before serving, drain well. Place an anchovy fillet on each piece; criss-cross with a strip of pimiento. This can be served on lettuce as a first course, or as a finger food atop long narrow crackers or strips of firm bread spread with a mixture of cream cheese and sour cream. Makes 3 to 4 dozen pieces.

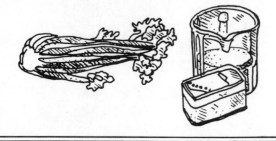

SWISS CHEESE-RIPE OLIVE DIP

Mrs. Keith V. Nylander, Di Giorgio Wine Company,

> *1 lb. process Swiss cheese,*
> *shredded*
> *6 Tbs. California Sauterne*
> *or other white table wine*
> *2 Tbs. mayonnaise*
> *2 (4½-oz.) cans chopped ripe olives,*
> *drained well between paper towels*
> *¼ cup chopped chives or parsley*
> *2 tsp. grated onion*
> *2 tsp. Worcestershire sauce*
> *Salt and paprika*

Have cheese at room temperature; place in a bowl. With a fork, gradually beat in wine; blend in mayonnaise. Add remaining ingredients, mixing well. Chill several hours to blend flavors. Bring to room temperature before serving. Heap in a bowl and dust with paprika. Serve with potato chips or corn chips, crisp crackers or melba toast. Makes about 3 cups.

CHICKEN PIROSHKI

Rodney D. Strong, Sonoma Vineyards, Windsor

> *PASTRY*
> *2½ cups sifted all-purpose flour*
> *1 tsp. salt*
> *¾ cup shortening*
> *5 to 6 Tbs. cold water*
> *Filling (see below)*

Sift flour with salt and cut in shortening until pieces are the size of small peas. Add cold water by teaspoonful, tossing with a fork until all the flour-coated bits are barely dampened. Shape dough into a ball; roll out to about ¼ inch in thickness and cut out circles with a 2 or 3 inch cutter.

> *FILLING*
> *2 Tbs. chopped onion*
> *¼ cup butter or margarine*
> *2 Tbs. flour*
> *½ cup California Burgundy or*
> *other red table wine*
> *½ cup chicken stock (canned or*
> *bouillon-cube chicken broth*
> *may be used)*
> *2 Tbs. chopped parsley*
> *½ tsp. Worcestershire sauce*
> *½ tsp. poultry seasoning*
> *Salt and pepper to taste*
> *2 cups ground, cooked chicken*
> *(giblets are good)*
> *2 hard-cooked eggs, grated or*
> *chopped*

Sauté onion gently in butter for 5 minutes. Blend in flour; add wine and stock; cook, stirring constantly, until mixture boils and thickens. Remove from heat. Add all remaining ingredients, blending well. Heap some of this mixture in the center of each pastry circle. Moisten edges of pastry with cold water; fold over to form semi-circles. Place on a baking sheet. Press edges of pastry together with a fork; prick with a fork; prick tops. Brush tops with unbeaten egg white or milk. Bake in a hot oven (450 degrees) for 15 to 20 minutes, or until delicately browned. Serve hot. Makes about 24 turnovers.

MELON AU PENACHE

Chef Jeanty, Domaine Chandon, Yountville

> *2 canteloupes*
> *1 honeydew melon*
> *Panache (Chandon's*
> *apertif wine)*

Halve melons, discard seeds. Make melon balls and refill half shells with balls. Sprinkle liberally with Panache and chill. Garnish with apple slices, and/or prosciutto if desired. Serves 8.

HIBACHI COCKTAIL SAUSAGE

Hibachi Cocktail Sausage is a delightful party novelty. Mrs. Joseph J. Fanzia of Franzia Brothers Winery, Ripon, puts cocktail sausages on skewers, brushes them with melted butter and then browns them over charcoal while brushing with California white table wine. They are served with hot mustard, right off the grill. If a hibachi is not available, broil sausage in the oven and serve immediately.

FRANKFURTERS BURGUNDY

Chunky Slices of Frankfurter can be heated in California Burgundy with a little chopped onion to be served as a "cocktail pick" hors d'oeuvre. Have some wine-flavored mustard for dipping, plus your favorite aperitif to sip.

BLUE CHEESE MEAT BALLS A LA LICO
Mrs. Frank Lico, San Martin Vineyards Company, San Martin

The first time I cooked these meat balls I was a little leery about trying something new, but when I saw the empty dish before dinner I knew they were a hit. My husband complains because he eats so many before dinner he hasn't room for anything else. They are especially good when company comes since they can be prepared early in the day and heated just before serving.

> *1 lb. lean ground beef*
> *6 ounces blue cheese, crumbled*
> *1 tsp. salt*
> *1 small clove garlic, minced*
> *½ cup bread crumbs*
> *¼ tsp. oregano*
> *¼ tsp. rosemary*
> *2 Tbs. chopped parsley*
> *¾ cup California white table wine*
> *¼ cup oil*

Combine beef, cheese, salt, garlic, bread crumbs, oregano, rosemary, parsley and ½ cup of the wine; mix well. Shape mixture into small bite-size balls (about 1 tsp. each). Brown well on all sides in heated oil; drain on absorbent paper. Refrigerate until ready to use. Before serving, place in shallow casserole or chafing dish. Add the remaining ¼ cup of wine. Heat thoroughly. (If using casserole, place in 350 degree oven for 15 minutes.) These meat balls can be made larger and served as a main dish with spaghetti. Makes about 75 bite-size meat balls.

GRAPEVINE CHICKEN LIVERS
Mrs. Harold Berg, University of California, Davis

> *½ cup bacon, diced*
> *2 Tbs. finely chopped onion*
> *2 Tbs. finely chopped green*
> * pepper*
> *1 lb. chicken livers*
> *½ cup California red table wine*
> *¼ cup chopped parsley*

Sauté bacon, onion and green pepper until lightly browned. Remove to chafing dish. In remaining fat, brown livers. Add wine, parsley; simmer 10 to 15 minutes. Combine all ingredients in chafing dish. Serve hot with picks. Serves 6 to 8.

GUN CLUB PHEASANT
Mrs. Ernest A. Wente, Wente Bros., Livermore

> *2 or 3 pheasants*
> *1 (4/5-qt.) bottle California white*
> * table wine*
> *2 medium onions, finely chopped*
> *2 tsp. celery seed*
> *1 tsp. garlic powder*
> *4 to 6 whole cloves*
> *2 bay leaves*
> *2 or 3 sprigs each: rosemary,*
> * oregano and tarragon*
> *Salt and pepper*
> *2 eggs*
> *Seasoned cracker crumbs*
> *3 Tbs. oil*

Cut meaty parts of pheasants into finger-size pieces (not bite-size); place in large bowl. Combine wine, onions, celery seed, garlic powder, cloves, bay leaves, herbs, salt and pepper; mix well. Pour over pheasant pieces. Marinate at least 12 hours. Remove pheasant from marinade; drain pieces on paper towels. Beat eggs with about ¼ cup remaining marinade. Dip pheasant pieces in egg mixture, then roll in seasoned crumbs. Cover bottom of flat baking pan (about 9x13 inches) with oil. Arrange pieces of pheasant in single layer; cover and bake in moderate oven (350 degrees) for about 1 hour, or until tender. If pan becomes too dry, add a little marinade. Uncover and allow pieces to brown and crisp. Serve warm, not hot. Makes about 24 servings.

CHOPPED LIVER MODERNE

Mrs. Emanuel B. Jaffe, E. & J. Gallo Winery, Modesto

This is my modernized variation of a centuries-old European delicacy. The broiling and grinding are time-savers; the utilization of the broiling juices and wine drastically reduces the amount of fat suggested in old-world recipes. The addition of a little mayonnaise helps to make a smooth blend. Serve with thinly-sliced rye bread or crackers.

1 lb. chicken or calf liver
¼ cup minced onion (or ½ tsp.
* onion powder)*
2 Tbs. oil or rendered
* chicken fat*
3 hard-cooked eggs
¼ cup California Sauterne or
* other white table wine*
Salt

In a lightly oiled pan without rack, broil liver under low heat until medium-well done. Cool. (If using calf liver, peel outer skin and remove as many veins as possible.) Brown onion in heated oil. Grind or chop liver and eggs with onion until very smooth and fine. Add wine and salt; mix well with fork. Texture should be of spreading consistency; if not, add broiling juices from liver and/or a little mayonnaise as needed. Pile high in a bowl and garnish with parsley. Makes about 1½ cups.

CRABMEAT CANAPES, SANTA CLARA

Mrs. Edward Pedrizzetti, Pedrizzetti Winery, Morgan Hill

3 Tbs. butter or margarine
3 Tbs. flour
½ cup cream or undiluted
* evaporated milk*
¼ cup chicken broth (canned or
* bouillon-cube broth may be used)*
¼ cup California Sauterne, Chablis,
* or other white table wine*
1 Tbs. minced parsley
1 Tbs. minced pimiento
1 cup flaked fresh or canned
* crabmeat*
Salt, celery salt, and pepper
Dash of cayenne
60 (1½-inch) rounds of white bread,
* approximately*
Paprika

Melt butter and stir in flour; add cream and chicken broth; cook, stirring constantly, until mixture is thickened and smooth. Remove from heat and add wine, parsley, pimiento, crabmeat and seasonings to taste. Chill mixture thoroughly. Toast rounds of bread on one side only; spread untoasted side with the crabmeat mixture; dust with paprika. Broil until delicately browned. Serve at once. Makes about 60 canapes.

CHICKEN LIVER SANDWICH

A. J. Handel, Guild Wine Co., Lodi

¼ cup chopped green onion
¼ cup butter or margarine
½ lb. chicken livers
Garlic salt
Paprika
¼ cup California Rosé or
* white table wine*
Thin slices tomato
Hot buttered toast
Chopped parsley

Cook green onion a few minutes in butter. Season chicken livers with garlic salt and paprika. Add to pan with onion; cook until golden brown on one side. Turn livers, add wine, cover pan and cook until tender. Arrange tomato slice on each piece of toast. Top with chicken livers and pan liquid. Sprinkle with parsley. Serves 3.

TRIPE HORS D'OEUVRE

Mrs. J. F. M. Taylor, Mayacamas Vineyards, Napa

2½ lbs. tripe
1 (4/5-qt.) bottle California
* white table wine*
2 carrots
1 onion
Handful of celery leaves
2 tsp. salt
1 tsp. powdered cloves
2 cloves garlic
2 cups mayonnaise
½ cup chopped sweet pickle
2 Tbs. chopped capers
2 Tbs. chopped fresh tarragon,
* or 1 tsp. dried tarragon*
1 sweet onion, sliced paper thin

At least 1 day before serving, rinse tripe several times in cold water. Place tripe in large kettle. Cover with wine; add carrots, whole onion, celery leaves, salt, cloves, garlic. Simmer several hours, until very tender. (Or, cook 30 minutes in a pressure cooker, allowing pressure to drop before opening cooker.) Meanwhile, mix mayonnaise with sweet pickle, capers and tarragon. Remove tripe from stock; when cool, cut into strips (¼-inch wide and 1-inch long). In a deep bowl, put a layer of tripe; top with layer of sweet onion slices. Continue this layering until tripe is used up. Add mayonnaise mixture; mix well. Taste and correct seasoning. Cover and refrigerate until needed. Serve on thin slices of buttered bread or crisp crackers. (Wine stock can be frozen and used again.) Makes about 1 quart of spread.

ROLLED CHICKEN SANDWICHES

Mario Trinchero, Sutter Home Winery, Inc., St. Helena

> 1 (8-oz.) package cream cheese
> 2 cups very finely ground cooked
>   chicken (firmly packed)
> ½ cup finely ground celery (firmly
>   packed)
> ¼ cup chopped parsley
> ½ cup California Sauterne or
>   other white table wine
> 2 tsp. grated onion
> 1 tsp. Worcestershire sauce
> Salt
> Softened butter or margarine
> 36 to 40 slices very fresh white
>   bread, crusts removed

Have cream cheese at room temperature; place in a bowl and mash with a fork. Add chicken, celery and parsley; blend well. Gradually beat in wine; add onion, Worcestershire sauce and salt to taste. Spread slices of bread with butter, then with the chicken mixture. Roll up. (Slices will roll more easily if you go over them lightly with a rolling pin before spreading them with the butter and filling.) Place sandwiches "seam" side down on a platter or in a shallow pan; cover with waxed paper, then wrap in a damp towel. Chill ½ hour or so before serving.

For smaller sandwiches, cut crosswise in halves after chilling.

For toasted sandwiches, omit softened butter. Chill sandwiches as directed, then just before serving, brush outside with melted butter and toast under the broiler. Turn to brown all sides evenly, watching carefully. Makes 36 to 40 sandwiches.

SHERRIED PICKLED MUSHROOMS

Mrs. Leonard Berg, Mont La Salle Vineyards, Napa

> 2 (4-oz.) cans button mushrooms
> ⅔ cup olive oil
> ½ cup lemon juice
> ¼ cup California Sherry
> 1 clove garlic, halved
> 1 medium onion, finely chopped
> ¾ tsp. dry mustard
> 3 small bay leaves
> 1 tsp. salt
> ¼ tsp. pepper

Combine all ingredients in quart jar, mix well. Cover and refrigerate for at least 24 hours. Discard garlic. To serve, arrange mushrooms on picks and insert picks in fresh orange, grapefruit or pineapple, if desired. Makes about 1½ cups.

COCKTAIL MEAT BALLS IN CURRY SAUCE

J. Leland Stewart, Souverain Cellars, St. Helena

> 1 lb. ground beef
> ½ cup grated soft bread crumbs
> ¼ cup milk
> ¼ cup California Sherry
> 1 egg, slightly beaten
> 2 Tbs. grated onion
> 1 tsp. salt
> ¼ tsp pepper
> 2 Tbs. bacon drippings
>   or other fat
> 1 (10½-oz.) can condensed cream of
>   mushroom soup
> ¼ cup California Sherry
> ½ tsp. curry powder
>   (or to taste)

Mix beef, bread crumbs, milk, ¼ cup wine, egg, onion, salt and pepper. Shape mixture into little balls, using 1 level teaspoon per meat ball Heat bacon drippings in a large, heavy skillet; add a single layer of meat balls and cook, not too fast, for about 10 minutes, or until meat balls are done, shaking pan gently from time to time to cook them evenly. Repeat until all meat balls are cooked. Combine soup, ¼ cup wine and curry powder; heat, piping hot. To serve, spear each meat ball with a toothpick. Accompany with a bowl of the curry sauce for dunking. Makes about 60 meat balls.

DEVILED EGGS IN ASPIC

Alice and Joseph Heitz, Heitz Wine Cellar, St. Helena

> 1 envelope unflavored gelatin
> ⅓ cup cold water
> ½ cup hot chicken stock
>   (canned or bouillon-cube
>   broth may be used)
> ¾ cup cold chicken stock
> ¼ cup California Sherry
> 1 Tbs. lemon juice
> ¼ tsp. Worcestershire sauce
> Dash of powdered cloves
> Salt and pepper
> 6 small shrimp
> 6 deviled egg halves

Soften gelatin in the cold water for 5 minutes. Dissolve in the hot chicken stock. Add cold chicken stock, wine, lemon juice, Worcestershire, and seasonings to taste. Pour a thin layer of this mixture into 6 oiled custard cups; chill until firm. Meantime, chill remaining gelatin mixture until syrupy. Press a shrimp into top of each deviled egg half; place halves "face down" on the firm aspic layer; pour in partially thickened aspic. Chill until firm. Unmold on crisp salad greens. Serve with mayonnaise or Thousand Island dressing. Serves 6.

AVOCADO AND GRAPEFRUIT COCKTAIL
*Mrs. Joe V. Kovacevich, Cresta Blanca Wine Company,
Delano*

> 2 (No. 303) cans grapefruit
> segments
> ½ cup strained honey
> ¼ cup California Muscatel or
> other dessert wine
> 2 Tbs. lime juice
> Generous dash of salt
> 1 to 1½ cups diced avocado
> Sprigs of fresh mint or
> maraschino cherries for garnish

Drain grapefruit thoroughly. Mix honey, wine, lime juice and salt; pour over grapefruit. Cover and let stand in the refrigerator several hours to chill thoroughly. Just before serving, add avocado to grapefruit; mix lightly. Spoon into sherbet glasses; garnish each serving with a mint sprig or a maraschino cherry. Serves 6.

TINY WINEY PIZZA PIES

Tiny Winey Pizza Pies, or pizzalinas, are different and fun as a cocktail-or-anytime snack. Mrs. Leo Demosteve, Soda Rock Winery, Healdsburg, finds that sliced French bread can be used instead of pizza dough for a just-as-delicious but easier version. She makes a thick, rich, meaty wine-tomato sauce, puts sliced bread on cookie sheets, and spreads with sauce. Pizzalinas are then sprinkled with Parmesan cheese and oregano, baked till bubbly (about 25 minutes in a slow oven) and served immediately.

CHEESE-FROST FRENCH BREAD
Mrs. Stanford J. Wolf

> 1 (5-oz.) jar American or Cheddar
> cheese spread
> ¼ cup California Sherry
> 2 Tbs. mayonnaise
> ½ tsp. prepared mustard
> ½ tsp. Worcestershire sauce
> 1 long loaf French bread

Put cheese spread in a mixing bowl, add Sherry and blend well with a fork. Add mayonnaise, mustard and Worcestershire sauce; mix thoroughly. Cut the loaf of French bread lengthwise in halves, then slice crosswise, cutting down to the crust but not through it. Spread cheese mixture over cut surfaces of bread and broil slowly until "frosting" is delicately browned. Serve piping hot. Serves 6 to 8.

FRUIT AND WINE APPETIZER
Edward Seghesio, Seghesio Winery, Cloverdale

> ½ cup California Port, Muscatel
> or other dessert wine
> ¼ cup California Sauterne or
> other white table wine
> 2 Tbs. lemon juice
> 1 Tbs. grenadine
> 1 (7-oz.) bottle chilled ginger ale
> 1 cup sliced seeded grapes
> 1 cup grapefruit segments
> ½ cup diced unpeeled red apple

Combine wines, lemon juice and grenadine; chill. Just before serving add ginger ale and pour over prepared fruits. Serves 6 to 8.

BLUE CHEESE BUTTER
*Mrs. Gerta Wingerd, University of California
Medical Center, San Francisco*

> ½ lb. blue cheese
> ¼ lb. soft butter or margarine
> ¼ cup California Port
> 2 Tbs. minced parsley
> ½ tsp. onion juice

Have cheese at room temperature. Place cheese and butter in a mixing bowl; blend well with a fork; gradually beat in wine. Set bowl in a pan of hot (not boiling) water; beat mixture with a fork just until smooth and creamy. Remove bowl from water. Add parsley and onion juice. Turn mixture into a serving dish. Chill several hours. Bring to room temperature before serving. Serve with crisp crackers or melba toast as an hors d'oeuvre. Makes about 1½ cups.

VICTORIAN SHERRIED CRAB FONDUE

Victorian Sherried Crab Fondue gives you a chance to polish up the chafing dish and let the guests dig in. This recipe, to be conveniently prepared beforehand, is warmed in a chafing dish at serving time, using the water jacket. Erma Tolstonage, Roma Wine Company, Fresno, uses a skillet for actual cooking. Melt ½ pound butter and brown 4 small chopped onions. Add 1 pound Cheddar cheese, cubed, ¾ cup catsup, 4 tablespoons Worcestershire sauce, ¼ cup California Medium Dry Sherry, cayenne pepper to taste. When cheese is melted and sauce is smooth, blend in 4 cups prepared crab meat. Refrigerate to be warmed later, or serve immediately from warm chafing dish. Let guests help themselves using toast points, Melba toast squares or small patty shells. A California Dry Sherry is excellent sipping with this.

Soups

"Drink a glass of wine after your soup, and you steal a ruble from the doctor."

—*Russian Proverb*

Start from scratch, or use cans or the frozen variety—you'll find that wine-flavored soup served hot or cold is a marvelously savory start to a meal, or a meal itself. A thick chowder, well-laced with California Sherry or white wine, and served with chunks of crusty hot bread, will warm the spirit as well as the body in winter. For summer's refreshment, serve a wine-fragrant chilled soup. And for a welcome change, try soup as a first course served in the living room with hors d'oeuvre before sitting down to the table. A hot wine-seasoned consommé, served in handled mugs, is easy for guests to manage and deliciously appetizing as well. You simply add one tablespoon of wine (either Sherry or Burgundy is perfect) for each cup of consommé as it simmers. The alcohol vanishes, leaving rich new flavor—sheer taste adventure!

VINTAGE TOMATO BOUILLON

Mrs. Earl A. Humphrey, Guild Wine Co., Lodi

This dish may be served as an appetizer with crackers before the main dinner on the patio, etc.

> *3 cups canned tomato juice*
> *1 thick slice onion*
> *1 stalk celery, sliced*
> *1 bay leaf*
> *4 whole cloves*
> *1 (10½-oz.) can condensed*
>   *consommé*
> *½ cup California red table wine*
> *Salt and pepper*
> *Thin slices of lemon for garnish*

Combine tomato juice, onion, celery, bay leaf and cloves in a saucepan. Bring to boil; cover and simmer for 20 minutes. Strain. Add consommé, wine, salt and pepper. Serve very hot in bouillon cups. Float slice of lemon in each cup. This bouillon is compatible with almost any menu. Serves 5 to 6.

NEAPOLITAN CLAM SOUP

Mrs. John B. Cella II, Cella Wineries, Fresno

> *48 small clams*
> *3 cups California white table wine*
> *½ cup olive oil*
> *¼ cup chopped leeks (white*
>   *part only)*
> *¼ tsp. marjoram*
> *¼ cup chopped onion*
> *2 cloves garlic, minced*
> *½ cup peeled chopped tomatoes*
> *2 stalks celery*
> *2 Tbs. minced parsley*

Scrub clams and combine in kettle with wine; cover and cook over high heat until clams open. Drain, reserving stock. (You may remove clams from the shells or not, as you prefer.) Heat oil in a saucepan; sauté leeks and onion until lightly browned. Add garlic, tomatoes, celery, marjoram and reserved stock. Cook over high heat 10 minutes. Discard celery. Add clams and parsley; cook 1 minute more. Serve in deep soup plates with sautéed sliced Italian or French bread. Serves 4 to 6.

POACHED EGG SOUP
Mrs. Dinsmoor Webb, University of California,
Department of Viticulture & Enology, Davis

> *1 quart rich chicken broth, salted*
>   *to taste*
> *½ cup California Dry Sherry*
> *Several sprigs parsley, finely*
>   *chopped*
> *1 lemon, thinly sliced*
> *½ sweet red pepper, finely chopped*
> *8 very fresh eggs*
> *Water*
> *2 Tbs. wine vinegar*

Bring broth to boil; add Sherry, parsley, lemon slices and chopped red pepper. Meanwhile poach eggs in boiling water to which vinegar has been added. Poach only four at a time, allowing three minutes cooking time. Lift eggs from poaching water into another container of hot, not boiling, water to rinse off vinegar flavor. Strain hot broth into soup bowls, add 2 eggs to each bowl, and serve immediately. This is a hearty soup, and goes well with bread and fruit for luncheons. Serves 4.

WINEMAKERS SOUP
Mrs. Edmund A. Rossi Jr., Italian Swiss Colony, Asti

This dish has no particular origin—we just like spinach!

> *1 pkg. potato soup mix*
> *1 pkg. frozen chopped spinach*
> *4 Tbs. California Dry Sherry*
> *1 Tbs. butter*
> *Salt and pepper*

Cook soup as directed on package. Cook spinach as directed on package and drain well. Add spinach to soup and bring to boiling point. Just before serving, add Sherry, butter and seasonings to taste. Serve piping hot. Since this is a rather rich soup, it is best with a light dinner, or served for luncheon, accompanied by a salad and rolls. Serves 4.

SOUP TICINESE
Mrs. William Bonetti, Charles Krug Winery, St. Helena

> *1 Tbs. butter*
> *4 eggs*
> *3 cups consommé*
> *¼ cup finely chopped parsley*
> *½ cup California Sherry*

Heat butter in 10-inch skillet. Beat 1 egg lightly with fork. Pour into very hot skillet; cook until golden and set. Remove from skillet. Repeat with remaining eggs. Cut the cooked eggs into ⅛-inch strips. Bring consommé to boil; add egg strips, parsley and Sherry. Serve hot. Serves 4.

FRESH MUSHROOM AND PARSLEY SOUP
Linda Hagen, Tasting Room Manager and Resident
 Chef at Chateau St. Jean, Kenwood

> *1 lb. fresh mushrooms, sliced*
> *¼ lb. butter (1 stick)*
> *¼ cup white wine*
> *1½ cups fresh parsley, chopped finely*
> *3 cups homemade beef broth or*
>   *2 cans beef broth*
> *2 cups half and half*
> *2 cups sour cream*
> *Salt*
> *Cracked pepper*

Sauté mushrooms in butter and wine, add parsley, sauté 5 minutes more. Add beef broth and half and half. Simmer 5-10 minutes. Remove from heat, stir in sour cream. Salt and pepper to taste. Can be reheated, but do not boil.

BAY CIOPPINO
Mrs. Joseph E. Digardi, J.E. Digardi Winery, Martinez

As host or hostess, it is your duty to "pitch in." Cioppino is best eaten with the fingers, with the aid of an oyster fork. The gravy may be eaten with a spoon. Furnish everyone with a napkin large enough to tie around his neck.

> *1 fresh cracked crab, uncooked*
> *12 fresh prawns*
> *12 small clams in shells*
> *3 Tbs. olive oil*
> *1 onion, chopped*
> *1 clove garlic, chopped*
> *⅓ cup California red wine vinegar*
> *1 (no. 2½) can solid-pack*
>   *tomatoes, undrained*
> *Salt and pepper*
> *Dash of celery salt*
> *½ cup chopped parsley*
> *1 lb. rock cod or halibut,*
>   *cut in 2-inch cubes*
> *¼ cup California Sherry*

Wash crab, prawns and clams thoroughly; set aside. Heat olive oil in Dutch oven; brown onion and garlic. Add vinegar; simmer a few minutes. Add crab, prawns, clams in their shells, undrained tomatoes, salt, pepper, celery salt and parsley. Cover and cook for 30 to 40 minutes. Add water, if necessary. Add rock cod or halibut; cook, covered, until fish is done. Add Sherry; simmer slowly for a few minutes. Serve in deep soup plates. Serves 4.

CIOPPINO ALLA GENOVESE
Mrs. Frank Franzia, Franzia Brothers Winery, Ripon

We serve this meal on a cold winter evening and invite a few families to help us eat it. It is a fun meal for a group.

> *2 medium-sized onions, chopped*
> *1 Tbs. chopped garlic*
> *1 Tbs. chopped parsley*
> *1 Tbs. chopped celery*
> *1 Tbs. chopped green pepper*
> *½ cup olive oil*
> *2 cups solid-pack tomatoes*
> *1 cup tomato sauce*
> *2 Tbs. salt*
> *⅛ tsp. pepper*
> *1 small sprig fresh basil,*
>   *or 1 tsp. dried basil*
> *1 Tbs. paprika*
> *½ cup California Sherry*
> *4 cups water*
> *2 large fresh crabs, cracked*
> *1½ lbs. raw shrimp (in shells)*
> *2 lbs. rock cod, sea bass, or*
>   *swordfish, cut in bite-size pieces*

Sauté onions, garlic, parsley, celery and green pepper in oil until golden brown. Add tomatoes and tomato sauce, salt, pepper, basil, paprika and Sherry. Cook 15 minutes over low heat. Add water; bring to boiling. Add cracked crabs, and shrimp and clams in their shells. Cook slowly for 1 hour, adding a little more water or Sherry, if necessary. Add raw fish; cook 20 minutes longer. Serve in bowls with plenty of garlic bread, accompanied with a tossed green salad with oil and wine vinegar dressing. For dessert have apples baked with California Chablis. Serves 10 to 12.

CHINESE CONSOMMÉ

Mrs. Cornelius Ough, University of California, Department of Viticulture & Enology, Davis

The soup is so quick and easy, yet delicious. Also, as the wine is added just a minute before serving, you can use the same wine that will be served at the table.

> 1 (No.2) can tomato juice
> 1 (10½-oz.) can beef consommé
> 1 Tbs. butter
> ¼ cup California white table wine
> Garnish of chopped chives, scallion
>   tops, green pepper, celery tops or
>   combination of these

Combine tomato juice and consommé in a saucepan; heat to boiling. Place butter and wine in soup tureen or other serving dish. Add boiling consommé mixture; serve immediately. Sprinkle 1 teaspoon of desired garnish on each bowl of soup as it is served. I prefer serving this before a beef and potato entrée, or what might be considered a "heavy" meal. Serves about 4.

CHINESE EGG FLOWER SOUP

Chinese egg flower soup is a delicate delight, yet nothing could be simpler. Start with any light clear soup, such as consommé or chicken broth (bouillon cubes may be used). Season to taste, with salt, pepper, California Sherry and chopped green onion. Just before serving, while broth is simmering, slowly stir in a lightly beaten egg. Egg will form thin ribbons, attractive as a garnish but also an appealing taste accent.

COLD TOMATO SOUP, LOS GATOS

Mrs. Michael J. Bo, Almaden Vineyards, Los Gatos

> 2 (11-oz.) cans condensed
>   tomato soup (undiluted)
> 1½ cups water
> 1 cup dairy sour cream
> 1 teaspoon bottled horseradish
> ½ cup California Dry Sherry
> ¼ tsp. curry powder (optional)
> Salt

Combine soup, water and sour cream, using electric beater or blender. Add horseradish, Sherry, curry powder and salt to taste. Chill thoroughly. Serve with a crab meat soufflé and steamed artichokes with mayonnaise. Serves 4.

SEAFOOD SOUP, GOLDEN STATE

Mrs. James Gott, United Vintners, Inc., San Francisco

> 1 cup raw regular rice
> 2½ cups boiling water
> 1 teaspoon salt
> 2 (10½-oz.) cans condensed
>   chicken soup with rice
> 2 (10½-oz.) cans pepper pot soup
> 2 (14½-oz.) cans evaporated milk
> ¾ cup California Dry Sherry
> ¾ tsp. curry powder, or
>   more to taste
> ⅔ lb. fresh cooked crabmeat
>   (canned may be used)
> ⅔ lb. fresh cooked shrimp
>   (canned may be used)

Pour rice into boiling salted water and steam about 25 minutes until water is absorbed and rice is tender. Meanwhile, heat soups, milk, Sherry and curry together. Add crab and shrimp and heat gently for a few minutes. Pour into warmed tureen. To serve, spoon about 4 tablespoons cooked rice into each soup bowl. Ladle soup over rice. This is an excellent luncheon or Sunday supper dish, served with a green salad and toasted French rolls. Serves 6 to 8.

ICED BORSCH

Mrs. Alfred Fromm, The Christian Brothers, Napa

> 4 cups concentrated, seasoned
>   beef stock
> 1 bunch raw beets, peeled and
>   grated (about 2 to 3 cups)
> ½ cup California Burgundy,
>   Claret or other red table wine
> 2 Tbs. tomato paste
> 2 bay leaves
> 3 egg whites, stiffly beaten
> 5 Tbs. dairy sour cream
> Salt
> Cayenne
> 1½ tsp. sugar
> Grated rind of 1 lemon

In a large kettle, combine beef stock (which may be made by adding 5 bouillon cubes to 4 cups boiling water,) beets, wine, tomato paste, bay leaves and stiffly beaten egg whites. Beat mixture over medium heat until it comes to boil. Remove from heat; let stand 10 minutes. Strain mixture through a fine, damp cloth; refrigerate until cold. Serve chilled with sour cream mixed with salt, cayenne, sugar and lemon rind as topping. This, with a large loaf of rye bread and the wine remaining in the bottle, becomes a meal in itself. Serves 6 to 8.

Barbecue & Basting

ALL FOUR SAUCES USE THESE INGREDIENTS:

California Wine Vinegar
California Wine or Broth (or other liquid)
Herbs and Spices
Garlic
Onion
Mustard (dry or prepared)
Catsup or Chili Sauce
Brown Sugar or Honey
Salt
Pepper or Paprika
Soy Sauce
Worcestershire Sauce
Oil

These easy sauce recipes make from 2½ to 3¼ cups. Heat each sauce to blend ingredients, and baste meat with warm sauce. You'll find each one simply delicious, used on its proper meat, whether barbecued or oven baked.

Ingredients

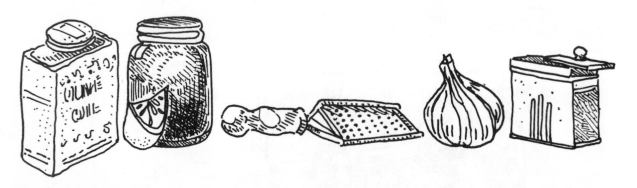

FOR BEEF OR VEAL

¼ cup California Wine Vinegar
1 cup California red table wine
1 cup consommé
2 teaspoons mixed thyme, rosemary, marjoram
1 clove garlic, crushed
¼ cup onion, grated
2 teaspoons mustard (dry or prepared)
¼ cup catsup or chili sauce
1 tablespoon brown sugar
1 teaspoon salt
½ teaspoon pepper
1 tablespoon Worcestershire sauce
½ cup oil

FOR CHICKEN, TURKEY OR LAMB

⅓ cup California Wine Vinegar
1 cup California white table wine
1 cup chicken broth
2 teaspoons mixed rosemary and oregano
1 teaspoon dried dill
1 clove garlic, crushed
2 tablespoons onion, grated
¼ cup catsup (optional)
2 tablespoons brown sugar or honey
1 teaspoon salt
½ teaspoon paprika
1 teaspoon soy sauce
1 teaspoon Worcestershire sauce
½ cup oil

FOR PORK

⅓ to ½ cup California Wine Vinegar
1 (8-oz.) can tomato sauce
½ cup California Dry Vermouth
½ cup chicken broth
1 teaspoon powdered ginger
¼ cup onion, grated
1 teaspoon mustard (dry or prepared)
3 tablespoons brown sugar or honey
1 teaspoon smoked salt
¼ teaspoon pepper
1 tablespoon soy sauce
1 tablespoon Worcestershire sauce
¼ cup oil

FOR FISH

¼ cup California Wine Vinegar
¾ cup California Sherry
¾ cup broth
½ teaspoon powdered ginger
1 clove garlic, crushed
2 tablespoons catsup or chili sauce (optional)
¼ teaspoon paprika
¼ cup soy sauce
1 teaspoon Worcestershire sauce
½ cup oil

Meats

"A roast without a bottle of wine is like a kiss from a man without a mustache."
—La Togna (The Italian
Grandmother of
Angelo Pellegrini)

When even the simplest of everyday meats—hamburger, stews—can become a culinary triumph enriched by California wine, then surely your "company best" deserves equally fine treatment. Marinate, season, baste or sauce that roast or steak with wine and you'll discover a superb new succulence and aroma—natural meat juices blended with the wine and herbs or spices into a symphony of flavor. For utter perfection, serve with a fanfare—California wine at the table.

CORNED BEEF & CABBAGE

Mrs. Robert Mondavi

Wash corned beef well. Place in a large kettle; cover with one-half California white table wine and one-half water. Add whole black peppercorns, bay leaves, and garlic cloves. Simmer several hours, depending on size of corned beef. When almost done, add small white onions, carrots, potatoes and cabbage. During last 15 minutes of cooking, add Corn Meal Dumplings.
CORN MEAL DUMPLINGS: Sift together 1 cup uncooked yellow corn meal, ½ cup sifted flour, 2 teaspoons baking powder and ½ teaspoon salt. Beat 1 egg with ½ cup milk; add dry ingredients. Stir in 1 tablespoon melted butter. Drop by spoonfuls into hot stock. Cover tightly; simmer 15 minutes. Remove at once. Makes 6 large dumplings.

GREAT GRAVY POT ROAST

Mrs. Robert J. Weaver, University of California, Department of Viticulture & Enology, Davis

Gravy is delicious. Don't be afraid to sop the bread!

1 (3 to 4-lb.) piece beef chuck or
*   boneless sirloin*
1 tsp. salt
Dash pepper
1 clove garlic, finely chopped
1 large carrot, cut in thin strips
1 large onion, sliced
¾ cup California red table wine
¾ cup dairy sour cream, at room
*   temperature*
½ cup water
2 to 3 Tbs. flour
1 Tbs. lemon juice

Rub meat with salt and pepper. Brown meat on all sides over high heat. Add garlic, carrot and onion; cook until onion is golden brown, about 3 minutes. Lower heat; stir in wine and sour cream. Cover tightly and cook over very low heat (liquid barely simering) for 2 to 2½ hours, or until meat is tender. Remove meat. Skim off fat from pan juices. Mix water and flour to a smooth paste. Add to pan juices, stirring until thickened. (Add a little more boiling water, if gravy is too thick.) Stir in lemon juice. Serve with fluffy mashed potatoes, tossed green salad. Serves 4 to 6.

BEEF IN SOUR CREAM

Earl Hoff, Mont La Salle Vineyards, Fresno

>4 slices bacon, diced
>2 pounds beef stew meat, cut in
>   1 inch cubes
>4 onions, chopped
>1 clove garlic, minced
>2 tsp. salt
>¼ tsp. pepper
>½ tsp. marjoram
>⅔ cup California white table wine
>1 pint dairy sour cream
>Chopped parsley
>Paprika

Cook bacon in heavy kettle or Dutch oven until browned. Remove bacon; set aside. Add beef to fat remaining in kettle; brown on all sides. Add onion and garlic; cook a few minutes. Stir in bacon, salt, pepper, marjoram and wine. Bring to boiling. Cover tightly and simmer 1½ hours, or until meat is tender. Add a little broth or water if mixture becomes dry. Skim off any excess fat. Slowly stir in sour cream; heat gently. Sprinkle with parsley and paprika. Serve with wild rice, peas with mushrooms and hot rolls. Serves 4 to 6.

LI'L OLE WINEMAKER POT ROAST

Mrs. Vincent L. Vandevert, United Vintners, Inc.
*   San Francisco*

This recipe is a composite of ingredients I've seen used in pot roasts. It seems there is no end to what you can do to a tough piece of meat to make it glamorous and tender if you use a little imagination, a few spices and, of course, California wine.

>¼ cup oil
>1 (4-lb.) rump roast
>1 cup soy sauce
>2½ cups water
>2 sticks cinnamon
>Pinch anise seed
>1 envelope dry onion soup mix
>½ cup sugar
>1 cup California Dry Sherry
>3 Tbs. cornstarch

Slowly heat oil in Dutch oven or large, heavy skillet. Brown meat on all sides. Combine soy sauce, 2 cups water, cinnamon sticks, anise seed, onion soup mix and sugar. Pour over meat. Simmer, covered, 3 or 4 hours, or until meat is tender. Add Sherry during last hour of cooking. When meat is tender, remove to heated platter. Reserve 2½ cups of cooking liquid in the skillet; bring to boiling. In a small bowl, make a smooth mixture of cornstarch and remaining ½ cup water. Stir into boiling liquid; simmer, stirring constantly, until thick and translucent. Serve with poppy seed noodles, carrots, and a tossed salad made with avocado, grapefruit sections and mandarin oranges. Serves 6 to 8.

SHERRIED BEEF DELIGHT

Mrs. Leonard Maullin, Paul Masson Vineyards, Saratoga

This recipe is a variation of an old-time East European one. It is very tasty and hearty, and good for cold weather, making an unusual and well-received "company" dish.

>3 lbs. lean beef, trimmed and
>   cut in 1-inch cubes
>2 tsp. salt
>½ tsp. pepper
>1 Tbs. flour
>2 Tbs. oil (not olive)
>3 Tbs. dry onion soup mix
>1 pound prunes
>2 cups hot water
>3 or 4 large sweet potatoes, pared
>   and quartered
>2 Tbs. lemon juice
>2 Tbs. brown sugar
>½ cup California Sweet Sherry
>¼ cup raisins
>¼ cup shelled almonds

Sprinkle beef with salt, pepper and flour. Brown in heated oil in a Dutch oven or large deep skillet. Add onion soup mix and enough water just to cover meat. Cook over low heat, covered, for 1 hour, adding small amounts of water, if necessary. Stir occasionally. Meanwhile, soak prunes for 1 hour in 2 cups hot water. Drain prunes, reserving liquid. Heat soaking liquid and add to meat; continue cooking 30 minutes longer. Add prunes, sweet potatoes, lemon juice, brown sugar, Sherry, raisins and almonds. Simmer, covered, ½ hour longer, or until meat and potatoes are tender. Serve with hot buttered rice, green salad and assorted cold relishes. For a real company treat, add sliced turkey to the menu. Serves 6 to 8.

VINEYARD ROAST BEEF

Michael Capaldo, Weibel Champagne Vineyards,
*   Mission San Jose*

>5 lbs. beef roast
>2 cups California Burgundy or other
>   red table wine
>1 clove garlic, minced
>1 large onion, quartered
>1 Tbs. oregano
>½ tsp. black pepper
>Salt
>½ cup California Dry Sherry

Prick roast deeply with ice pick on all sides, reaching to the center. Mix marinade in a glass or plastic bowl, preferably a narrow, deep one capable of holding the roast plus about 1½ quarts liquid. Combine remaining ingredients. Mix the potion well. Place roast in wine mixture. Add more Burgundy, if necessary, to bring level to within two inches from top of roast. Cover and refrigerate over night. Turn meat several times. Place roast and marinade in covered baking dish. Bake in moderate oven (350 degrees) for about 2½ hours. Serves 8 to 10.

B.B.Q. STEAK SPECIAL

Michael Capaldo, Weibel Champagne Vineyards,
Mission San Jose

This exotic dish is almost impossible to buy in any restaurant, and it will be worth your trouble, I can assure you.

> *1-inch thick good quality steaks*
> *Onion salt*
> *Garlic salt*
> *Black pepper*
> *Cayenne*
> *Oregano, crushed*
> *California Burgundy or Rosé*

Ignite charcoal in barbecue with grill adjusted close to coals. While coals reach highest heat, prepare meat as follows: Place steak on cutting board and with large fork or ice pick, pierce it with holes throughout. Sprinkle on seasonings and wine evenly. Encourage all seasonings to penetrate the meat by piercing steak again. Turn steak over; repeat piercing and seasoning on other side. When fire is very hot, sprinkle over it 2 handfuls of hickory chips or 2 small pieces of hickory that have been soaked in water for at least one hour. Immediately place steak on grill, as close to fire as possible. Drop barbecue cover down, allowing only small amount of air to enter. Fire should be semi-active. Time cooking carefully. Turn steak after 3½ minutes. Cook second side for 2 minutes for medium rare, 3½ minutes for well done.

DAUBE DE BOEUF SAUVIGNON

Mrs. Thomas Jordan, Jordan Winery, Healdsburg

> *2½ lbs. filet of beef or top sirloin*
> *2 cups Jordan Cabernet Sauvignon*
> *2 Tbs. chopped shallots*
> *3 carrots*
> *3 medium onions*
> *2 cloves of garlic*
> *½ lb. diced ham*
> *1 cup rich beef stock,*
> *(homemade preferred)*
> *1 stalk celery*
> *Parsley sprig*
> *Bay leaf*
> *Pinch of thyme*
> *12 firm, white mushrooms*
> *1 cup green peas,*
> *(fresh preferred)*

Trim any fat from the beef and set aside. Cut the beef into about 12 pieces and season with salt and pepper. Place in a bowl with the Cabernet Sauvignon and the chopped shallots, then marinate for two hours. Drain and reserve the marinade. Dry each piece of meat well and brown a few at a time in 3 tablespoons of the beef fat. In a heavy casserole (with lid), place one half of the browned meat, 2 sliced carrots, 2 chopped medium onions, 2 crushed cloves of garlic, and ¼ pound diced ham. Tie together the celery, parsley, bay leaf, and thyme. Add this faggot to the meat and vegetables and then add on top the remaining browned meat, another sliced carrot, another chopped onion, the remaining ¼ cup diced ham, 2 cups of the reserved marinade and the 1 cup of beef stock. Cover the casserole with a lid that has a small hole in it and seal the edges with a stiff paste made of flour and water. Bring it to a boil and then cook in a slow oven (300 degrees) for 3 to 3½ hours. Remove the cover, skim the fat from the juices and discard the faggot. Quickly sauté the mushrooms in butter or margarine. Add these plus the green peas to the casserole. Re-heat thoroughly to just barely cook the peas and mushrooms. Salt and pepper to taste. Garnish each serving with freshly chopped parsley. Serves 4.

CONTRA COSTA FLANK STEAK

Mrs. Joseph E. Digardi, J.E. Digardi Winery, Martinez

> *1 cup fine dry bread crumbs*
> *⅓ to ½ cup grated Romano or*
> *Parmesan cheese*
> *2 Tbs. finely chopped parsley*
> *¾ tsp. salt*
> *⅛ tsp. pepper*
> *2 eggs, beaten*
> *2 Tbs. milk*
> *1 (1½-lb.) flank steak, tenderized*
> *and cut in 4 pieces*
> *1 clove garlic, finely chopped or*
> *¼ tsp. garlic salt*
> *¼ cup olive oil*
> *½ cup California Sherry or Marsala*

Combine bread crumbs, cheese, parsley, salt and pepper; mix well. Combine beaten eggs with milk. Dip meat in egg mixture, then in bread crumb mixture; repeat until all eggs and crumbs are used. Cook garlic in oil. Brown meat slowly in seasoned oil. When well browned, lower heat and add wine. Cover and simmer 10 minutes. Serves 3 to 4.

GREEN PEPPER STEAK GILROY

Green Pepper Steak Gilroy can be prepared with either a California Sauterne or Burgundy according to Mrs. Louis A. Bonesio, Bonesio Winery, Gilroy, who added wine to the original recipe for a tastier dish. To serve 4 or 5, cut 1 pound round steak into cubes; dredge with seasoned flour. Brown in ¼ cup oil in large skillet. Combine 1 cup diced celery, 2 or 3 green peppers, diced, 1 clove garlic, mashed, with 1 cup water and 2 teaspoons soy sauce. Add to meat and bring to simmer; add 1 cup wine and simmer until tender (about 1½ hours). Serve with boiled rice, tossed salad and a bottle of California Grenache Rosé, Zinfandel or Cabernet.

VALLEY CHATEAUBRIAND
Mrs. Greg Goorigian, Vie-Del Company, Fresno

I needed a sauce for Chateaubriand that would suit my family. I wasn't too successful in all the cook books that I searched. Finally I asked my butcher (who was a Frenchman) if he could help me. After several trials, omission of certain ingredients, replacement with others and addition of California wines, I came up with a sauce that not only my family but my guests have raved about.

> 1 (2-lb.) beef fillet
> Salt and pepper
> ½ lb. fresh mushrooms, sliced
> 3 Tbs. butter
> 1 Tbs. chopped chives
> 1 Tbs. chopped parsley
> 1 bunch shallots or green onions,
>   chopped
> ½ tsp. salt
> Dash of pepper
> 1 tsp. red meat sauce or
>   Worcestershire sauce (optional)
> ½ cup California Sherry
> 2 Tbs. California Brandy

Have butcher prepare beef fillet. Cook whole fillet seasoned with salt and pepper over hot coals (or broil, or sauté in butter). This meat is usually served rare or medium rare. (However, if a guest should prefer his meat well done, slice off one serving from the whole fillet. Cook until almost done, then add the remaining part of the fillet and cook it to desired doneness.) Place meat on a heated platter and slice to desired thickness. Serve immediately with mushroom-wine sauce. Menu might include a rice pilaf; green beans blended with sour cream; tossed green salad garnished with sliced avocado and tomato; fresh sliced peaches marinated in Brandy.
TO PREPARE SAUCE: Sauté mushrooms in butter, add chives, parsley and shallots; simmer 5 minutes. Add salt, pepper and meat sauce; stir well. Add Sherry and simmer to blend flavors. Stir in Brandy and keep warm until ready to serve. If sauce should thicken on standing, thin with a little Sherry. (If a smooth sauce is preferred, cool the cooked sauce, strain and reheat before serving.)

TENDERLOIN STEAKS WITH ROYAL MUSHROOM SAUCE
James Lawrence, Lawrence Winery, San Luis Obispo

> 6 Beef tenderloin steaks,
>   cut 1-½ inches thick
> 2 Tbs. butter
> 1 tsp. salt
> dash of pepper
> ½ cup chopped fresh mushrooms
> ¼ cup sliced green nion with tops
> 4 tsp. cornstarch
> 1 cup Lawrence Winery Red Table Wine
> ½ cup water
> 2 Tbs. snipped parsley

In heavy skillet, cook steaks in butter over medium-high heat to desired doneness, turning occasionally. Allow 9-10 minutes total cooking time for rare; 11-12 minutes for medium. Season with salt and pepper. Transfer steaks to serving platter; keep hot.
In same skillet, cook mushroom and green onions till tender, but not brown. Blend in cornstarch. Stir in Lawrence Winery Red Table Wine, water, parsley, 1 tsp. salt and dash of pepper; cook and stir till thickened and bubbly. Cook and stir one minute more. Serve sauce over steaks. Serves 6.

RED WINE POT ROAST
James E. Woolsey, Roma Wine Company, Fresno

> 3 to 4 lbs. lean beef
> 1½ cups California Claret or other
>   red table wine
> 2 large onions, sliced
> 1 lemon, sliced
> 2 Tbs. sugar
> 1 Tbs. salt
> 1 tsp. ginger (optional)
> 12 whole black peppers
> 4 Tbs. fat
> 2 Tbs. flour

The day before it is to be cooked, buy a solid piece of lean beef-rump, bottom round, shoulder or chuck. Place meat in deep bowl, and add all of the above ingredients except fat and flour. The meat should be more than half covered with Claret. Let stand 18 to 24 hours in a cold place, turning occasionally during the day. Remove meat from liquid, drain thoroughly, then brown all over in 2 tablespoons hot fat in heavy kettle. Strain wine marinade and add to meat. Cover kettle and let simmer 3 to 4 hours, adding a little water if it cooks dry. When tender, lift meat out, pour off and reserve remaining liquid. In kettle melt 2 tablespoons fat, stir in flour and brown lightly. Add the liquid and cook, stirring, until slightly thickened. (If too thick, thin with hot water to desired consistency.) Taste, add more salt if needed, put meat back into gravy and heat 5 minutes longer. Serve sliced on platter, pouring gravy over roast. Serves 6 to 8.

DAVIS TERIYAKI

Mrs. Vernon Singleton, University of California
Department of Viticulture & Enology

The basic recipe, with a few changes of my own, was given to me when we lived in Hawaii. The word teriyaki immediately makes us think of Hawaii and the beaches. One never went on a drive or picnic without smelling that wonderful smell of teriyaki cooking. I soon found myself cooking teriyaki instead of hot dogs.

> *1¼ pounds sirloin tip*
> *½ cup soy sauce*
> *¼ cup California red table wine*
> *1 clove garlic, finely grated*
> *2 Tbs. finely grated fresh ginger*
> *2 Tbs. sugar, or to taste*

Slice meat in ¼-inch thick slices across the grain. Combine remaining ingredients; mix well. Pour over meat; marinate at least 1 hour. To broil, line cookie sheet with foil; grease lightly. Add meat and broil about 5 minutes, or until lightly browned. Turn and brown other side. When using charcoal fire, meat may be basted with remaining marinade during cooking, about 5 minutes per side. Menu might include: steamed rice; asparagus with sour cream horseradish sauce; tossed salad; hot rolls; banana cream pie or fresh fruit. Serves 5 to 6.
Mrs. Singleton suggests, "Fresh ginger is easier to grate if frozen, and keeps several months. I wash the ginger, dry it and put into a plastic bag and freeze. I then grate the amount needed and immediately return the ginger to the freezer."

TERIYAKI STEAK STRIPS

Paul H. Huber, E. & J. Gallo Winery, Fresno

> *2 pounds flank steak or top round*
> *¼ cup chopped green onions*
> *½ tsp. salt*
> *1 cup canned beef consommé,*
> *   undiluted*
> *¼ cup California red table wine*
> *⅓ cup soy sauce*
> *1 clove garlic, mashed*
> *2 Tbs. lime juice*
> *2 Tbs. brown sugar or honey*

Cut meat into 1-inch wide strips diagonally across grain. Layer meat strips, green onions and salt in large bowl. Mix remaining ingredients; pour over meat. Let stand overnight, or at least 5 to 6 hours. Drain meat, reserving marinade. Grill strips quickly over hot coals, brushing with marinade; turn once. (Don't overcook, as meat will become tough.) Serves 4 to 6.

ROLATINI

Mrs. Fred A. Lico, San Martin Vineyards Company,
San Martin

> *12 thin slices sirloin tip roast*
> *¾ cup seasoned bread crumbs*
> *½ lb. mushrooms, sliced*
> *2 onions, chopped*
> *⅓ cup butter*
> *½ cup pine nuts*
> *1 cup California Sauterne*
> *3 Tbs. butter*

Sprinkle each slice of meat with 1 tablespoon bread crumbs. Sauté mushrooms and onions in ⅓ cup butter until tender; add pine nuts. Divide the mixture onto meat slices; roll up and secure with picks. Place rolls in roaster; add wine and the 3 tablespoons butter. Bake in a moderate oven (350 degrees) for 25 minutes. Serve with rice or buttered egg noodles, green beans or spinach, and tossed salad. Serves 6.

ROLLED STEAKS LIVERMORE

Mrs. James Concannon, Concannon Vineyard, Livermore

> *1 medium-sized onion, finely chopped*
> *1 medium-sized green pepper, finely*
> *   chopped*
> *½ cup butter or margarine*
> *1 (6-oz.) can tomato paste*
> *1 cup cracker crumbs*
> *1 tsp. salt*
> *½ tsp. pepper*
> *6 cube steaks (about 1½ pounds)*
> *½ cup California Burgundy*
> *½ cup water*

In an electric skillet set at 250 degrees, sauté onion and green pepper in ¼ cup of the butter until golden brown. Combine half the tomato paste with the cracker crumbs, salt and pepper; add the sautéed mixture. Divide mixture onto steaks. Roll up each steak and fasten with string. Brown steaks on all sides in remaining ¼ cup butter in electric skillet. Blend remaining tomato paste with wine and water. Pour over browned steaks. Cover and simmer 40 to 60 minutes at 150 to 180 degrees. Serve with rice or mashed potatoes (with accompanying meat sauce as gravy), green salad and hot vegetable. Serves 5 to 6.

BEEF BRACIOLA (BEEF ROLLS)

Livia Vercelli, Healdsburg

6 large pieces of Sirloin Tip,
 cut ¼ inch thick
¼ lb. Italian salami
½ cup Parmesan cheese
2 Tbs. butter, softened
1 cup white bread, soaked
 in milk, wrung dry
1 egg, beaten
2 Tbs. minced parsley
6 slices (football size) Mortadella

Sauce

2 Tbs. oil
2 Tbs. butter
1 large clove garlic, chopped fine
1 large onion, chopped fine
2 medium carrots, chopped fine
1 can tomato sauce

Mix salami, cheese, butter, bread, parsley and egg. Taste mixture and season with salt and pepper. Place pieces of Mortadella over the meat, leaving ½ inch margin so as not to squeeze filling out. Spread mixture over Mortadella and roll slice tightly and tie with string.Brown rolls in skillet and then transfer to simmering sauce.

Sauce: Heat oil, butter, add garlic and onion. When limp, add carrot and allow to simmer for a minute before receiving rolls. Simmer rolls for plus or minus one hour (or till tender). Remove rolls and put sauce through a mill or sieve to produce a velvety sauce. Spoon over top of roll when serving.

FRESNO HASH

*Richard Norton, Fresno State University,
 Department of Viticulture & Enology*

⅓ cup butter
2½ cups leftover roast beef, cut in
 ¼-inch cubes
2 cups raw potatoes, cut in ¼-inch
 cubes
1 medium onion, chopped
½ cup thick beef gravy or ½ (10-oz.)
 can of beef with barley soup
⅛ tsp. thyme
Dash garlic powder
½ cup California red table wine
½ tsp. salt
⅛ tsp. freshly ground pepper

Melt butter in heavy skillet. Mix remaining ingredients; turn into skillet. Place skillet in a moderate oven (350 degrees); bake 1½ hours, turning 3 to 4 times with spatula. Serve with crisp green salad. Serves 4 to 5.

BEEF SUKIYAKI

Mrs. Jim Tanaka, Louis M. Martini, St. Helena

The best method of serving this is in bowls. Put some rice into the bowl, and arrange some of the ingredients on it.

2 lbs. lean beef (sirloin tip or fillet)
1 lb. fresh spinach, cut in
 2-inch pieces
6 green onions, cut in 1½-inch
 pieces
2 onions, thinly sliced
2 lbs. shirataki (Japanese
 mushrooms)
1 (4-inch square) piece tofu (soy
 bean curd), cut in small cubes
1 cup sliced fresh mushrooms
1 cup dashi no moto (Japanese
 seasoning)
1½ cups soy sauce
1 cup California Sherry or white
 table wine
2 Tbs. sugar
1 tsp. monosodium glutamate
¼ cup rendered beef fat

Slice beef as thin as possible; arrange on a platter with spinach, both kinds of onions, shirataki, tofu and mushrooms. In a bowl, combine the dashi no moto, soy sauce, wine, sugar and monosodium glutamate. Put platter and bowl on table with an electric skillet. The dish is cooked at the table. Heat fat until smoking. Put in beef slices, turning when cooked on one side. Add both kinds of onions and mushroom slices; stir until cooked. Push to one side of skillet. Add dashi mixture to pan. When hot, add spinach, tofu and shirataki; stir until the spinach is cooked, about 3 minutes. Mix meat, onions and mushrooms into other ingredients and the sukiyaki is ready to eat. Serves 4 to 6.

FLANK STEAK PACIFIC

*Mrs. Alvin Ehrhardt, United Vintners'
 Community Wineries, Lodi*

1 cup soy sauce
1 cup California Sherry
⅓ cup peanut or olive oil
3 small cloves garlic, minced
⅓ cup chopped or grated fresh
 ginger or ½ tsp. ground ginger
2 flank steaks

Blend soy, Sherry, oil, garlic and ginger. Marinate the flank steaks (or any other steak) in the mixture for several hours, turning occasionally. Grill over brisk coals three to four minutes per side for rare, five minutes per side for medium. Serve with tossed salad, steamed rice and berry pie baked with California Port. Serves 3 to 4.

MEAT BALLS IN CAPER SAUCE (KLOPSE)

Mrs. Lewis A. Stern, E. & J. Gallo Winery, Modesto

German food is always substantial; seldom does one encounter a dish that can possibly be described as frivolous. Here is a meat dish that will satisfy those who come to the table seeking hearty fare.

4 Tbs. butter
3 onions, chopped medium fine
6 slices white bread
1 cup light cream
1½ lbs. ground beef
½ lb. ground veal
½ lb. ground pork
4 anchovy fillets
3 eggs
2 tsp. salt
1 tsp. pepper
½ cup California Sauterne or other
    white table wine (chilled)
3 cups boiling water
¼ tsp. marjoram
3 sprigs parsley
3 stalks celery
2 Tbs. flour
2 Tbs. lemon juice
¼ cup capers, drained

Melt 2 tablespoons of the butter in an electric frying pan; add onions. Sauté 10 minutes, stirring occasionally. Soak bread in cream for 10 minutes; press out excess liquid. Grind bread, sauteed onions, ground beef, veal and pork, and anchovies in a food grinder. Add eggs, 1 teaspoon of the salt, ½ teaspoon of the pepper and chilled wine. Mix together; shape into 2-inch balls. In a deep saucepan, combine the boiling water, remaining salt and pepper, marjoram, parsley and celery. Drop meat balls into boiling liquid; boil 20 minutes. Melt the remaining 2 tablespoons butter in a saucepan; mix in flour to form a smooth paste. Remove meat balls from liquid; strain liquid. Add strained liquid to the flour-butter mixture, stirring constantly until it boils; lower heat and cook 5 minutes. Add lemon juice and capers; stir well. Place meat balls on heated platter; pour over sauce. Garnish with sprig or two of parsley. Serve piping hot with plain boiled potatoes, buttered green beans, lettuce and tomato salad with French dressing. Serves 8 to 10.

SKILLET SPECIAL

Skillet Special is described as a popular, economical and speedy entrée of about 4 servings by Mrs. Larry Cahn, Wine Institute, San Francisco. In a large frying pan, sauté 1 pound ground lean beef with 1 large onion, chopped, and ½ pound fresh mushrooms, sliced, in 2 tablespoons butter. Add 1 (10-oz.) package chopped frozen spinach, thawed and well drained. Combine 3 beaten eggs and ¼ cup California red table wine; add to meat mixture. Cook, stirring, until eggs set. Serve immediately with crusty buttered French bread, and a hearty California red table wine.

HAMBURGERS WITH CHILI RABBIT

Justin Meyer, Franciscan Vineyards, Rutherford

1 (1-lb.) can chili con carne with
    beans
1½ cups shredded process American
    cheese
⅓ cup California Burgundy or other
    red table wine
1¼ lbs. ground beef
1 tsp. salt
2 Tbs. grated onion
4 slices toast or toasted buns

In a saucepan, combine chili con carne, cheese and wine. Stir over low heat until cheese melts and mixture is hot. Season beef with salt and onion Shape meat into 4 patties; pan-fry or broil to desired doneness. To serve, place meat patties on toast or buns; cover with hot chili mixture. Serve immediately with a green salad. Serves 3 to 4.

BUFFET MEAT BALLS

Mrs. Walter E. Staley, Western Grape Products, Kingsburg

3 lbs. ground lean beef
3 cups dried bread crumbs
3 small onions, minced
1 Tbs. cornstarch
3 eggs, beaten
2 cups evaporated milk
4 cups California Burgundy or Claret
3 tsp. salt
⅛ tsp. allspice
½ cup fat or oil
1 cup sifted flour
1 quart water
5 beef bouillon cubes
1 tsp. pepper
1 Tbs. sugar
About ¼ cup soy sauce

(If desired, this dish may be made the day before.) Combine meat, crumbs, onion, corstarch, beaten eggs, evaporated milk, 1 cup of the wine, 2 teaspoons salt and allspice. Shape into small balls with floured hands. Heat fat in a large heavy skillet. Brown balls on all sides in hot fat; remove balls to a Dutch oven. Stir flour into fat remaining in skillet; add water, remaining 3 cups of wine, bouillon cubes, remaining 1 teaspoon salt, pepper, sugar and enough soy to lightly brown. Cook, stirring, until smooth. Pour sauce over meat balls; simmer, covered, for 30 minutes. (If made a day ahead, cool and then refrigerate. Reheat at serving time.) An elegant buffet service might include the meat balls kept warm in chafing dish, accompanied by fluffy rice, green beans topped with crisp onion rings, crisp bread sticks and a fresh fruit salad. Makes about 45 meat balls, 2-inch size.

DELANO STROGANOFF

Mrs. Chet Steinhauer, Cresta Blanca Wine Company,
Delano

2 Tbs. butter
1 lb. ground beef
1 Tbs. instant minced onion
1 clove garlic, minced
½ lb. mushrooms, sliced
¼ cup California red table wine
Juice of 1 lemon
2 beef bouillon cubes
1 cup water
2 cups uncooked wide noodles
Salt and pepper
½ cup dairy sour cream
Paprika
Chopped parsley

Melt butter in large heavy skillet or Dutch oven; add beef, onion, garlic and mushrooms. Cook until meat loses its red color, stirring with fork to break up meat. Add wine, lemon juice, bouillon cubes and water. Simmer, uncovered, 10 minutes. Add noodles; cover and simmer about 15 minutes, or until noodles are tender, adding more water if necessary. Season with salt and pepper. Stir in sour cream; heat genlty. Sprinkle with paprika and parsley. Serves 3 to 4.

QUICK SPICY CASSEROLE

Richard Norton, Fresno State University,
Department of Viticulture & Enology

1 cup quick-cooking rice
1 lb. lean ground beef
2 Tbs. margarine
¾ cup chopped onion
⅛ tsp. each: garlic powder, thyme
    and sage
1 (10¾-oz.) can condensed Scotch
    broth soup
1 (4-oz.) can small mushroom caps,
    undrained
¾ cup California Burgundy
1 cup grated sharp Cheddar cheese
¼ cup sliced stuffed olives

Cook rice following package directions. Brown meat in heated margarine. Add onion and sauté until tender. Add cooked rice and all remaining ingredients except cheese and olives. Simmer 5 minutes. Turn into 1½-quart casserole. Cover and bake in moderate oven (350 degrees) for 30 minutes. Remove from oven; sprinkle with cheese and sliced olives. Return to oven until cheese begins to melt. Serves 6 to 8.

WILD RICE CHUCKBALLS

Mrs. Russel Overby, United Vintners, Inc., San Francisco

This is the kind of dinner to throw together when your favorite out-of-towners drop in unexpectedly, and the butcher had a sale on ground beef the day before.

2 cups boiling water
½ cup wild rice, washed thoroughly
½ cup brown rice
1½ tsp. salt
1 lb. ground chuck
1 egg, unbeaten
½ cup wheat germ
1 medium onion, finely chopped
1½ cups dairy sour cream
1 clove garlic, finely chopped
¼ tsp. monosodium glutamate
⅛ tsp. seasoned pepper
3 dashes Tabasco sauce
¼ cup California Sweet Sherry
3 Tbs. oil
6 large mushrooms, sliced
¼ green pepper, chopped
1 tsp. fresh oregano, or
    1½ tsp. dried oregano
Freshly ground nutmeg (optional)

Combine boiling water, wild rice, brown rice and 1 teaspoon salt in a heavy covered pot. Cover and simmer slowly 40 minutes. Do not uncover until all water has evaporated. Meanwhile, combine chuck, egg, wheat germ, onion, ½ cup sour cream, garlic, remaining ½ teaspoon salt, monosodium glutamate, seasoned pepper, Tabasco and Sherry. Mix thoroughly. Shape into 8 balls. Roll in a little extra wheat germ (about 3 to 4 tablespoons). Heat oil in large heavy skillet. Cook chuckballs until well browned; push to one side. Add mushrooms, green pepper and oregano; cook gently until mushrooms are limp. Add vegetables to rice; mix well. Turn off heat; drain off oil from skillet. Add remaining 1 cup sour cream to pan, mixing gently with chuckballs. Sprinkle with nutmeg, if desired. Spoon immediately over rice. Serve with sourdough French bread and avocado salad (made with oil and California wine vinegar dressing). Serves 3 to 4.

BEEF KIEV

Beef Kiev is a back-yard barbecue hamburger version of the classic "Chicken Kiev". Mrs. Chet Steinhauer, Cresta Blanca Wine Company, Delano, suggests that these might be broiled if desired. For filling, blend ¼ cup butter with 1 tablespoon capers, drained. Form into 4 mounds; turn out on waxed paper or foil. Freeze until firm. Season 1½ pounds ground beef adding ½ cup California Burgundy; divide into 4 portions. Make a depression in center of each burger, pressing down to just ½ inch from the bottom. Place a mound of frozen caper-butter in each depression; mold meat mixture over to cover butter completely. Brush burgers with Worcestershire sauce and barbecue over medium-hot coals about 10 minutes. Turn carefully (so butter doesn't leak out) and cook about ten minutes longer.

PORK CHOPS IN WINEY PLUM SAUCE

Mrs. Nina Concannon Radisch, Concannon Vineyard
* Livermore*

4 thick loin pork chops
1 tsp. salt
⅛ tsp. pepper
⅛ tsp. sage
2 tsp. flour
1 (5-oz.) jar strained plums for babies
½ cup California Port
1 tsp. grated lemon peel
½ tsp. cinnamon
¼ tsp. ground cloves

Trim fat from chops. Season chops with salt, pepper and sage; flour lightly. Render trimmed fat in heavy skillet and brown chops on both sides. Remove chops to a shallow buttered dish. Mix remaining ingredients; pour over chops. Bake in a moderately-slow oven (325 degrees) for 50 minutes, or until tender, adding more wine if necessary. Serve with rice and green salad. Serves 3 to 4.

GOURMET PORK CHOPS

Mrs. C. Dudley Warner, Jr., Cresta Blanca
* Wine Company, Livermore*

This is a delightful buffet dish and is much improved if prepared the day before, which allows the flavors to "mellow".

8 center-cup pork chops (with all
    fat removed)
Butter or shortening
1 (2¼-oz.) can button mushrooms
1 envelope dry onion soup mix
1 cup California white table wine
1 cup chicken broth
2 tsp. bottled garlic spread
½ pint dairy sour cream
Chopped parsley

Brown chops in very small amount of butter or shortening; remove from pan. Add mushrooms to pan; brown lightly. Add dry soup mix, wine, broth and garlic spread; stir until well blended. Return chops to pan. Cover and simmer slowly about 45 minutes, or until chops are tender. Add sour cream; heat gently (do not boil). Garnish with chopped parsley; serve. Serves 6 to 8.

LEG OF PORK

Mrs. Robert Mondavi, Robert Mondavi Winery, Oakville

1 leg of fresh pork (about 5 lbs.)
1 large bunch green finocchio (fennel)
    leaves and stems, chopped
2 or 3 cloves garlic, minced
Salt and pepper
1 cup California white table wine

Make small slits in pork and insert mixture of finocchio and garlic. Season with salt and pepper. Roast in slow oven (325 degrees) basting frequently with wine. Allow about 55 minutes per pound, or roast pork to 185 degrees on meat thermometer inserted in thickest part of roast, but not touching bone. Serves 6 to 8.

APPLE-STUFFED CROWN OF PORK

Mrs. Bernard C. Hoag, Guild Wine Co., Lodi

1 onion, chopped
¼ cup diced celery
2 cups diced tart apples
2 Tbs. butter or margarine
¼ cup light molasses
¼ cup California Sherry, heated
1 tsp. grated lemon rind
Juice of ½ lemon
1 tsp. salt
½ tsp. sage
4 cups bread cubes, toasted
1 (7-lb.) crown pork roast

Cook onion, celery and apple in butter for 5 minutes, until soft but not browned. Remove from heat; add all remaining ingredients except pork roast. Fill roast lightly with stuffing, heaping in center. Roast, uncovered, in moderate oven (325 degrees) about 4 hours. (To be fancy, fasten paper frills to the roast's rib tips.) Serves 6 to 8.

BEANS AND FRANKFURTERS
Mrs. Michael J. Bo, Almaden Vineyards, Los Gatos

It is only a 40-minutes drive to the ocean from our home in Gilroy. When we spend the day there it involves two meals—a mid-day barbecue and supper before we return. This casserole dish, made at home, heats well on a barbecue pit.

> 1 (10-oz.) package frozen lima beans
> 1 (1-lb.) can pork and beans
> 1 (1-lb.) can red kidney beans,
>   drained
> ½ cup catsup
> ½ cup California Dry Sherry
> 1 tsp. dry mustard
> ½ tsp. Worcestershire sauce
> ½ envelope dry onion soup mix
>   (the 1¾-oz. size)
> 1 lb. frankfurters, cut in 1-inch pieces

Cook lima beans following package directions. Drain and mix with remaining ingredients. Bake in greased 1½ or 2-quart casserole in moderate oven (350 degrees) for 40 to 50 minutes. Serve with summer picnic salad (see below), celery and carrot stick with pickles, French rolls, and for dessert-fresh fruit. Serves 6 to 8.

PORK SCALLOPINI
Mrs. Robert H. Meyer, Allied Grape Growers, Asti

> 1½ lbs. pork tenderloin, sliced about
>   1 inch thick
> ½ cup sifted flour
> 2 Tbs. butter
> 2 Tbs. oil
> ½ cup California Dry Sherry
> ¼ cup water
> ½ cup chopped onion
> 1 clove garlic, minced or pressed
> 1 tsp. salt
> ¼ tsp. pepper
> ¼ tsp. each: thyme, rosemary,
>   and oregano
> 2 cups fresh mushrooms, sliced

Dredge meat in flour. In electric frying pan set at 420 degrees, brown meat quickly in butter and oil. Stir in Sherry and water. Add onion, garlic, salt, pepper and herbs. Cover and cook over low heat (225 degrees) for 30 minutes, adding a little more water, if needed. Add mushrooms; cook, covered, 15 minutes longer. Since this entrée is well-seasoned, I prefer to serve baked potatoes, a mild vegetable and a citrus fruit and avocado salad with it. Serves 3 to 4.

PORK SAN JOAQUIN
Mrs. John George Franzia, Sr., Franzia Brothers Winery, Ripon

This is my husband's original recipe. His first hobby is raising vegetables and second, cooking.

> 2 lbs. pork steak, cut into 1-inch
>   pieces
> ½ tsp. allspice
> ½ tsp. garlic salt
> ½ tsp. seasoned salt
> ¼ tsp. seasoned pepper
> 3 stalks celery, cut crosswise into
>   ¼ inch pieces
> ½ cup California Sauterne, Chablis or
>   other white table wine

Fry pork slowly (without added fat or oil) in heavy skillet until golden brown. Add all remaining ingredients. Cook quickly about 5 minutes so that celery remains crisp. Serve warm with candied yams, pickled beets, green salad and crusty French bread for a colorful as well as tasty meal. Serves 5 to 6.

APRICOT HAM STEAK

Apricot ham steak the California way combines a cup of California Sauterne or other white table wine with a cup of apricot jam. Trim rind from a 1-inch center slice of uncooked ham, slashing fat around edge to prevent curling. Place ham in shallow baking pan; pour wine-jam mixture over it. Bake in moderate oven (350 degrees) about one hour, basting often.

SHERRY PORK CHOPS AND APPLES
Mrs. James A. Cook, University of California, Department of Viticulture & Enology, Davis

> 6 pork chops
> 3 medium-large unpared apples,
>   cored and sliced
> ¼ cup brown sugar (packed)
> ½ tsp. cinnamon
> 2 Tbs. butter
> Salt and pepper
> ½ cup California Sherry

Preheat oven to 350 degrees. In heavy skillet, brown chops on both sides in a little hot fat. Arrange apple slices in greased baking dish (9x13 inches). Sprinkle with brown sugar and cinnamon; dot with butter. Top with browned pork chops; sprinkle with salt and pepper. Pour over Sherry. Cover and bake in preheated oven (350 degrees) for 1½ hours, or until meat is tender. With this dish-baked rice, broccoli or peas, hot rolls and a green salad. Serves 6.

BURGUNDY GRILLED SPARERIBS

Mrs. Theodore Cadlolo, Cadlolo Winery, Escalon

> *1 cup California Burgundy*
> *½ cup olive oil*
> *1 small onion, chopped*
> *1 tsp. salt*
> *⅛ tsp. pepper*
> *2 tsp. oregano*
> *1 bay leaf, crushed*
> *Garlic salt*
> *5 to 6 lbs. spareribs*

Combine all ingredients except spareribs. Place spareribs in shallow dish. Pour marinade over meat; cover and refrigerate at least 2 hours. When ready to grill, remove meat from marinade. Place ribs on grill over hot coals. Cook, turning constantly, until brown; salt and pepper lightly. Continue cooking, turning constantly, until meat is done. Serves 5 to 6.

OVEN BARBECUED SPARERIBS

Mrs. Harold Roush, Lodi

> *1 Tbs. chili powder*
> *½ tsp. salt*
> *1 Tbs. celery seed*
> *¼ cup brown sugar, firmly packed*
> *1 tsp. paprika*
> *3 to 4 lbs. spareribs*
> *½ cup California red table wine*
> *1 (10-oz.) can condensed tomato soup*

Combine chili powder, salt, celery seed, brown sugar and paprika; rub over spareribs. Broil 5 minutes on each side, about 6 inches from heat. Place bone side down in roasting pan. Combine wine and undiluted soup; brush spareribs with part of sauce. Bake in a moderate oven (350 degrees) for 1½ hours. Baste and turn ribs every 30 minutes. Reduce heat to 325 degrees during last half hour of cooking. Menu might include baked potato; sweet and sour cabbage; molded fruit salad; hot biscuits. Serves 4 to 6.

LA CHOUCROUTE GARNIE

Mrs. Harold Berg, University of California, Davis

Ask enologist Lewis Stern of E. & J. Gallo Winery for his reaction to this recipe. This is a wonderful winter-time dish.

> *24 whole cloves*
> *2 small onions*
> *2 carrots, pared and cut in half*
> *   lengthwise*
> *1 (2-inch thick) piece bacon (about*
> *   ¾ lb.), cut in half and scored*
> *3 lbs. sauerkraut, washed and*
> *   squeezed dry*
> *1 lb. smoked pork (butt, shoulder,*
> *   loin, and/or spareribs)*
> *1 (1 to 1¼-lb.) slice ham*
> *¾ lb. sausages (Alsatian or*
> *   German), not spicy hot ones*
> *6 juniper berries (optional)*
> *8 peppercorns*
> *1 cup consommé*
> *¾ cup California white table wine*
> *1 jigger (1½-oz.) gin (2 jiggers if*
> *   juniper berries are not used)*
> *¾ lb. knackwurst*

Stick 12 cloves into each onion. Place onions, carrots and bacon in the bottom of a large kettle. Add sauerkraut, smoked pork, ham and sausages in layers. Sprinkle with juniper berries, if desired, and peppercorns. Pour over consommé, wine and gin. Cover tightly. Place in a slow oven or simmer very slowly on top of stove (over asbestos) for no less than 3 hours and not more than 5 hours. (This must be very slow, so you can just hear a whisper of simmering when you bend close.) Do not stir. One-half hour before serving, bury the knackwurst in the top of the kettle. To serve, make a mound of the sauerkraut in the center of a large, handsome serving dish. Arrange the meat and sausage around it. To serve with this hearty dish: a really flavorful mustard, tossed green salad and sourdough French bread to mop up the broth. Serves 6 to 8.

PORK-AND-SAUERKRAUT CASSEROLE

To prepare this flavorful country dish serving 6 to 8—line the bottom of a large casserole with 8 thick slices of bacon. Add 2 quarts sauerkraut; arrange 6 to 8 pork chops on top. Add either small white onions or large onions cut into sections. If desired, add some large Italian sausages. Cover with additional bacon slices. Add enough California white table wine to cover. Cover casserole and bake in slow oven (300 degrees) for 1¾ to 2 hours. (Frankfurters may be added the last 15 minutes of cooking, if desired.

SMOKED BRATWURST IN SAUTERNE

Mrs. Herman Ehlers, East-Side Winery, Lodi

> *4 links of bratwurst sausage*
> *½ cup water*
> *½ cup California Sweet Sauterne or*
>   *other white table wine*
> *¼ cup oil*

Preheat electric frying pan to 420 degrees. Add sausages; pour over water, wine and oil. Simmer until liquid has boiled down. Lower heat; brown sausages as desired. Good with macaroni and cheese, tossed salad, rolls and any dessert. Serves 4 to 6.

TROPICAL HAM

Tropical ham looks like a luau, is quick to fix. Brown a thick slice of raw ham in a little heated fat cut from edge of slice. Drain a No. 303 can of cling peach halves; peel and quarter 1 banana. Place ham in shallow casserole; top with fruit. Sprinkle with ¼ cup brown sugar, ¼ cup shredded coconut, nutmeg; dot with 1 Tbs. butter. Pour over ⅓ cup California Sherry and 2 Tbs. wine vinegar. Bake in a moderately hot (375 degrees) oven for about 20 minutes. Serves 4 to 5.

SUNDAY MORNING SAUSAGE

David E. Gallo, E. & J. Gallo Winery, Modesto

This recipe is a Gallo family favorite for Sunday morning brunch.

> *4 lbs. pork loin (boned, medium fat)*
> *1 Tbs. fennel seed*
> *1 tsp. crushed dry hot red chili pepper*
> *Salt and pepper*
> *¼ cup California Sauterne*

Coarsely grind pork loin. Season with fennel, chili pepper and liberal amounts salt and pepper. Add wine; mix thoroughly. Cover and let stand at room temperature 1 hour. Pack in foil, rolled tightly like a casing. Store in refrigerator 12 hours. When ready to cook, form sausage into patties and fry over low heat. Baste with Sauterne during last 5 minutes of cooking. Serve piping hot.

SPICY PEACH HAM RING

Harry Baccigaluppi, Calgrape Wineries, Inc., Delano

> *1 can (1 lb. 13-oz.) cling peach slices*
> *4 cups ground cooked ham*
> *1 cup cracker crumbs*
> *½ cup chopped onion*
> *2 eggs, lightly beaten*
> *¾ cup white table wine*
> *½ cup water*
> *1¼ tsp. salt*
> *1 tsp. dry mustard*
> *¼ tsp. crushed tarragon*
> *⅛ tsp. pepper*
> *1 Tbs. cornstarch*
> *Dash ground cloves*
> *1 Tbs. lemon juice*

Drain peaches, saving 1¼ cups syrup. Combine ½ cup peach syrup in bowl with ham, crumbs, onion, eggs, ½ cup wine, water, 1 teaspoon salt, ½ teaspoon mustard, tarragon and pepper; toss lightly. Press into greased 5 or 6 cup ring mold; unmold into shallow baking pan. Bake in 350 degree (moderate) oven 45 to 50 minutes until well browned. When ring is almost done, combine in saucepan cornstarch, cloves and remaining mustard and salt; blend in remaining peach syrup and wine. Cook, stirring constantly, until thickened and clear. Stir in peach slices and lemon juice. Place ham ring on serving platter; spoon sauce over ring. Serve at once. Serves 5 to 6.

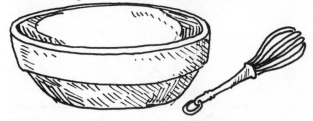

SHERRIED TROPICAL HAM

Brother Timothy, The Christian Brothers, Napa

> *1 (3-to-4-lb.) whole canned ham*
> *½ cup California Cream Sherry*
> *½ cup Tropical Sherry Glazer*
>   *(see below)*

Place ham in shallow, uncovered baking pan. Score ham with sharp knife. Pour Sherry over ham. Bake in moderately-slow oven (325 degrees) for 1 hour. Baste every 15 minutes with additional Sherry. Spread Tropical Sherry Glaze over top of ham; continue baking for 20 minutes longer.
TROPICAL SHERRY GLAZE: In a saucepan, combine 1 (9-oz.) can crushed pineapple (undrained), ½ cup orange marmalade, 1 cup California Cream Sherry, 2 tablespoons cornstarch, ⅛ teaspoon mace and ¼ teaspoon tumeric. Heat, stirring constantly, until sauce thickens and clears. Use ½ cup to glaze ham; serve remaining sauce, hot or cold, as an accompaniment to the ham. Serves 6 to 8.

NAPA MACARONI-HAM BAKE

Justin Meyer, Franciscan Vineyards, Rutherford

> 2 cups uncooked elbow macaroni
> 4 cups boiling water
> 1 Tbs. salt
> 2 Tbs. minced onion
> ½ cup butter or margarine
> ¼ cup flour
> 1 cup milk
> 1 cup chicken stock
> ½ cup California Sauterne or other
>   white table wine
> ½ lb. American cheese, grated
> Dash of nutmeg
> Salt and pepper
> 1 (12-oz.) can chopped ham
> 2 Tbs. chopped parsley
> Buttered fine bread crumbs
> Paprika

Cook macaroni in boiling salted water until tender, about 7 minutes; drain. Saute onion in butter for 5 minutes. Blend in flour. Add milk and stock; cook, stirring, until mixture boils and thickens. Add wine and cheese; stir over low heat until cheese melts. Season with nutmeg, salt and pepper. Combine sauce, cooked macaroni, ham (cut into ½-inch chunks) and parsley. Pour into greased casserole. Sprinkle with crumbs and paprika. Bake in a moderate oven (350 degrees) for 1 hour. Remove from oven; let stand 5 to 10 minutes before serving. Serves 4 to 6.

CRANBERRY-ROSÉ HAM GLAZE

Cranberry-Rosé ham glaze tops a festive dish with a happy, zesty glow. Mrs. Robert Mondavi scores a ham, bakes as usual, basting frequently with a mixture of 1 can jellied cranberry sauce heated with 2 cups California Rosé.

PICCATA DI VITELLO

Dante Bagnani, Geyser Peak Winery, Geyserville

> 1½ lbs. veal round, sliced
>   ⅛ inch thick, and pounded
> ½ cup flour
> 6 Tbs. butter or margarine
> ½ cup Johannisberg Riesling
> Juice of ½ lemon

Flour the thin meat sliced by pressing them into the flour and patting them gently. Melt butter over medium heat and add veal. Turn them the minute the edges begin to whiten. When both sides have been cooked, pour in wine, add juice of lemon and stir gently. Taste broth. If needed, add salt or lemon juice. Serve with a sprinkling of fresh chopped parsley if a third flavor interest is desired.

VEAL PICCANTE

Bruno C. Solari, Italian Swiss Colony, Asti

> 12 very thin fillets of veal
> Flour
> ¼ cup butter
> ¼ cup olive oil
> ½ cup California Dry Vermouth or
>   white table wine such as Chablis
> Rind of 1 small lemon, finely
>   chopped
> 3 Tbs. chopped parsley
> 1 Tbs. chopped fresh oregano
> 1 Tbs. chopped fresh thyme or
>   marjoram
> Salt and pepper
> Lemon slices

Coat veal fillets with flour. Heat butter and oil in heavy frying pan; sauté fillets until golden brown, about 4 or 5 minutes. Remove and keep warm. Add wine to pan drippings and bring to simmering. Return meat to pan. Add lemon rind, herbs, salt and pepper; simmer 3 or 4 minutes. Serve with slices of lemon. Menu might include vichysoisse; rice cooked in chicken broth; fresh peas; green salad with oil and vinegar dressing; fresh peaches poached in California Port on vanilla ice cream. Serves 3 to 4.

WINE WONDERLAND HAM

Doris Paulsen, Wine Institute, San Francisco

> 1 (1-inch thick) center-cut slice
>   of ham
> ½ cup peanut butter (either chunky
>   or cream-style)
> ¼ cup orange marmalade
> ½ cup California red table wine

Place ham in shallow baking pan. Spread peanut butter over ham; then spread with orange marmalade. Pour in wine. Bake in moderate oven (350 degrees) for one hour. Serves 3 to 4.

VEAL SCALLOPS, NIÇOISE

Mrs. Bernard C. Hoag, Guild Wine Co., Lodi

> 3 cloves garlic
> 1/3 cup olive oil
> 8 thin veal scallops (about 1½ lbs.)
> Flour
> Salt
> Freshly ground pepper
> ½ cup California white table wine
> 1 small can anchovy fillets
> ¼ cup chopped parsley

Peel garlic; chop very fine. Sauté garlic in olive oil until brown and crackly. Discard garlic. Dust veal with flour; sauté in garlic-flavored oil until nicely browned on both sides. Season with salt and pepper; add wine. Continue cooking until the wine is reduced a little and the meat is tender. Turn scallops to bathe thoroughly. Coarsely chop anchovy fillets; add to pan along with parsley. Heat through, turning scallops. Serves 4 to 5.

MOUNTAIN VIEW VEAL WITH EGGPLANT

Mrs. A. Jensen, Gemello Winery, Mountain View

My husband and I are very fond of veal, and came up with this recipe trying veal combined with other foods.

> 6 boned veal cutlets (about 2 lbs.)
> 1/3 cup flour
> 1 tsp. salt
> 1/8 tsp. pepper
> 3 Tbs. oil
> 1 large eggplant
> 2 eggs, slightly beaten
> Seasoned bread crumbs
> 6 slices Mozzarella or Monterey Jack
>   cheese
> 1 cup dairy sour cream
> 2 (8-oz.) cans tomato sauce
> ½ cup California Dry Sherry, Sauterne,
>   or other white table wine
> Slivered almonds

Dip veal in flour seasoned with salt and pepper; brown in heated oil. Cut eggplant crosswise in 1-inch slices; parboil about 5 to 7 minutes in boiling, salted water. Dip parboiled eggplant slices in slightly beaten egg, then coat with seasoned bread crumbs; brown in oil. Place slices of eggplant in a 9x12-inch baking pan. On each slice of eggplant, place a slice of cheese, then a browned veal cutlet. Combine sour cream, tomato sauce and wine; mix well. Pour over meat. Bake in a moderate oven (350 degrees) for 30 minutes, or until tender. Just before serving, sprinkle with slivered almonds. Serve with tossed green salad, slivered green beans, French bread. Serves 6 to 8.

LODI VEAL SAUTÉ

Reginald Gianelli, East-Side Winery, Lodi

This is a recipe that my father brought from his birthplace in the province of Genoa, Italy. The story told was that it was best prepared by the *male* members of the family. (Males, have friend wife handy to do shopping, washing, etc., but don't allow any women to cook this sauté.)

> 2 large white or yellow onions, finely
>   chopped
> 1 cup chopped parsley
> 1 clove garlic, peeled and crushed
> 2 (2-inch) sprigs rosemary or
>   ¼ tsp. dried rosemary
> 2 (3 to 4-inch) sprigs oregano or
>   ¼ tsp. dried oregano
> ¼ cup olive oil
> 2 lbs. top round veal steak, sliced
>   ½ x ½ x 1½-inch strips
> 1½ tsp. salt
> 1/8 tsp. ground black pepper
> 1 (5¾-oz.) can green olives, drained
> 1 (4-oz.) can button mushrooms,
>   drained
> 1 cup California white table wine
> 1/8 tsp. allspice
> 1 lemon, sliced

Sauté onions, parsley, garlic, rosemary and oregano in heated oil until slightly cooked but not browned. Add veal strips, salt and pepper. Sauté slightly, about 5 minutes, mixing well. Add olives, mushrooms, wine and allspice. Cover and simmer until veal is tender, 5 to 10 minutes. Top with lemon slices. Cover and simmer 5 minutes longer. Discard lemon slices and serve. With this I enjoy Italian noodles cooked "al dente," steamed zucchini, tossed salad, with chicory. Dessert might include fruit and cheese served with California Tawny Port. Serves 4 to 6.

VEAL CHOPS PARMESAN

Mrs. George Al Berry, Roma Wine Company, Fresno

> 4 loin veal chops with kidney attached
> Juice of 1 fresh lime
> Salt and pepper
> 4 Tbs. butter
> 2 Tbs. flour
> 6 Tbs. grated Parmesan
>   cheese
> ¾ cup California white table wine

Brush veal chops and kidney with fresh lime juice; sprinkle with salt and pepper. Dip chops in 2 tablespoons melted butter. Coat with flour; cover both sides liberally with grated Parmesan cheese. Let chops stand in refrigerator about 1 hour. Sauté in remaining 2 tablespoons butter until browned on both sides. Pour wine around chops. Cover and simmer slowly for 30 to 40 minutes. Serve with buttered noodles, green vegetable in season and tossed salad. Serves 2.

HERB VEAL CHOPS ST. HELENA

*Mrs. Ivan Schoch, St. Helena Cooperative Winery,
St. Helena*

>6 large veal chops, cut 1-inch thick
>2 Tbs. butter
>1 Tbs. oil
>Salt and pepper
>3 Tbs. minced shallots or
>   green onion
>½ cup California Dry Vermouth or
>   white table wine
>1 tsp. mixed basil and thyme
>   or tarragon
>½ cup beef stock or cream

Dry chops on paper towels. Heat butter and oil in skillet until butter has almost stopped foaming. Brown chops for 3 to 4 minutes on a side. Season with salt and pepper. Arrange chops in a casserole, overlapping them slightly. Remove all but 3 tablespoons of fat from skillet. (If fat has burned, discard and add additional butter.) Add shallots; cook slowly for 1 minute. Add wine and herbs; simmer a few minutes, scraping up browned bits from pan. Pour over chops. Cover casserole; place below oven center. Bake in moderately-slow oven (325 degrees) for 30 to 35 minutes, basting and turning chops 2 or 3 times. Remove to hot platter. Skim off and discard any fat. Add stock or cream to pan juices; boil rapidly a few minutes until thickened slightly. Pour over chops. Serve with sautéed potatoes, broiled tomatoes and green beans. Serves 4 to 6.

VEAL ROAST WITH WINE SAUCE

Mrs. Tulio D'Agostini, D'Agostini Winery, Plymouth

This roast makes a particularly delicious gravy.

>3 Tbs. olive oil
>1 (6-lb.) rump roast of veal
>6 medium onions, sliced very thin
>3 Tbs. flour
>1 cup boiling water
>3 strips suet
>1 cup California white table wine
>¼ tsp. rosemary
>1½ tsp. salt
>Pepper

Heat olive oil in roasting pan; brown roast on all sides. Remove roast. In same pan, add onions and brown lightly. Make paste of flour and a little cold water; add to roasting pan and brown. Add boiling water, stirring constantly to make a smooth sauce. Place strips of suet over roast; place in roasting pan along with wine and seasonings. Cover tightly and cook in moderate oven (350 degrees) about 2½ hours. Add more wine as needed. Stir frequently to prevent sticking. Slice roast and serve with the pan sauce. Foil-wrapped baked potatoes are a grand accompaniment. Serves 6 to 10.

BRAISED VEAL MODESTO

Mrs. Richard Peterson, E. & J. Gallo Winery, Modesto

>2½ lbs. veal, cut into 1½-inch cubes
>1½ tsp. salt
>½ cup sifted flour
>3 Tbs. bacon fat or butter
>12 tiny white onions
>12 small carrots
>1 shallot or 3 green onions
>1 Tbs. flour
>½ cup California red table wine
>1 cup chicken broth
>1 small stalk celery
>Sprig of parsley
>Pinch of thyme

Dredge veal in mixture of salt and ½ cup flour. Brown in bacon fat or butter. Remove veal to 2-quart casserole. Arrange onions and carrots around edge. Combine remaining ingredients in blender; blend until shallot and celery are finely chopped. Pour over meat and vegetables in casserole. Bake in moderately-slow oven (325 degrees) for 1½ hours, or until veal is very tender. Serves 6 to 8.

VELVETY VEAL

Mrs. J. F. M. Taylor, Mayacamas Vineyards, Napa

>4 medium-sized artichokes
>10 to 12 medium-sized mushrooms
>1 egg
>½ pint dairy sour cream
>1 tsp. savory salt
>1 lb. veal steak, thinly sliced
>   and pounded
>10 to 12 crisp salty crackers, rolled
>   to crumbs
>¼ cup butter
>½ tsp. salt
>1 cup California white table wine
>1 Tbs. fresh tarragon, or
>   ½ tsp. dried tarragon

Cook artichokes, removing leaves. (Put them in refrigerator and serve at a later meal with melted butter or mayonnaise.) Discard chokes; slice artichoke hearts. Slice mushrooms and add to artichokes; refrigerate until ready to use. Beat together egg, sour cream and savory salt. Dip each piece of veal (on one side only) first in cracker crumbs, then in egg-cream mixture; stack like pancakes. Cover with a bowl; refrigerate. When ready to cook, heat large skillet over medium heat (or heat electric frying pan to 300 degrees); melt butter. Cook meat quickly (no more than 3 or 4 minutes a side), sprinkling each side with salt. Place on hot platter and keep warm in oven. Sauté artichoke and mushroom slices in same pan, adding a little more butter, if necessary; add a little wine. When vegetables are nicely browned, spoon over meat. Pour remaining wine in skillet. Add tarragon. Bring to rapid boil, scraping all the brown crispy bits loose from bottom of skillet. Pour over meat. Serves 3 to 4.

BREAST OF VEAL GENOVESE

Mrs. Joe Boragno, Sanger Winery Association, Sanger

The flavor of this dish improves a great deal if prepared and refrigerated for a day or two, then reheated just before serving. A little more wine may be added when reheating, if the meat seems dry.

> 4½ lbs. breast of veal, cut in
>   serving-size pieces
> ⅓ cup olive oil
> 2 Tbs. minced parsley
> 5 cloves garlic, minced
> 1 Tbs. minced onion
> 1 Tbs. minced celery
> ¼ tsp. finely chopped fresh
>   rosemary
> 3 or 4 bay leaves
> ⅔ cup California Sauterne or other
>   white table wine
> ½ cup California Sherry
> 1 tsp. salt
> 1 (4-oz.) can sliced mushrooms,
>   drained
> 1 Tbs. butter
> 1 (9-oz.) can pitted green-ripe
>   olives, drained

In large heavy skillet or Dutch oven, lightly brown meat in olive oil. Combine parsley, garlic, onion, celery and rosemary; sprinkle over meat. Add bay leaves and wines. Cover and bring to boiling; reduce heat and simmer gently for about 1 hour. Add salt and mushrooms which have been sautéed in butter until golden brown. Continue simmering for another 30 minutes or until tender. Add olives during last 15 minutes of cooking. Menu might include rice pilaf, green vegetables, carrot-pineapple gelatin salad, French bread, sherbet. serves 4 to 6.

LEG OF LAMB MARSALA

Paul U. Frei, Italian Swiss Colony, Asti

> 1 (6 to 8-lb.) prime leg of lamb
> 1 small onion
> 1 clove garlic
> ¼ tsp. pepper
> 2 tsp. salt
> ¼ tsp. marjoram
> 1 sprig fresh rosemary
> 1 cup California Marsala

Cut 5 or 6 deep gashes, crosswise, in leg of lamb to the bone. With mortar and pestal, grind onion, garlic, pepper and salt. Add marjoram and rosemary; crush. Moisten with a little Marsala. Stuff mixture into gashes; distribute evenly and rub in. Bake in slow oven (300 degrees) about 30 to 35 minutes per pound. After first 2 hours, baste every 30 minutes with remaining Marsala. Serves 6 to 8.

VEAL POCKET

Mrs. Raymond V. Paolucci, Petri Wineries, Escalon

This recipe was prepared by the grandparents of my husband back in Spain. Such a good recipe could hardly be left behind when they came to this country. Of course, when veal wasn't available, lamb or goat was used instead; but veal makes the best meat for this dish by far. The young bones are especially savory for crunching.

> 1 (3-lb.) breast of veal
> 2 cups cooked spinach or chard
> 1 small carrot
> 1 small onion
> 1 stalk celery
> 1 Tbs. parsley
> 1 clove garlic
> ¼ cup olive oil
> 2 Tbs. catsup
> 1½ tsp. salt
> 1 tsp. oregano or poultry
>   seasoning
> 1 chicken bouillon cube
> 1 Tbs. water
> 1 cup bread crumbs
> 1 raw egg
> 1 cup California white table wine

Have butcher cut a pocket or slit in veal for stuffing. Grind or chop very fine the spinach or chard, carrot, onion, celery, parsley and garlic. Heat olive oil. Add vegetables and sauté; add catsup, salt, oregano (or poultry seasoning), and chicken bouillon cube dissolved in 1 tablespoon water. Cover and simmer until vegetables are tender-crisp. Stir in bread crumbs; remove from heat. Stir in egg until smooth. Stuff this mixture into the prepared pocket of veal. Sew with heavy thread to close opening (or skewer). Rub veal with oil; place in a covered roasting pan. Add wine. Roast in moderate oven (350 degrees) about 15 to 20 minutes. Reduce heat to 275-300 degrees. Continue cooking for 1¾ to 2 hours, basting often with additional wine. With this I like to serve baked potatoes with sour cream, hot vegetable, and a tossed salad with plenty of good aged California wine vinegar. Serves 3 to 4.

VEAL CASSEROLE A LA SWISS

*Mrs. William V. Cruess, University of California,
Department of Food Science & Technology, Berkeley*

> 3 lbs. thin veal cutlets, pounded
>   as for scallopini
> 1 lb. Swiss cheese, thinly sliced
> ⅓ cup butter
> 1 (8-oz.) package broad noodles
> 1 lb. fully-cooked ham
> 2 (10¾-oz.) cans beef gravy
> 1 cup light cream
> ⅓ cup sifted flour
> 1 Tbs. paprika
> 1 cup California white table wine

The day before serving, cut veal slices in half. Place slice of cheese on one half of veal slice; top with other half. Melt butter in frying pan; brown veal. Remove veal from pan and set aside. Cook noodles according to package directions; drain. Cut ham into 24 chunks. Brown ham slightly in skillet; remove from pan and set aside. In same skillet, combine gravy, cream, paprika and flour. Cook, stirring, about 10 minutes, or until smooth and thickened. Stir in wine. In a 2-quart casserole, layer drained noodles, sauce, veal and ham; repeat until all ingredients are used. Refrigerate, covered, overnight, or at least 2 hours before baking. Bake in a moderately-hot oven (375 degrees) for 1½ hours, or until tender. Serve with peas and tossed salad. Serves 8 to 10.

LAMB CHOPS BAKED IN WHITE WINE
Mrs. Keith Walker, Paul Masson Vineyards, Saratoga

> 6 shoulder lamb chops
> Garlic
> Salt and black pepper
> 4 Tbs. butter
> 1 onion, chopped
> 2 Tbs. chopped shallots
> 1 Tbs. chopped parsley
> 1½ Tbs. flour
> 1 cup California white table wine

Rub lamb chops with garlic, salt and pepper. Brown chops over moderate heat on both sides in 3 tablespoons of the butter. Transfer chops to baking dish and keep hot. In remaining 1 tablespoon butter, sauté onion, shallots and parsley until onion is soft. Stir in flour, blending well. Gradually add wine and cook until sauce is thickened, stirring continuously. Pour sauce over lamb chops, cover the casserole with a buttered brown paper, and bake in moderate oven (350 degrees) for 20 minutes, or until chops are tender. Add additional wine if sauce becomes too thick. Remove paper and cook 10 minutes longer. Serves 4 to 6.

BARBECUED LAMB CHOPS VERMOUTH

Brother Timothy, The Christian Brothers, Napa

If you're looking for a truly different way to serve lamb, try this recipe. Vermouth imparts an unusual flavor.

> 1 cup California Dry Vermouth
> 1 cup oil
> 1 Tbs. lemon juice
> 3 shallots, or 1 medium onion,
>   chopped
> 2 cloves garlic, minced
> 1 tsp. chopped tarragon
> 1 tsp. chopped basil
> 1 tsp. salt
> 10 peppercorns, crushed
> 6 thick lamb chops

Combine all ingredients except lamb; mix well. Pour over lamb chops. Let stand at room temperature at least 4 hours, turning chops from time to time. Grill lamb about 30 minutes, turning frequently and basting with marinade. Serves 4 to 6.

LAMB RACK BURGUNDY

Mrs. Julius L. Jacobs, Wine Institute, San Francisco

> 4 double-thick large loin lamb chops,
>   split
> ¼ tsp. salt
> ¼ tsp. coarse-ground black pepper
> ¼ tsp. paprika
> 3 Tbs. soy sauce
> ½ cup California Burgundy or
>   other red table wine
> ¼ tsp. dry mustard
> ¼ tsp. garlic powder
> ⅓ cup water
> 8 large button mushrooms,
>   peeled

Trim all excess fat from chops. Season with salt, pepper and paprika. Thread chops on long skewer to resemble rack of lamb, and place in shallow baking dish. Bake in moderate oven (350 degrees) ½ hour. Pour off melted fat. Mix soy sauce, wine, mustard and garlic powder; pour over chops, coating well. Bake ½ hour longer, basting two or three times. Add water and mushrooms and bake 15 minutes more. (Cooked whole baby carrots, peas, and tiny cooked new potatoes may be added last 15 minutes, if desired.) Serve with tossed green salad and dessert of cheese and/or fruit. Serves 3 to 4.

LAMB CHOPS CATHY

Mrs. Steve Riboli, San Antonio Winery, Inc., Los Angeles

> 1 onion, chopped
> 1 shallot, or 1 clove garlic, chopped
> 1½ tsp. dry mustard
> 1 tsp. salt
> ¼ tsp. pepper
> 1½ Tbs. butter, melted
> ½ cup California Sherry
> ½ cup California red table wine
> 6 small loin lamb chops

Combine onion, shallot (or garlic), mustard, salt, pepper and melted butter. Add to combined Sherry and red dinner wine. Pour over lamb chops in a shallow dish; marinate about 1½ hours, turning several times. Remove chops and strain marinade. Broil chops, basting several times with strained marinade. Serve with baked potatoes, green salad and fresh fruit dessert. Serves 4 to 6.

CURRIED LAMB OR BEEF

Fred Perelli-Minetti, A. Perelli-Minetti & Sons, Delano

Curry is an exotic Indian dish and should always include many unique (and generally unavailable) herbs and spices. After spending considerable shopping time in the pursuit of some of these ingredients, I realized that we had all we wanted right on the shelf—in the Vermouth bottle. There are over 200 botanicals listed and variously used in the production of Vermouth, which is a wine infusion of herbs and spices.

> ¼ cup olive oil
> ¼ cup butter
> 2 large onions, diced
> 3 to 4 lbs. lean lamb or beef, cut in
>   1 to 2-inch cubes
> 3 cloves garlic, crushed
> 2 tsp. salt
> 1 tsp. coarsely ground black pepper
> 1 cup chicken broth
> 1½ cups California Sweet Vermouth
> 1 Tbs. cornstarch or arrowroot
> 4 Tbs. curry powder
> 3 Tbs. water

Heat oil and butter in large, heavy skillet. Sauté onions until browned. Add meat; sauté 20 minutes. Add garlic, salt, pepper, broth and Vermouth. Bring to a boil; lower heat and simmer, covered, 1 hour. Make a paste of cornstarch, curry powder and water. Remove cover, and blend paste thoroughly with meat mixture. Continue simmering for 5 to 10 minutes, until liquid is slightly thickened. Serve over steamed rice, accompanied by such condiments as chutney, shredded coconut, chopped parsley, peanuts and raisins. Serves 8.

SHERRIED LAMB HAWAII

Mrs. Ernest C. Haas, East-Side Winery, Lodi

> 6 lb. leg of lamb, boned
> 1 lemon
> 1 clove garlic
> 1 Tbs. grated onion
> 2 Tbs. melted butter
> 2 Tbs. chopped parsley
> ½ tsp. ground ginger
> 1 tsp. curry powder
> 1 cup fresh pineapple pulp
> 1 Tbs. brown sugar
> 1 cup California Sherry
> 1 cup shredded coconut
> Basting Sauce (see below)

Skewer boned leg of lamb so that it can be broiled flat. Cut lemon; brush meat with juice and rub with cut rind. Crush garlic and mix with onion, butter, parsley, ginger, curry powder, pineapple, sugar, Sherry and coconut. Pour sauce over lamb in a glass or porcelain container and marinate several hours. Then scrape all marinade into saucepan and simmer gently while broiling meat. Place lamb, fat side down, on grill over medium hot coals. Turn and baste occasionally with Basting Sauce. (below). Meat will be medium rare in about 45 minutes. Serve hot marinade as accompanying sauce. Good with fluffy rice, broccoli and tossed salad. Serves 5 to 6.
BASTING SAUCE: Combine ½ cup each: pineapple juice California Sherry and olive oil. Season with ½ teaspoon ginger, 1 teaspoon curry powder, 1 clove garlic, crushed, salt and pepper.

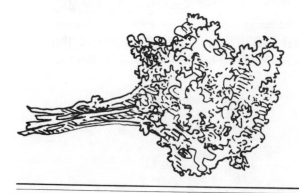

LEG OF LAMB IN WINE MARINADE

For leg of lamb that is just a bit different, and easy to do, Mrs. Robert Mondavi suggests this interesting treatment: Cover leg of lamb with California red table wine; add 1 onion (sliced) 2 cloves garlic (halved) and 2 bay leaves. Marinate several hours. Drain, reserving marinade. Sprinkle lamb with salt and freshly ground pepper. Place bacon strips over lamb. Roast in moderately-slow over (325 degrees) about 30 to 35 minutes per pound, basting with reserved marinade.

VARIATION: Make slits in meat; insert rosemary and garlic. Sprinkle with salt and pepper; top with strips of salt pork. Roast (as above), basting with California white table wine.

STUFFED LEG OF LAMB ROYALE

*Dr. James F. Guymon, University of California,
Department of Viticulture & Enology, Davis*

This procedure for roasting and basting is recommended for leg of lamb, beef roast, etc., with variations in herbs such as rosemary or mint for lamb; thyme and savory, singly or in combination, for other roasts.

> 1 (6 ot 7-lb.) leg of lamb
> ¼ lb. smoked ham
> ¼ lb. veal
> ¼ lb. fresh pork
> ½ tsp. marjoram
> ⅛ tsp. nutmeg
> ¼ cup fine dry bread crumbs
> 1 egg
> 2 cloves garlic, minced
> Salt
> ½ lb. fresh mushrooms
> Butter
> Pepper
> Flour
> 1 cup beef bouillon, consommé or
>   broth
> ⅔ cup California red table wine
> ½ tsp. thyme
> ½ tsp. savory

Bone leg of lamb, keeping cavity as intact as possible for easy stuffing. Last few inches of shank bone should be left in. Finely grind together ham, veal and pork; add marjoram, nutmeg, bread crumbs, egg, 1 clove of minced garlic and salt to taste. Blend thoroughly, using hands. Chop mushrooms; sauté a few minutes in butter; add to meat mixture, blending well. Stuff meat mixture inside cavity of lamb until completely filled. Close cavity by sewing with twine or using skewers. (Flaps of skin should be left on for sewing, but if not, a piece of smoked bacon rind can be used to patch opening. It also adds flavor.) Rub roast with butter; season with salt and pepper; dredge with flour. Place in roasting pan and roast in hot oven (450 degrees) for about 15 minutes to brown. Then reduce heat to 325 degrees, and continue roasting for 35 minutes per pound. Baste every 30 minutes with mixture of bouillon, wine, thyme, remaining clove of garlic (minced), pepper and savory. Heat basting mixture in saucepan and simmer a few minutes. When all of it is used, baste with pan juices. Serves 8 to 10.

MELT-IN-YOUR-MOUTH LAMB

Melt-in-your-mouth lamb, a boned leg roasted on a rotisserie but treated to a marinade similar to Blossom Hill Lamb With Wine is a version by Mrs. J. F. M. Taylor, Napa. She uses Zinfandel Rosé with curry powder, honey and seasoned salt.

LAMB BLOCKS WITH POTATOES

*Mrs. William V. Cruess, University of California,
Department of Food Science & Technology, Berkeley*

> ½ cup California red table wine
> 2 Tbs. olive oil
> 1 cup chicken or beef broth
> ½ of 8-oz. can tomato sauce
> ½ tsp. minced rosemary
> 1 clove garlic, minced
> ⅓ of a small onion, minced
> 1 tsp. salt
> ¼ to ½ Tbs. chili pepper with
>   seeds
> 5 lamb blocks (about 1 lb. each,
>   cut up)
> Butter or oil
> Salt and pepper
> Flour
> 5 medium-sized potatoes, pared and
>   halved lengthwise

Combine wine, olive oil, broth, tomato sauce, rosemary, garlic, onion, 1 teaspoon salt, and chili pepper in a saucepan. Heat to boiling and cook 5 minutes. Meanwhile, rub meat with butter or oil, salt, pepper and flour. Place in roasting pan; brown in a very hot oven (500 degrees). Reduce heat to 325 degrees. Place potatoes around meat; season with salt and pepper. Bake in (325 degree) oven for 1 hour, basting frequently with heated wine sauce. Serve with broccoli. Serves 8 to 10.

LEG OF LAMB ACAPULCO

Mrs. George Al Berry, Roma Wine Company, Fresno

> 1 (5 to 6-lb.) leg of lamb
> 1 cup California red table wine
> ½ cup orange juice
> ¼ cup chili sauce
> ¼ cup water
> 1 Tbs. chili powder
> 2 Tbs. olive oil
> 1 medium onion, finely chopped
> 2 cloves garlic, minced
> ¾ tsp. dried oregano
> 1 tsp. cumin seed, crushed
> 1 Tbs. brown sugar
> Salt and pepper

Place meat in deep glass or enamel pan. Combine remaining ingredients; pour over meat. Let stand in refrigerator 24 hours, turning occasionally. Remove meat from marinade; drain. Place on rack in a baking pan. Roast in very hot oven (450 degrees) for 15 minutes. Reduce oven temperature to 350 degrees. Spoon marinade over meat in 2 or 3 portions (to help keep mixture from sticking to bottom of pan). Continue cooking about 2½ hours, or until meat is tender, basting frequently. Add a few tablespoons of hot water to pan juices if they tend to cook down too quickly. Skim off fat and serve pan sauce with meat. Serves 8 to 10.

SANTA CLARA VALLEY SHANKS

Mrs. Peter Mirassou, Mirassou Vineyards, San Jose

> *6 lamb shanks*
> *1 lemon, cut in half*
> *½ cup sifted flour*
> *2 tsp. salt*
> *½ tsp. pepper*
> *¼ cup shortening or oil*
> *1 medium onion, chopped*
> *2 cloves garlic, minced*
> *1 cup California red table wine*
> *1 (10½-oz.) can condensed*
> *   consommé*
> *1 cup each: sliced carrots and celery*
> *1 bay leaf*
> *1 sprig fresh mint (optional)*

Rub meat all over with cut lemon, squeezing out juice; let stand about 10 minutes. Combine flour, salt and pepper in paper bag. Put in meat and shake until well coated. Heat shortening and sauté meat until browned; transfer to a deep 3-qt. casserole. Add onion and garlic to pan drippings and sauté until onion is limp; stir in any remaining flour and brown lightly. Gradually add wine and consommé, stirring until smooth, then pour over meat. Add carrots, celery, bay and mint. Cover and bake in moderate oven (375 degrees) for about 2 hours or until meat is tender. Serve with rice and a green salad. Serves 5 to 6.

FRESNO LAMB SHANKS

Paul H. Huber, E. & J. Gallo Winery, Fresno

These lamb shanks, with their rich and subtle sauce, have an international air—with dill, as used by Scandinavians, rosemary by Italians, and oregano by Mexicans and Westerners.

> *4 lamb shanks*
> *1 tsp. dill*
> *½ tsp. oregano*
> *1 tsp. rosemary*
> *1 large clove garlic*
> *1 large onion, thinly sliced*
> *1 (8-oz.) can tomato sauce*
> *¼ cup brown sugar*
> *1 cup California white table wine*
> *1½ tsp. salt*
> *⅛ tsp. pepper*

Place lamb shanks in roaster; add remaining ingredients. Cover roaster and cook 3 hours in moderately-slow oven (300 degrees). (If shanks are large, raise temperature to 325 to 350 degrees). Remove cover; continue cooking for 30 minutes. Pour sauce into saucepan; reduce to half over high heat. Pour over meat. Serves 4 to 6.

SIMPLY A MUST FOR MEATS

Simply a must for meats is the best way to describe how James E. Woolsey, Roma Wine Company, Fresno, feel about wine and cooking. To get the full delicious flavor of a leg of lamb, baste it while roasting with a white table wine like California Chablis or Sauterne. And to give roast beef an extra special flavor, try a California Burgundy wine baste. What wine alone does for meats is really magic, basic as salt and pepper.

BLOSSOM HILL LAMB WITH WINE

Mrs. E. Jeff Barnette, Martini & Prati Wines, Inc., Santa Rosa

I cook the lamb as directed and when ready to serve, set the Brandy aflame at the table. Then it is ready for carving and delicious eating.

> *1 (5 to 6-lb.) leg of lamb*
> *1 clove garlic, crushed*
> *3 Tbs. lemon juice (fresh,*
> *   frozen or canned)*
> *¼ tsp. each: curry powder, ground*
> *   ginger and dry mustard*
> *Salt and pepper*
> *3 Tbs. tart jelly (currant,*
> *   mint-flavored apple, etc.)*
> *1 cup California Burgundy or other*
> *   red table wine*
> *⅓ to ½ cup California Brandy*
> *   (optional)*

Wipe leg of lamb with a damp cloth; do not remove fell (the thin paper-like covering over meat). Rub the meat with crushed garlic; spread lemon juice over evenly. Mix together curry powder, ground ginger and dry mustard; rub evenly over meat. Cover lamb with aluminum foil or place in a large paper bag; refrigerate several hours or overnight. Season with salt and pepper. Roast, uncovered, in moderately-slow oven (325 degrees) 30 to 35 minutes per pound, or until meat thermometer registers 180 degrees. Mix jelly and wine together. About 45 minutes before lamb is done remove lamb from pan; pour off excess fat. To glaze lamb, brush with jelly-wine mixture at least 3 times. For a very festive occasion, warm Brandy over hot water or very low heat. When ready to serve, spoon a little Brandy over the meat. Set aflame and baste with remaining Brandy until flame dies. Serve pan juices with meat. Menu might include; fruit cocktail; au gratin potatoes; buttered peas with green onions; tossed green salad; peppermint mousse, ice cream or sherbet for dessert. Serves 6 to 8.

BEEF TONGUE IN PORT WINE SAUCE

Mrs. David B. Ficklin, Ficklin Vineyards, Madera

I think the most interesting thing about this recipe is that it was shared with us a number of years ago, when we first started marketing our Port. Mr. James P. Howe, a wine-grower of Gopher Gulch Ranch, Walnut Creek, sent it to us and it has been a favorite with all of us since.

> *Slices of cooked beef tongue*
> *Butter*
> *1 cup beef gravy (leftover home-made*
>   *gravy, or canned)*
> *1 Tbs. red currant jelly*
> *½ cup California Port*
> *Juice of ½ lemon*

Heat slices of tongue in small amount butter. Keep hot while preparing sauce. Blend gravy, jelly, Port and lemon juice. Heat just to boiling point, stirring to melt jelly. Strain and serve at once with hot tongue. Serves 3 to 4.

OXTAILS IN SAVORY SAUCE

Mrs. George Al Berry, Roma Wine Company, Fresno

> *3 lbs. oxtails, cut in 1½-inch pieces*
> *2 Tbs. butter*
> *¼ cup instant minced onion*
> *¼ cup water*
> *1 Tbs. dry mustard*
> *1 Tbs. arrowroot*
> *1 Tbs. dried mushrooms*
> *1 (10½-oz.) can condensed beef*
>   *bouillon*
> *1 cup California red table wine*
> *2 Tbs. tomato paste*
> *1 tsp. seasoned salt*
> *1 tsp. salt*
> *½ tsp. monosodium glutamate*
> *Dash cayenne*
> *½ cup dairy sour cream*
> *Chopped parsley*

Brown oxtails in butter; remove from skillet. Soak onion in water for 5 minutes; stir into pan drippings. Add dry mustard, arrowroot, mushrooms, bouillon and wine. Cook over low heat, stirring constantly, until thickened and smooth. Stir in tomato paste, seasoned salt, salt, monosodium glutamate and cayenne. Return browned oxtails to sauce. Cover and simmer 3 hours, or until oxtails are tender. Just before serving, stir in sour cream and sprinkle with parsley. Heat through and serve with noodles or steamed rice, buttered carrots, tossed green salad. Serves 4 to 5.

BOILED TONGUE DANTE

Dante Bagnani, American Industries Corp., San Francisco

> *1 or 2 large beef tongues*
>   *Water*
> *1 cup California white table wine*
> *1¾ teaspoons salt*
> *3 cloves garlic*
> *1 teaspoon whole peppercorns*
> *1 carrot*
> *2 stalks celery*
> *1 large onion, sliced*
> *½ cup California wine vinegar*
> *½ cup olive oil*
> *¼ cup chopped parsley*
> *3 green onions, chopped*
> *⅛ teaspoon freshly ground pepper*

Cover tongue with water and at least 1 cup wine; add 1½ teaspoons salt, 2 cloves garlic, peppercorns, carrot, celery, and onion slices. Bring to boiling; simmer 3 to 3½ hours, or until fork-tender. When done, remove from cooking liquid and slice. In a jar, combine wine vinegar, oil, parsley, remaining clove garlic (mashed), green onions, remaining ¼ teaspoon salt and pepper. Shake well to blend. Serve over warm tongue, accompanied by a tossed green salad, crusty French bread, and cheese for dessert. Serves 6.

ITALIAN LIVER LODI

Mrs. Charles J. Welch, Guild Wine Co., Lodi

We happen to be fond of liver, but it isn't easy to find much variety of preparation. In our early married days, liver was very inexpensive. I found this recipe—minus the wine—and used it frequently. Later we discovered the addition of wine was a natural—and the dish was even better.

> *1 pound beef liver*
> *3 tablespoons flour*
> *3 tablespoons bacon drippings*
> *1 onion, chopped*
> *1 clove garlic, minced*
> *1 green pepper, chopped*
> *¼ pound mushrooms, sliced*
> *1 (1-lb.) can whole tomatoes*
> *¼ teaspoon oregano*
> *1 teaspoon salt*
> *½ cup California red table wine*
> *Spaghetti*
> *Grated Parmesan cheese*

Cut liver into ½-inch cubes; dredge with flour. Heat bacon drippings in large frying pan. Add liver, onion, garlic, green pepper and mushrooms. Sauté until liver is browned. Add tomatoes, seasonings and wine. Cover and simmer 25 minutes. Meanwhile, cook spaghetti, following package directions; drain well. Serve the liver over the spaghetti; pass the cheese. Serve with a tossed salad, sourdough French bread, and stuffed zucchini. Serves 4 to 6.

SAVONA TRIPE STEW
Mrs. Frank Franzia, Franzia Brother Winery, Ripon

This recipe has been handed down to the fourth generation in our family, from way back in Italy. Everyone enjoys it; the children love it.

> *3 lbs. tripe*
> *¼ cup olive oil*
> *2 large onions, sliced*
> *2 tsp. salt*
> *¼ tsp. pepper*
> *¾ cup California Sauterne or other*
> *   white table wine*
> *3 or 4 fresh tomatoes*
> *   or 1 cup canned tomatoes*
> *2 stalks celery, diced*
> *2 carrots, diced*
> *1 (1-lb.) can garbanzos, drained*
> *2 to 3 cups diced potatoes (optional)*

Rinse tripe in cold water several times. Cut tripe into strips about 3 inches long and ½ inch wide. Heat oil in kettle; add tripe, watching carefully that it doesn't stick. Add onions; cook and stir until soft. Add salt, pepper, wine, and tomatoes; simmer a few minutes. Add water to cover tripe (about 2 to 3 cups); simmer 1½ to 2 hours. Add celery and carrots; cook 30 minutes longer. Add more water, if necessary. Add garbanzos; cook another 15 minutes. If potatoes are desired, add and cook 30 minutes. Serve with plenty of fresh French bread. Serves 4 to 6.

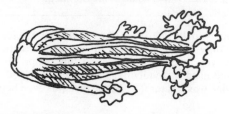

TONGUE WITH WHITE WINE ASPIC
Mrs. Louis P. Martini, Louis M. Martini, St. Helena

> *1½ lbs. sliced cooked tongue*
> *Stuffed large green olives*
> *2 envelopes plain gelatin*
> *⅓ cup cold water*
> *2 (10½-oz) can condensed*
> *   consommé*
> *1 cup California white table wine*

Arrange overlapping slices of tongue in 2 rows along sides of a shallow serving dish. Arrange stuffed green olives in center. Soften gelatin in cold water. Bring 1 can of the consommé to boil; add gelatin, stirring until the gelatin is dissolved. Stir in wine and remaining can of consommé. Chill until mixture is slightly syrupy. Pour over tongue; chill for at least 2 hours, or until set. A simple summer menu might include: potato salad, sliced tomatoes, hot rolls, fruit in season and coffee. Serves 6 to 8.

KIDNEYS IN SHERRY
Mrs. Herbert Cerwin, Cerwin Vineyard, Sonoma

> *4 lamb kidneys*
> *3 shallots (or 3 Tbs. chopped onion)*
> *2 Tbs. butter*
> *12 fresh or canned mushrooms*
> *1 cup California Dry Sherry*
> *Chopped parsley*

Devein kidneys and cut in mushroom-size pieces. Rinse well in salt water; dry. Sauté shallots in butter. Add kidneys and mushroom; sauté until kidneys are nicely browned. Add Sherry. Simmer, covered, 5 to 10 minutes over low heat until kidneys are tender. Sprinkle with chopped parsley and serve. Serves 2 to 3.

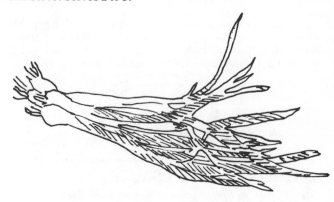

KIDNEYS BURGUNDY
Ed Schuh, The Christian Brothers, Napa

There are many fine Italian cooks in the Napa Valley. Eating in their homes is a rare experience. Here is an unusual recipe which has become a favorite of mine.

> *4 lamb kidneys*
> *2 cups boiling water*
> *¼ cup butter*
> *1 onion, sliced*
> *¼ tsp. salt*
> *⅛ tsp. pepper*
> *½ cup California Burgundy or other*
> *   red table wine*
> *2 tsp. chopped parsley or*
> *   sweet basil*

Cut kidneys in half; remove fat and outer membrane; cut kidneys into ½-inch slices. Cover with cold salted water; let stand 1 hour; drain. Clean kidneys well by placing in saucepan and pouring 2 cups boiling water over them; drain. Melt butter in shallow saucepan; add kidneys and onions. Cover and simmer until tender, about 20 minutes. Season with salt and pepper. Pour over wine; simmer several minutes longer. Sprinkle with parsley or basil and serve at once. Serves 3 to 4.

Poultry

"...and we meet with Champagne
and a chicken at last!"
—Lady Mary Wortley Montagu

A chicken in every pot can be just plain old boiled chicken—but add the one touch of glamour—California wine, cooked at a low simmer along with your favorite herbs and a bit of onion, and the result—pure taste magic. Such a dish may well deserve Champagne served at the table; a salute to the vast versatility of poultry cooked with wine. All methods of preparation, all manner of sauces lend themselves to this joyous teaming—easy, adventurous and utterly delectable.

CHICKEN A LA GALLO
Mrs. Ernest Gallo, E. & J. Gallo Winery, Modesto

1 large fryer, cut in pieces
1 Tbs. olive oil
2 Tbs. butter
2 tsp. flour
Salt and pepper
½ cup California Sauterne
½ cup chicken broth
2 tsp. chopped parsley
1 small clove garlic, minced (optional)
½ tsp. coarsely grated lemon rind
1 Tbs. chopped rosemary
2 Tbs. California Sherry

Brown chicken in oil and butter in heavy saucepan or skillet. Sprinkle on flour, salt and pepper; brown a few minutes longer. Add Sauterne, stirring constantly; boil rapidly until almost all wine has been absorbed. Add broth, simmer until chicken is almost done, then add finely chopped herbs and Sherry. Cook 10 to 15 minutes longer; serve immediately on warm plates. Serves 4 to 5.

SQUABS SAUTÉED IN WHITE WINE
H. Peter Jurgens, Almaden Vineyards, Los Gatos

6 small squabs
½ cup butter
Salt and pepper
3 Tbs. chopped shallots
1¼ cups California white table wine
3 Tbs. finely chopped parsley
1 Tbs. finely chopped tarragon

Singe, clean, and split squabs. Melt butter in a large skillet. Lightly brown squab halves on both sides over high heat. Season with salt and pepper. Add shallots and ¾ cup of wine. Reduce heat. Cover skillet tightly and simmer gently for 15 minutes. Add parsley, tarragon and remaining ½ cup wine. Cook, uncovered, for 5 minutes longer. Serve on toast triangles with a little sauce spooned over each squab. Serves 4 to 6.

53

LIMED CHICKEN WITH SHERRY

Ernest C. Haas, East-Side Winery, Lodi

2 whole broiling chickens, about
   1½ or 2 lbs. each
½ cup raisins or currants
3 medium onions, sliced thin
1 green pepper, finely chopped
½ cup bread crumbs
1 tsp. salt
⅛ tsp. cracked black pepper
3 limes
1 cup butter
2 dashes Angostura bitters
⅓ cup chopped walnuts
12 large almond-stuffed olives, or
   ripe olives, coarsely chopped
2 tsp. cinnamon
2 bay leaves, crumbled
½ cup California Sherry

Wipe chickens inside out. Mix raisins, onions, green pepper and bread crumbs; season with salt and pepper. Stuff into cavities of chickens. Sew up neatly. Cut 1 lime, brush birds with juice; dust with additional salt and pepper. Brown birds in hot butter, turning frequently. Slice the 2 additional limes very thin, and cover bottom of a buttered baking dish with them. Add bitters, then successive layers of walnuts and olives, sprinkled with cinnamon and crumbled bay leaves. Lay chickens on top and pour remaining frying butter over them. Cover tightly; roast very slowly (275 degrees) for 1 to 1½ hours, until tender. A few minutes before removing from oven, sprinkle on Sherry. Serves 3 to 4.

GINGER CHICKEN

Mrs. Thomas Leong, Paul Masson Vineyards, Saratoga

The Chinese take great pains to preserve or enhance natural flavors. This is one of the traditional sauces used for frying chicken.

¼ cup California Dry Vermouth
¼ cup soy sauce
1 Tbs. sugar
⅛ tsp. black pepper
Pinch of salt
¼ tsp. monosodium glutamate
1 Tbs. fresh ginger, minced
1 (2½-lb.) fryer, cut into serving-
   size pieces
Flour
Oil

Combine Vermouth, soy sauce, sugar, pepper, salt, monosodium glutamate, minced ginger and garlic. Marinate chicken in this mixture 3 to 4 hours, or overnight. Drain chicken; flour lightly. Fry in oil until brown and tender. Or, if desired, grill over coals. Menu might include: prawns with asparagus (or any other Chinese dish combining meats and vegetables) and steamed rice. Makes about 2 servings.

CHICKEN VERMOUTH

Mrs. John L. Tribuno, Vermouth Industries of California, Delano

1 broiler fryer cut into quarters
¾ cup California Dry Vermouth
Juice of 2 limes
Salt

Place chicken in pan, skin side down. Mix Vermouth and lime juice; pour over chicken. Place chicken in pre-heated broiler, 8 inches from source of heat. Baste frequently until chicken is brown. Turn to brown second side. Remove from broiler; cover pan with aluminum foil. Bake browned chicken in slow oven (250 degrees) for 1 hour. Serve with risotto a la Milanese, sautéed mushrooms, mixed green salad, and for dessert a chocolate soufflé. Serves 3 to 4.

CHICKEN IN SOUR CREAM

Mrs. Adolf L. Heck, Korbel Champagne Cellars, Guerneville

4 chicken breasts
6 Tbs. butter
¾ cup California Sauterne or
   other white table wine
1 small onion, finely chopped
1 cup dairy sour cream
Salt and white pepper

Remove skin from chicken breasts. In heavy skillet, brown chicken breasts lightly in 4 tablespoons of the butter. Turn occasionally. Sprinkle ½ cup of the wine over chicken. Cover and simmer 20 to 25 minutes, or just until tender. Meanwhile, melt remaining 2 tablespoons butter in a saucepan. Cook onion until soft but not browned. Add remaining ¼ cup wine; slowly stir in sour cream. Season with salt and white pepper. Heat only long enough to warm cream. Pour over chicken. Serves 3 to 4.

CHICKEN WITH ARTICHOKES
Mrs. Louis A. Petri, United Vintners, Inc., San Francisco

2 Tbs. olive oil
1 large frying chicken
1 small onion, minced
1 clove garlic, minced
1 tsp. flour
1 cup hot chicken broth
1 Tbs. tomato paste
¼ cup chopped parsley
Few sprigs rosemary
6 raw artichokes, trimmed and halved
1 tsp. salt
¼ tsp. pepper
1 cup California Sauterne or other
  white table wine

In large Dutch oven, heat olive oil and brown cut-up fryer in it. Remove chicken when browned. Cook onion and garlic in oil until onion is transparent. Stir in flour, then add hot chicken broth, and tomato paste and bring to boil. Add parsley, rosemary and artichokes, and simmer 5 to 10 minutes. Then place browned chicken on top of artichokes, add salt and pepper and pour wine over all. Bring to boil, then cover and bake in slow oven (325 degrees) about 45 minutes chicken and artichokes are tender. Serves 3 to 4.

CHICKEN MARENGO STYLE
Mrs. Pete Peters, Fresno

1 broiler-fryer, about 2½ lbs. cut up
½ cup flour
1½ tsp. salt
½ tsp. ground pepper
½ cup fat for browning
2 Tbs. water
12 small white onions, parboiled
½ lb. mushrooms, sliced
1 clove garlic, crushed or pressed
1 cup broth or water
1½ cups drained canned tomatoes
½ cup California Sherry
Salt and pepper

Coat chicken with blended flour, salt and pepper, setting aside any left-over flour for the sauce. Cook chicken slowly to a *light golden* brown in the fat. Reserve 4 tablespoons of the fat for the sauce. Add water to chicken; cover tightly and cook over low heat until fork-tender, 20 to 25 minutes. Meanwhile prepare sauce: cook onions, mushrooms and garlic in reserved fat. Cook stirring occasionally 8 to 10 minutes or until mushrooms are softened. Sprinkle any left-over flour mixture over top and blend in thoroughly. Add broth and water and tomatoes all at once. Cook stirring constantly until uniformly thickened. Add wine. Cover and simmer 5 to 10 minutes. Season to taste. Pour sauce over cooked chicken arranged on hot platter. Good with rice pilaf and a tossed green salad. Serves 3 to 4.

BLUE MOON CHICKEN
Mark Gouig, Sonoma Vineyards

1 chicken, cut up
3 slices bacon
4 cloves garlic
1 tsp. thyme
1 head Cyree cabbage
1 onion, yellow
1 cup Gewurztraminer or
  Johannisberg Riesling

Brown chicken with bacon and garlic. Salt and pepper to taste. Add thyme. Simmer for 15 minutes; add onion and quartered cabbage. Add wine; cook for ½ hour over medium heat. Serve with rice and corn bread.

CHICKEN ORIENTAL
Dr. Emil M. Mrak, University of California, Davis

We consider this recipe quite original as well as delicious. We have yet to find someone who hasn't liked it.

½ cup California Burgundy or
  other red table wine
½ cup Japanese soy sauce
3 Tbs. honey
1 pressed clove garlic
1 frying chicken, cut in serving
  pieces
¼ cup butter
2 Tbs. olive oil

Mix wine, soy sauce, honey and garlic juice; pour over chicken pieces in a glass or porcelain container. Refrigerate 24 hours. Then drain and fry chicken in butter and oil until brown in a teflon pan. Place chicken in a covered casserole and finish cooking in a moderately-slow oven (325 degrees) for 45 minutes to 1 hour, until chicken is tender. (The real trick is in the initial browning, and I can assure you that if this is done in an ordinary frying pan, trouble lies ahead. Because of the density of the honey and soy sauce, the material will burn; but with teflon, the chicken won't stick to the pan. In browning, therefore, we use a teflon frying pan, an abundance of butter and some olive oil.) Serves 3 to 4.

POLLO SCHIACCIATO

Mrs. Enrico Prati, Martini & Prati Wines, Inc., Santa Rosa

> 2 (1 to 1½-lb.) chickens, split down
>   the front
> 1½ Tbs. olive oil
> 1 clove garlic, unpeeled
> 2 leaves fresh sage
> Salt and pepper
> ¼ cup California Sauterne or other
>   white table wine

Place split chickens, bone side down, on hard surface and flatten by hitting a few quick, hard strokes with the heel of the hand. Over medium low heat, warm a heavy 10-inch skillet containing olive oil, garlic and sage. Season chickens with salt and pepper and place in pan as flat as possible. Cover with a small lid only 8 or 9 inches in diameter so that it fits flat directly on the chicken. Put a weight on top of the lid. (I use an old-fashioned flatiron.) Cook chicken about 30 minutes until golden brown on both sides, turning as necessary. Remove and discard garlic and sage. Reduce heat. Add wine, a small amount at a time, to keep skillet moist. Turn chickens occasionally; continue adding wine as needed, until chicken is tender and glazed. This is a nice luncheon dish, served with your favorite salad, hot rolls and your favorite white table wine. Serves 4 to 6.

SMOTHERED CHICKEN

Mrs. John Franzia Sr., Franzia Brothers Winery, Ripon

> 2 frying chickens or 1 roasting chicken,
>   cut in serving-size pieces
> 3 to 4 Tbs. olive oil
> 1 large onion, finely chopped
> 1 tsp. chopped parsley
> 1 clove garlic, finely chopped
> 2 small bay leaves
> 2 whole cloves
> ¾ cup California Sauterne, Chablis or
>   other white table wine
> Salt and pepper
> 2 (2½-oz.) jars button mushrooms,
>   undrained
> 1 (8-oz.) can ripe black olives, drained

Fry chicken slowly in heated oil until golden brown. Add onion; sauté until golden. Add parsley, garlic, bay leaves, whole cloves and wine. Season with salt and pepper. Cover tightly and cook slowly for about 30 minutes. Add undrained mushrooms and olives. Cook 10 minutes longer, or until chicken is tender. Skim off any excess fat from pan sauce. This dish is also good the next day and reheats very well. With this recipe I like buttered noodles and green beans. For dessert—apples baked in Claret. Serves 4 to 6.

CHICKEN NAPA VALLEY

Chicken Napa Valley is a fork-tender bake of the parts you like the best. Mrs. Otto Gramlow, Beaulieu Vineyard, Rutherford, suggests using 3 pounds chicken parts of your choice. Dredge in seasoned flour, then brown in butter in large skillet. Put chicken in covered 2-quart casserole. In same skillet, combine 1 cup catsup, ½ cup California Sherry, ½ cup water, 2 tablespoons lemon juice, 1 tablespoon Worcestershire sauce, 1 medium onion, minced; bring to boil. Pour mixture over chicken, cover; bake in moderately-slow oven (325 degrees) about 1¼ hours, or until tender. Serve with a complement of California white table wine at the table.

CHICKEN SAUTERNE

Mrs. A. Jensen, Gemello Winery, Mountain View

> 3 whole chicken breasts
> 1½ tsp. salt
> 1 pkg. frozen green peas with onions
> 1 (6-oz.) can button mushrooms
> 5 Tbs. butter
> 3 Tbs. flour
> 1 Tbs. instant minced onion
> ½ tsp. each: celery salt,
>   paprika, Italian herbs and
>   Worcestershire sauce
> ¼ tsp. monosodium glutamate
> 1 cup broth from cooking chicken
>   breasts
> ½ cup California Sauterne or other
>   white table wine
> 1 cup light cream

One hour before serving, place chicken breasts in water to cover; add 1 teaspoon salt. Simmer, covered, until tender (about 30 minutes). Remove skin and bones from chicken, leaving meat in large pieces. Reserve 1 cup of chicken cooking broth. Cook frozen peas with onions, following package directions. Sauté mushrooms in 2 tablespoons of butter in heavy skillet. Remove mushrooms. In same pan, melt remaining 3 tablespoons butter; stir in flour, instant minced onion and seasonings. Stir in reserved chicken broth and wine; cook, stirring constantly, over low heat until thickened. Cool slightly; stir in cream, mushrooms, peas and onions, and chicken. Heat through (do not boil). Serve over wild rice along with a tossed green salad and hot rolls. For dessert—fresh fruit and a sweet California dessert wine. Serves 6 to 8.

CHICKEN KIEV
Mrs. S. Hall, Bandiera Wines, Cloverdale

> 4 medium chicken breasts
>   (double or whole)
> Salt
> ¼ lb. butter
> ½ cup each: *chopped green onion*
>   *and parsley*
> Flour
> 2 eggs, well beaten
> 1 cup fine cracker meal
> ⅓ cup flour

Cut chicken breasts in half lengthwise. Remove skin and cut away bone. Don't tear the meat—each half should be all in one piece. Place each piece of chicken, boned side up, between 2 pieces of saran wrap. Working out from center, pound with wooden mallet to form cutlets not quite ¼-inch thick. Peel off saran. Sprinkle meat with salt. Measure 1 tablespoon each onion and parsely and sprinkle over each cutlet. Cut the chilled butter into 8 sticks. Place small stick of butter near end of cutlet. Roll as for jelly roll, tucking in sides of meat. Press to seal well. Dust with flour; dip in beaten egg; roll in fine cracker meal. Chill chicken rolls thoroughly—at least one hour. Fry in deep, hot fat (340 degrees) about 15 minutes or until golden brown. Drain on paper toweling. Serve Sauterne Sauce (below) over chicken. A good menu might include: Zucchini Italienne, tossed salad with oil and vinegar dressing, garlic bread. Serves 6.
SAUTERNE SAUCE: Melt 6 tablespoons butter in heavy sauce pan. Stir in 6 tablespoons flour; cook over low heat, without browning flour, about 5 minutes. Gradually add 2 cups chicken broth to flour mixture, stirring constantly until thickened and smooth. Add 1½ cups California Dry Sauterne, 2 sprigs chopped parsley, garlic powder, Worcestershire sauce and horseradish to taste, and simmer 30 minutes; stir occasionally. Strain. This sauce will keep in refrigerator in covered jar one week.

CHICKEN BREASTS FLAMBÉES

Chicken Breasts Flambées can be your secret to successful hostessing, simply done. Sauté chicken breasts in butter until tender; keep hot. Prepare a rich cream sauce flavored with wine and onion. To serve, follow the simple directions of Mrs. Ronald G. Hanson, Mt. Tivy Winery, Reedley: Have ready ½ cup California Brandy. Place chicken on heated platter. Pour some of the Brandy into a small ladle and the rest over the chicken. Warm the Brandy in the ladle over a match, then light it and pour over the chicken. Spoon the blazing Brandy over the chicken so the flavor penetrates. Serve with sauce.

SUMMER CHICKEN LOAF
Arthur Accomazzo, Cucamonga Winery, Cucamonga

> 1 (4-lb.) stewing chicken
> 1 quart boiling water
> 2 tsp. salt
> 1 Tbs. instant minced onion
> 1 carrot
> 1 stalk celery
> 2 envelopes plain gelatin
> ½ cup California Chablis or
>   other white table wine
> 1 Tbs. lemon juice
> Ripe olives, green pepper, and
>   pimiento for garnish
> ½ cup finely chopped celery
> 2 Tbs. finely chopped green
>   pepper
> 2 Tbs. chopped pimiento
> ¼ cup sweet pickle relish
> 4 hard-cooked eggs

Cut chicken in pieces and add boiling water, salt, onion, carrot and celery. Cover and simmer about 2 hours, or until meat is tender. Cool in broth, then remove skin and bones, and chop meat fine (there should be about 3 cups meat). Skim fat from broth, and boil broth down to 2½ cups. Soften gelatin in wine, and dissolve in the 2½ cups broth. Blend in lemon juice and additional salt, if needed. Cool. Spoon a little of the gelatin mixture into bottom of 1½ quart mold, and arrange a pattern of ripe olive slices, green pepper and pimiento pieces in it. Chill until set. Then fold chicken, celery, green pepper, pimiento and well drained pickle relish into remaining gelatin. Spoon into mold to fill it half way. Arrange whole shelled eggs in mold, and cover with remaining gelatin mixture. Chill several hours or overnight. Unmold, and slice to serve. Serves 8 to 10.

POULET AU MOMENT MÊME
Mrs. Norman Fromm, Fromm & Sichel, Inc., San Francisco

My mother was seven years old when she came here from the German Rhineland. She inherited this recipe from her mother in a handwritten cookbook.

> 2 whole chicken breasts, boned and split
> ½ cup butter
> ⅓ cup Sherry
> 1 lb. mushrooms, sliced
> 1 cup cream
> 4 egg yolks
> Salt and pepper

Cook chicken breasts in butter and Sherry, well covered over low heat, until almost tender, 10 to 20 minutes. Add mushrooms and cook 3 minutes more. Beat cream and egg yolks together briefly, then pour over chicken and stir until sauce thickens. Season with salt, pepper and an additional tablespoon or two of Sherry, if desired. Serve with rice and green bean salad vinaigrette. Serves 3 to 4.

WINE-MUSHROOM CHICKEN MIX

Wine-Mushroom Chicken Mix is a custom-made mélange of chicken parts that's easy to prepare and delectable. Use chicken breasts for elegance, try it with drumsticks and wings for economy. Maynard A. Joslyn, Department of Nutritional Sciences, University of California, Berkeley, starts out with a cup of chopped onions and a cup of sliced mushrooms, browned in butter. Add 2 pounds chicken parts to this mix, salt and pepper to taste, and put in casserole. Pour over 1 cup California white table wine; bake in a moderate oven (350 degrees) until tender (about 1 hour). Serves 3 to 4. A good accompaniment to this dish—wild rice. An economical approach—mix ⅓ wild rice with ⅔ brown rice. To make the best of your approach, serve with a chilled California white table wine.

HUNTINGTON CHICKEN
Mrs. Kenneth R. Spencer, Mirassou Vineyards, San Jose

This dish is a special dish I have served through the years to large groups of guests. Everyone has enjoyed it, I know, for they want second helpings. That, to me, is a sign of a good recipe. This dish is better when made the day before, and it can be frozen.

> 2 (2-lb.) young chickens
> 1 cup California Pinot Blanc or
>   other white table wine
> Salt and pepper
> 1½ cups small shell macaroni, uncooked
> ½ cup chopped green pepper
> ½ cup chopped pimientos
> 2 (4-oz.) cans button mushrooms,
>   drained
> 1 (10½-oz.) can cream of chicken or
>   mushroom soup, undiluted
> 4 or 5 dashes Tabasco sauce
> 1 cup cheese cracker crumbs
> 1 cup grated sharp cheese

Cook chicken in wine and enough water to cover (about 2 to 3 cups) until tender, seasoning with salt and pepper. Pour off and reserve liquid from chicken. Measure cooking liquid from chicken; add enough water to make 1¼ quarts. Cook macaroni and green pepper in chicken liquid for 10 minutes. Drain, reserving liquid. Cut chicken meat into bite-size pieces. In a large mixing bowl, combine chicken, cooked macaroni, green pepper, pimientos, drained mushrooms, soup, chicken liquid and Tabasco sauce. In an 8 x 12-inch glass baking dish, place a layer of chicken mixture; top with cracker crumbs, then grated cheese. Repeat layers until all ingredients are used, ending with cheese. Bake in moderate oven (350 degrees) until cheese has melted. Serves 8 to 10.

POLLO EN GRAPPA
Mrs. Louis A. Petri, United Vintners, Inc., San Francisco

> 2 Tbs. olive oil
> 1 large roasting chicken, cut in pieces
> 1 tsp. salt
> ¼ tsp. pepper
> ½ cup chopped onion
> 1 clove garlic, minced
> 2 or 3 oranges, peeled and cut
>   into segments
> 1 small pineapple, hulled and
>   cut in eighths
> 1 stick fresh ginger root
> 2 tomatoes, quartered
> 2 tsp. brown sugar
> 1 cup California Grappa Brandy

Heat oil in large Dutch oven. Brown chicken pieces in oil, then add salt, pepper, onion and garlic. Heat until onion is transparent. Remove from heat and add all other ingredients except Grappa. Cover and bake in slow oven (325 degrees) 1 to 1½ hours until chicken is tender. Ten minutes before serving, remove cover and add Grappa. Serves 4.

BRUNSWICK STEW, CALIFORNIA STYLE
J.W. Fleming, Lockeford Winery, Lodi

Place 1 (4 to 5-lb.) stewing chicken in a large kettle. Add 1 cup California Sauterne or other white table wine and enough boiling water so that chicken is barely covered. Season with 1 tablespoon salt and onion, celery, parsley and peppercorns to taste. Cover and simmer for 2½ to 3 hours, or just until chicken is tender. Let cool in broth, then remove meat from bones and cut in good-sized pieces. Strain broth and skim off fat. Prepare remainder of dish as follows:

> ⅓ cup chicken fat, butter or
>   margarine
> 1 large onion, minced
> ⅓ cup flour
> 2 cups chicken broth
> 1 (No. 2) can stewed tomatoes
> 2 tsp. Worcestershire sauce
> Salt and pepper to taste
> 1 (No. 303) can lima
>   beans, drained
> 1 (12-oz.) can whole kernel corn
> 1 (No. 303) can okra, drained
> 2 cups diced raw potatoes
> 2 Tbs. California Sherry

Heat fat in heavy kettle. Add onion and cook gently for 5 minutes. Blend in flour; add chicken broth and tomatoes; cook, stirring constantly, until mixture boils and thickens. Add seasonings and vegetables. Cover, simmer gently for 30 minutes, stirring occasionally. Add chicken and Sherry; continue cooking 15 minutes longer. Serves 8.

BAKED TURKEY SANDWICHES

Baked Turkey Sandwiches are ideal for a Sunday night supper because all the makings may be prepared ahead of time. At the last minute, build and bake the sandwiches, toss a salad and open a bottle of California white table wine for a perfect informal meal. To serve 4, first prepare a flavorful Sherried mushroom sauce. To assemble sandwiches, place 2 slices toast side by side in each of 4 shallow, oval individual baking dishes. Spread toast with some of the mushroom sauce; top with 4 servings sliced, cooked turkey, then with 8 slices crisp-cooked bacon. Distribute remaining sauce over sandwiches, sprinkle with ½ cup grated Cheddar cheese and dust with paprika. Bake in a hot oven (450 degrees) 10 minutes, or until bubbly. Serve at once. (Lacking individual baking dishes, arrange and bake sandwiches in one large shallow baking pan, then carefully remove them to heated plates.)

CHICKEN WINGS IN LEMON SAUCE
Maxine Mabry, Landmark Vineyards, Sonoma County

> 12-16 chicken wings, cut in half and
>   with tips removed
> Salt and freshly ground white pepper
> 5 Tbs. butter
> 1 Tbs. vegetable oil
> 4 shallots, finely minced
> ½ cup white wine
> 1 cup chicken stock
> 1 bouquet garni
> ½ lb. mushrooms, finely sliced
> 1 tsp. cornstarch
> Juice of 1 lemon
> 2 egg yolks
> ¾ cup heavy cream or crème fraiche
> 2 Tbs. finely minced fresh parsley

Season the chicken wings with salt and pepper and set aside. Heat 3 tablespoons of the butter and the oil in a large, heavy skillet. Add the wings, a few at a time, and cook, partially covered, over medium heat until nicely browned on all sides. When all the wings are done, remove them to a side dish. Add the shallots to the pan and cook for 1 to 2 minutes or until they are soft and lightly browned. Add wine and stock. Bring the mixture to a boil, then add salt, pepper and the bouquet garni. Scrape the bottom of the pan well. Reduce the heat. Return the wings to the skillet, cover, simmer for 20 to 25 minutes or until tender but not falling apart. While the wings are cooking, heat the remaining butter in a small, heavy skillet. Add the mushrooms and cook over high heat until they are lightly browned. Season with salt and pepper and set aside. In a small mixing bowl, combine cornstarch, lemon juice, egg yolks and cream. Whisk the mixture until it is smooth and well blended. Season with salt and pepper and set aside. As soon as the chicken wings are done, with a slotted spoon remove them and the mushrooms to a warmed serving dish. Add the egg yolk and cream mixture to the pan juices. Whisk the sauce over low heat without letting it come to a boil. Taste and correct the seasoning. Spoon the sauce over the chicken wings. Sprinkle with parsley and serve immediately. Serves 4 to 6.

FRUITED CHICKEN SALAD
Dolores Cakebread, Cakebread Cellars, Rutherford

> 1 (28-oz.) can pears
> 1 (12-oz.) pkg. frozen rice pilaf
> 4 chicken breasts, (skinned)
> 1½ cups dry white wine
> ¼ cup chopped green pepper
> ¼ cup diced celery
> ¼ cup salted peanuts
> 2 Tbs. chopped green onion
> ¼ cup mayonnaise
> ½ tsp. curry powder

Chill the canned pears. Prepare the package of rice pilaf according to package directions. Cool. Poach the chicken breasts, (skinned), in half white wine and half water, until tender. Cool. Cube the chicken and mix with the rice pilaf, chopped green pepper, diced celery, peanuts, chopped green onion and curry powder. Mix the mayonnaise with 2 tablespoons dry white wine, and gently mix with the salad, (use more or less mayonnaise to your taste). Salt and pepper to taste. Mound onto lettuce lined plates, arrange canned pears around salad and garnish with small clusters of grapes or Mandarin orange slices. Serve with slightly chilled Cakebread Cellars Sauvignon Blanc.

TURKEYAKI
Mrs. Maury Baldwin, Sacramento

My husband and I tasted turkeyaki at the California State Fair several years ago, and have served it many times since then. We have never been able to decide if turkeyaki is more delicious hot or served cold the next day. Either way, it is superb.

> 4 lbs. boned turkey meat
> 2 cups California Sauterne or
>   other white table wine
> 1 cup soy sauce
> 1 cup olive oil
> 1 clove garlic, minced
> Juice of ½ lemon
> ½ tsp. powdered ginger (optional)

Cut turkey meat into 1½-inch cubes. Combine remaining ingredients; pour over turkey. Marinate at least 1 hour before cooking, stirring occasionally to expose all meat to marinade. Remove from marinade; place cubes on bamboo or metal skewers. Dip in remaining marinade. Broil over hot coals, turning skewers frequently, until meat is evenly browned, about 20 minutes. Do not overcook. Serve with rice pilaf. (If it's an unusual holiday dinner, the typical "all the trimmings" menu can be used.) When serving a large group, I bone the turkey the day before, since that is the most difficult part in preparing the recipe. Serves 6 to 8.

YOUNG TURKEY IN ITS JUICES

Mrs. Herbert Cerwin, Cerwin Vineyard, Sonoma

> 1 (6-lb.) young turkey
> Salt and pepper
> 2 Tbs. butter, melted
> ¼ lb. salt pork, sliced
> ¼ lb. veal, thinly sliced
> 1 cup California white table wine
> Herb bouquet (tie together parsley,
>   1 or 2 sprigs celery and 1 small
>   sprig thyme)

Season turkey with salt and pepper; place in large Dutch oven or small roaster. Brush with melted butter. Place in hot oven (450 degrees) for about 10 minutes, or until lightly browned. Remove from the oven; reduce heat to 300 degrees. Line a large casserole or terrine with alternating slices of salt pork and veal. Put in bird, breast side up. Add wine and herb bouquet; cover tightly, Place in slow oven (300 degrees); cook about 1½ hours, or until turkey is tender. Remove turkey from oven. Skim off excess fat from pan gravy; pour gravy over turkey placed on hot platter. If desired, gravy may be thickened with a little cornstarch mixed with cold water. Serve with hot purée of chestnuts and mixed green salad. Serves 6 to 8.

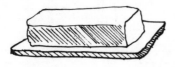

ROAST DUCKLING VERMOUTH

Bernice T. Glenn, Wine Advisory Board, San Francisco

> 1 (5-6 lb.) roasting duckling
> ¾ cup California Vermouth
>   (dry or sweet)
> 1 clove garlic
> ⅛ tsp. black pepper
> ¼ tsp. paprika
> ¼ tsp. salt
> 1 large orange

Wipe outside and cavity of duck with ¼ cup of wine; let stand several hours. Mash garlic clove and blend in pepper, paprika, and salt to make a stiff paste. If liquid is needed, add a few drops of Vermouth. Rub paste over duck, outside and inside, and prick fatty surface with a fork. Place orange inside the cavity. Roast in very hot oven (500 degrees) for ½ hour, draining off fat accumulating in pan. Lower heat to moderate (350 degrees) and continue roasting until tender, about 1½ to 2 hours longer. Baste duckling with remaining ½ cup Vermouth until ½ hour before done. Discard orange from cavity and serve. Menu might include: fresh grapefruit-apple-walnut salad; green rice; orange sherbet for dessert. Serves 3 to 4.

PORTED GAME HENS

Mrs. Ann H. Burton, Roma Wine Company, Fresno

> 6 Rock Cornish game hens
> About 4½ cups wild rice stuffing
> Butter or margarine
> ½ cup currant jelly
> 2 Tbs. butter or margarine
> Juice of ½ lemon
> 4 whole cloves
> Dash of salt
> ½ cup California Port

Stuff each game hen with about ¾ cup wild rice dressing. Rub hens with butter. In a saucepan, combine jelly, 2 tablespoons butter, lemon juice, cloves and salt. Bring to boiling and simmer 5 minutes. Remove from heat; add the Port. Roast hens in very hot oven (450 degrees) for 10 minutes. Reduce heat to 350 degrees; continue cooking for 1½ hours, basting with wine sauce. If desired, just before removing birds from oven, brown under broiler for a minute or two. Asparagus and spiced crabapples are a colorful and appropriate accompaniment. Include a Caesar salad, hot rolls and frozen lime pie for dessert. Serves 4 to 6.

SHERRIED CHICKEN LIVERS

E. M. Cobb, California Growers Wineries, Cutler

> 1 lb. chicken livers
> 4 Tbs. butter or margarine
> 2 Tbs. chopped onion
> 2 Tbs. flour
> 1 (10¾-oz.) can beef gravy
> ¼ cup California Sherry
> 1 Tbs. canned tomato paste
> Salt and pepper
> 1 (4-oz.) can mushroom stems and
>   pieces, drained
> 2 Tbs. chopped parsley

Cut chicken livers in halves. Melt butter in a large, heavy skillet; sauté onion until golden. Add chicken livers; sauté gently about 5 minutes, or until lightly browned, turning frequently. Remove livers from pan. Add flour to drippings, blend well; add gravy and wine; cook, stirring, until mixture boils and thickens. Blend in tomato paste; season with salt and pepper. Just before serving, add livers, mushrooms and parsley to sauce; heat gently but thoroughly. Serve on toast, or with rice or noodles. Serves 4.

PIGEONS WITH PEAS

Mrs. Leo Trentadue, Trentadue Winery, Geyserville

>   *4 young pigeons (squab)*
>   *Salt*
>   *freshly ground black pepper*
>   *2 Tbs. butter*
>   *2 Tbs. oil*
>   *1 medium onion, chopped*
>   *5 bacon slices, chopped*
>   *⅔ cup dry white wine*
>   *1¼ cups chicken stock*
>   *3 cups shelled green peas*
>   *1 tsp. sugar*

Wash and dry the pigeons. Season inside and outside with salt and pepper. In a large flameproof casserole, heat the butter and oil and fry the onion and bacon gently until the onion is soft and golden. Increase the heat, add the pigeons and cook, turning frequently, until golden brown all over, about 15 minutes. Add the wine and allow to bubble briskly until reduced to half the quantity: add the stock, bring to the boil, cover tightly and simmer very gently for 1¼ to 1½ hours or until the pigeons are almost tender. Check the pan from time to time to make sure there is enough liquid, adding more stock if necessary. Stir in peas with sugar and a little salt. Cover and simmer gently for another 20 minutes or until peas and pigeons are tender. Serves 4.

CORNISH HEN BAKED IN WINE

Rudolf Weibel, Weibel Champagne Vineyards, Mission San Jose

>   *½ cup shortening*
>   *2 small onions, minced*
>   *2 whole cloves*
>   *1 tsp. peppercorns*
>   *2 cloves garlic, cut fine*
>   *½ bay leaf*
>   *6 cornish hens, cleaned and trussed*
>   *2 cups California white table wine*
>   *(Chablis, Grey Riesling, etc.)*
>   *½ tsp. salt*
>   *⅛ tsp. pepper*
>   *Few grains cayenne*
>   *1 tsp. minced chives*
>   *2 cups cream or evaporated milk*
>   *(undiluted)*

Melt shortening, add onions, cloves, peppercorns, garlic and bay leaf. Cook for several minutes. Add birds and brown on all sides. Add wine, salt, pepper, cayenne and chives. Simmer until birds are tender, about 30 minutes. Remove to hot serving dish. Strain pan sauce. Add cream and heat to boiling point. Pour over birds. Serve with wild rice. Serves 6.

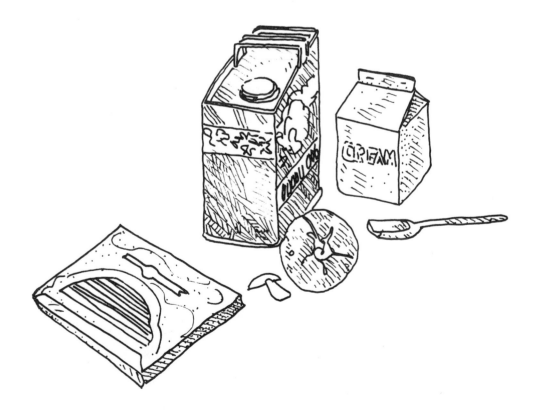

Wild Game

"Then charge your glasses merrily round, since we're supplied with hare and hound, while cheerful Bacchus leads us on."
— *Anonymous English hunting poem*

Seldom is food more rewarding than that which the hunter himself has bagged for the feast. And you'll find that game flavor reaches its peak when marinated in wine, which acts as a meat tenderizer as well. Game birds, which are usually dry, will benefit from the extra juiciness as well as the richly mellow flavor of a wine braise or baste. To really bring out the best in your sights, sit down to the feast with a bottle of California wine.

ROAST PHEASANT VERMOUTH

Mrs. John L. Tribuno, Vermouth Industries of California
Delano

3 Tbs. butter
3 green onions, chopped
½ cup canned mushrooms, drained
¼ cup chopped pecans
1 apple, chopped
¾ cup bread crumbs, soft but
   slightly dry
Salt and pepper
California Dry Vermouth
1 pheasant
½ cup butter
1 cup California Dry Vermouth

Melt butter, add onions and mushrooms. Sauté until onions are tender. Add pecans, apple, bread crumbs, seasonings and enough Vermouth to bind together. (Amount of Vermouth depends on dryness of bread.) Stuff pheasant with bread crumb mixture and place in roasting pan. Melt butter, mix with 1 cup of Vermouth and pour over bird. Roast in slow oven (300 degrees) for 1 hour, basting frequently. Slow cooking is very important to keep the bird moist. Pour pan sauce over pheasant before serving. Serve with broiled tomatoes, Boston lettuce and watercress salad with oil and wine vinegar dressing. For dessert, Brandied peaches or sugared strawberries with lemon peel in dry red wine. Serves 2 to 3.

20-MINUTE VENISON STEW

Mrs. Edward Prati, Martini & Prati Wines, Inc.,
Santa Rosa

1 to 1½ lbs. venison or beef
   (use a tender cut)
2 Tbs. olive oil
2 green peppers, cleaned and
   cut into 1½-inch squares
1 tsp. garlic salt
½ tsp. pepper
3 Tbs. California red
   table wine
2 medium tomatoes, peeled and
   quartered
1 (10¾-oz.) can beef gravy

Cut meat ¼ inch thick and into 1½ inch squares. Heat Dutch oven over very high heat. Add oil, coating sides and bottom of pan; pour out excess. Add venison, peppers, garlic salt and pepper. Stir rapidly and constantly for about 5 minutes. Add wine; continue stirring vigorously until wine is absorbed, about 5 minutes. Reduce heat to simmer. Add tomatoes and beef gravy. Cover tightly and simmer 10 minutes. Serve at once, over rice, with tossed salad. For dessert-fruit and cheeses. Serves 4 to 6.

GUINEA HEN IN WHITE WINE
Mrs. Herbert Cerwin, Cerwin Vineyard, Sonoma

> *2 young guinea hens*
> *Flour*
> *6 Tbs. butter*
> *Salt, pepper, nutmeg*
> *2 cloves shallot, finely chopped*
> *1 cup California white table wine*
>   *(Riesling or Traminer)*
> *2 tsp. prepared mustard*
> *Juice of 5 lemons*
> *1 Tbs. grated lemon rind*

Cut guinea hens in pieces at joints. Flour and brown in 5 tablespoons of the butter. Sprinkle on salt, pepper and nutmeg. Transfer to covered roasting pan or casserole. Chop hearts and livers and sauté in remaining 1 tablespoon butter along with shallots. Pour in wine, add mustard, lemon juice and rind, and heat to simmering. Pour over guinea hen in casserole. Cover and bake in slow oven (325 degrees) about 1½ hours, until tender. Serves 4.

ROAST PHEASANT
Mrs. J. F. M. Taylor, Mayacamas Vineyards, Napa

> *1 pheasant*
> *Savory salt*
> *2 pieces celery*
> *1 small apple, quartered*
> *Pheasant liver*
> *4 strips bacon*
> *1 cup canned consommé or*
>   *chicken broth (undiluted)*
> *½ cup California white table wine*
> *8 mushroom caps*

Sprinkle the inside of pheasant liberally with savory salt. Stuff with celery, apple and the bird's liver. Lay bacon on a rack in bottom of roasting pan and place bird on it, breast side up. Pour in mixture of consommé and wine. Place mushroom caps, hollow side up, around bird and sprinkle additional savory salt in each. Roast pheasant in hot oven (450 degrees) 40 to 60 minutes, depending on size of bird. Baste every 10 minutes with pan juices. Serve with wild rice.

WILD RICE:
> *½ cup wild rice*
> *1½ cups water*
> *Salt*
> *12 chopped almonds*
> *¼ cup dried currants*

Wash rice thoroughly and let soak in water for at least an hour. Drain. Bring salted water to boil, add rice and simmer, uncovered, until dry and fluffy. Add almonds and currants. To serve: Put pheasant on platter. Place rice around it, and spoon remaining basting sauce over all. Lay crisp bacon strips on top at the last minute. Serves 2.

WILD GAME POT ROAST

Wild Game Pot Roast is the way **Mrs. H. L. Wente, Wente Bros., Livermore**, answered the challenge: "What can you do with a piece of moose?" Place a 3 to 4 pound cut of moose, elk or venison in a mixture of 4 cups California Claret, 1 medium onion, sliced, 1 large bay leaf, ½ teaspoon dried rosemary, 3 or 4 crushed peppercorns, 3 or 4 juniper berries. Marinate for at least an hour, turning meat; remove meat and dry. Heat 4 tablespoons olive oil in a Dutch oven, brown meat lightly, then cover and bake in slow oven (300 degrees) 30 minutes to the pound. If more baste is needed, use heated wine. Serve pot roast with the same Claret used in preparing the dish.

BURGUNDY VENISON STEW

Burgundy Venison Stew is hearty fare, fully-flavored. **Mrs. Otto Beringer, Beringer Bros., Inc., St. Helena**, dredges meat in seasoned flour, browns it in hot olive oil with chopped onion. She then adds California Burgundy to the pot along with carrots, parsley, garlic, rosemary, Italian seasoning. Thin tomato sauce and mushroom gravy with equal parts of water and pour over meat. Simmer 3 to 3½ hours; ½ hour before serving add button mushrooms, garlic, chopped parsley and more California Burgundy. Serve stew on top of polenta with soft Monterey Jack cheese, or over steamed rice. Wine choice for this dish would be a California Burgundy or Pinot Noir.

VENISON SPARERIBS
Mrs. Frank J. Pilone, Cucamonga Vineyard Company, Cucamonga

This is my own recipe.

> *12 venison ribs*
> *Salt and pepper*
> *1 cup chili sauce*
> *½ cup lemon juice*
> *½ cup California Sherry*
> *1 onion, chopped*
> *1 stalk celery, chopped*
> *½ green pepper, chopped*

Cut ribs into serving pieces; if large, cut in half. Place ribs in roaster; brown, uncovered, in hot oven (400 degrees) for 20 minutes. Drain off all fat. Combine all remaining ingredients in saucepan; bring to boil. Pour over ribs. Reduce oven heat to 325 degrees. Bake ribs, covered, about 2½ hours or until done. Baste frequently with additional Sherry, Sauterne or water. Venison requires a lot of basting, for it is a dry meat. With this dish I like to serve risotto, zucchini and tossed green salad. Serves 3 to 4.

SAVORY VENISON
Mrs. Tulio D'Agostini, D'Agostini Winery, Plymouth

The secret of enjoyable venison is to marinate the meat thoroughly. That, in addition to slow *covered* cooking, will produce a meal "fit for the gods". I always use a white wine when cooking venison. It imparts a good flavor, yet does not cause the meat to darken.

> 2 cups wine vinegar
> 4 cups water
> 1 clove garlic
> 3 Tbs. chopped parsley
> 1 whole clove
> 1 tsp. oregano
> 4 lbs. venison chops, steaks or ribs
> 4 strips salt pork
> 2 large onions, sliced
> 1 cup diced carrots
> 1 cup peas, fresh, frozen or canned
> 1 cup California white table wine
>   (Dry Muscat or Sauterne)

Combine vinegar and water and bring to boil; add garlic, parsley, clove and oregano. Cool. Pour into glass or porcelain container. Place venison in this marinade and refrigerate overnight. Turn occasionally. When ready to cook, remove venison from marinade and dry off with paper towels. In heavy kettle, such as Dutch oven, fry salt pork briefly, then put in venison and top with onion slices. Cook over moderate heat about 30 minutes until meat is well browned on both sides. Add vegetables plus a small amount of liquid from canned peas or some of the strained marinade. Bake, covered, in a slow oven (300 degrees) about 1½ hours. When meat is tender, add wine and continue cooking another 15 minutes. Serves 4 to 6.

WILD DUCK POACHED IN WINE SAUCE
Aldo Fabbrini, Beaulieu Vineyard, Rutherford

> ½ lb. butter
> 2 Tbs. Worcestershire sauce
> 1 Tbs. red currant jelly
> 2 cups California Burgundy or
>   other red table wine
> 1 jigger (2 Tbs.) Benedictine
> Breasts of wild duck
> Salt and pepper

Melt butter and add all ingredients except duck. Mix well. Cut raw duck breasts and simmer in sauce 12 minutes if small, up to 20 minutes, if large. Add salt and pepper. Serves 2.

GRAPE-STUFFED WILD DUCK
Mrs. E. L. Barr, Western Grape Products, Kingsburg

This is a favorite recipe which I obtained from Mr. Abe Rodder of Fresno.

The night before cooking, season inside of ducks with generous amount of salt and pepper; stuff them with Emperor or Tokay grapes. With a 30-guage physician's hypodermic needle, insert California Burgundy into breasts and legs. (This gives the meat an unusual flavor, and if you like ducks well done, the meat will be soft and juicy, and not stringy as is the case without this process.) Rub meat portion of ducks with considerable garlic; then paint entire ducks generously with hot butter (this seals the duck). Refrigerate until ready to roast. Roast in a moderate oven (350 degrees) about 2 hours, or use your own judgement as to how well done you like ducks. To serve, cut down center and place one half with skin-side up, the other half skin-side down. A little trimming of parsley, wild rice and mint jelly will give you a gourmet's delight. Apple sauce is also good served as a side-dish.

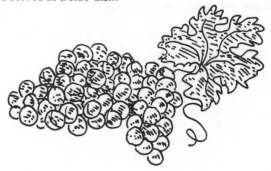

QUAIL CAROLINA
J. C. Russell, Almaden Vineyards, Los Gatos

> 4 quail (or squab)
> 4 stalks celery
> 8 slices carrot
> 2 Tbs. butter
> 2 Tbs. olive oil
> 1 onion, sliced
> 6 ripe black olives
> 1 cup California white table wine
> ¼ cup California Dry Sherry
> ¼ cup California Dry Vermouth
> ½ cup chicken stock
> Salt and pepper
> Pinch of oregano
> 2 Tbs. finely chopped parsley

Insert in cavity of each quail, 1 stalk celery and 2 slices carrot. Sauté quail in butter and olive oil until lightly browned. Add onion to pan and sauté lightly. Add olives, wines, chicken stock, salt, pepper and oregano. Cover and cook slowly until quail are tender, about 1 hour. Just before serving, add parsley. Serve quail over spoon bread, with string beans and fresh okra broiled in butter. Serves 3 to 4.

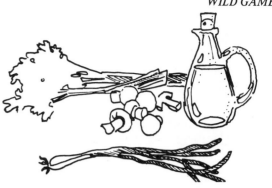

PHEASANT WITH BRANDY AND CREAM

Mrs. Everett T. Estes, Sanger Winery Association, Sanger

> *3 pheasants*
> *6 slices bacon*
> *¼ cup butter*
> *8 shallots, thinly sliced (or 2*
> *Tbs. minced onion and 1*
> *clove garlic, crushed)*
> *½ cup California Brandy*
> *2 cups chicken stock*
> *½ tsp. freshly ground*
> *black pepper*
> *1 tsp. salt*
> *1 pint heavy cream*
> *¼ cup prepared horseradish*

Cover breast of each pheasant with 2 bacon slices; truss birds to keep shape while cooking. In large heavy skillet, brown birds in butter along with shallots (or onion and garlic); remove to baking pan along with juices from skillet. Pour Brandy over birds; set aflame. When flame dies, add chicken stock, pepper and salt. Roast, uncovered, in moderate oven (375 degrees) for 30 to 45 minutes (depending on size of birds), basting frequently. Add cream and horseradish to pan juices; continue roasting for 15 minutes, basting frequently. Test for doneness. Serve with sauce from pan. This dish would go well with wild rice, any vegetable, green salad, hot rolls and currant jelly. Serves 6.

BARBECUED WILD DUCK

Barbecued wild duck is outstanding in flavor, yet simple to prepare as done by Mrs. Walter H. Sullivan Jr., Beaulieu Vineyard, Rutherford. She explains as follows: Rub each duck inside and out with lemon juice and olive oil. Put into each cavity 1 stalk of celery and 4 or 5 juniper berries. Place ducks on large barbecue skewer, alternating them, one breast-side up, the next breast-side down. Season with salt and pepper; roast over coals. (I always use either oak or vine stumps from old grape vines, when we have them.) After 20 minutes, put ducks close to fire so that skins become crunchy. Remove birds from skewer to fire-proof platter or dish. Pour California Brandy over and set aflame. Serve with a risotto mixed with slivered almonds, and a salad made with equal parts of sliced oranges and sliced sweet onions, with a vinaigrette dressing. I like a full-bodied California Burgundy with this.

SHERRIED ROAST PHEASANT

Mrs. Joseph Concannon Jr., Concannon Vineyard,
Livermore

This recipe is not an original, but we think it is the finest pheasant recipe we have ever encountered. If properly cooked, the breast can be sliced much easier than turkey. It can be prepared early in the morning, thus cutting kitchen time if company is coming. Since pheasant season happily coincides with Thanksgiving (and Joe is a hunter), this recipe is usually used as our traditional Thanksgiving dinner. Amount can be easily doubled or tripled.

> *½ medium-sized, mild onion,*
> *finely chopped*
> *2 Tbs. butter or margarine*
> *1 (4-oz.) can mushrooms (stems*
> *and pieces)*
> *½ cup raw regular rice*
> *2 Tbs. chopped fresh parsley*
> *or 2 tsp. dried parsley*
> *Salt and pepper*
> *1 pheasant, washed and drained*
> *4 thick slices bacon*
> *½ cup California Dry Sherry*
> *¼ cup melted butter*
> *Sherry Sauce (see below)*

Sauté onion in butter about 5 minutes, until limp. Measure liquid from can of mushrooms and add water to make 1 cup. Add to cooked onion and bring to boil. Slowly add rice, stirring constantly. Cover and cook over low heat until all liquid is absorbed, about 20-25 minutes. Stir in mushrooms and parsley; season to taste. Stuff pheasant loosely with rice mixture; truss and place in baking pan, breast up. Lay slices of bacon over breast and legs. Roast, uncovered, in a moderate oven (350 degrees) for about 1½ hours or until pheasant is tender. Baste often with warmed mixture of Sherry and butter. Remove pheasant to heated platter and keep warm while preparing Sherry Sauce. Since pheasant itself is so rich, we usually serve peas, a simple green salad and a light dessert such as fresh fruit or sherbet.
SHERRY SAUCE: Pour off and discard all except 3 tablespoons of drippings from roasted pheasant. Stir in 3 tablespoons flour and add chicken broth made by dissolving 2 chicken bouillon cubes in 1½ cups boiling water. Stir until sauce thickens. Add 2 tablespoons California Dry Sherry. Adjust seasoning. Serve sauce hot with pheasant. Serves 2 to 4.

ROSEMARY RABBIT
*Mrs. John George Franzia Sr., Franzia Brothers Winery
  Ripon*

To cook rabbit slowly and evenly, without burning, I like
to use an 11¾-inch cast iron skillet.

> 1 frying rabbit, cut in serving-size
>   pieces
> Salt and pepper
> 2 eggs, slightly beaten
> About 2 cups dry bread or fine
>   cornflake crumbs
> Oil
> 1 Tbs. fresh rosemary leaves
> ¾ cup California Sauterne, Chablis,
>   or other white table wine

Season rabbit pieces with salt and pepper. Dip each piece
in beaten egg, then in bread crumbs. Fry quickly in heated
oil, about 10 minutes on each side. Sprinkle with rosemary
leaves, salt and pepper; add wine. Cover and cook slowly
about 30 minutes, or until tender. (Chicken may also be
prepared this way.) Serve with mashed potatoes, green
peas, sliced tomatoes and French bread, with fruit-flavored
gelatin for dessert. Serves 3 to 4.

ROAST BRACE OF RABBIT
Mrs. James Concannon, Concannon Vineyard, Livermore

> 1 cup California Burgundy or
>   other red table wine
> 6 pitted prunes
> 1 small bay leaf
> 1 whole clove
> 6 thin onion slices
> 1 clove garlic, mashed
> 1 carrot, thinly sliced
> 1 parsnip, chopped
> ¼ cup mushroom stems and pieces
> ¼ cup margarine
> 2 young rabbits (including livers),
>   cut in serving-size pieces
> 1 cup cream

Combine wine, prunes, bay leaf, clove, onion slices, garlic,
carrot, parsnip, mushrooms, margarine and rabbit livers
in roasting pan. Add rabbit pieces; sear in very hot oven
(500 degrees) for 10 minutes, without basting. Reduce heat to
350 degrees. Cover and cook about 35 minutes, or until
tender, adding a little water, if necessary; baste frequently.
Arrange rabbit pieces on platter and keep warm. Strain pan
drippings into a saucepan. Slowly stir in cream; bring to a
boil. Correct seasoning. Pour half the sauce over the rabbit
pieces; serve remainder in a sauceboat. Menu could include
mashed potatoes, steamed zucchini and fruit compote.
Serves 4 to 6.

RABBIT IN WHITE WINE
Mrs. Steve Riboli, San Antonio Winery, Inc., Los Angeles

> 1 (3 to 3½-lb.) young rabbit
> ½ tsp. salt
> ⅛ tsp. pepper
> ⅛ tsp. allspice
> 2 Tbs. butter
> 1 Tbs. olive oil
> 2 bay leaves
> 2 cups California white table wine
> 3 Tbs. canned condensed cream
>   of mushroom soup or consommé
>   undiluted

Cut rabbit into small serving pieces; sprinkle with salt,
pepper and allspice. Heat butter and olive oil in a large
heavy skillet; brown rabbit slowly on all sides, about 30
minutes. Add bay leaves, wine and soup. Cover and
simmer about 1 hour, or until done. Serve with steamed
rice and tossed green salad. Serves 6 to 8.

RABBIT SWEET AND SOUR
Ed Schuh, The Christian Brothers, Napa

I first ate this delicious dish in the home of Italian friends,
and was so intrigued by it that I asked Zoe, my wife, to
take the recipe home. We have it frequently, with artichoke
hearts, rice pilaf, and glasses of Sauterne.

> 1 (3 to 4-lb.) rabbit
> ¼ cup olive oil
> 1 Tbs. chopped salt pork
> 1 Tbs. chopped parsley
> 1 clove garlic, minced
> ¼ tsp. crushed red pepper seeds
> Salt and pepper
> 1 tsp. sugar
> 1 Tbs. California wine vinegar
> 1 cup California Sauterne or
>   other white table wine
> 2 Tbs. tomato paste
> ½ cup warm water
> 2 Tbs. pine nuts
> 2 Tbs. raisins

Cut rabbit into small serving pieces. Heat olive oil in
heavy skillet; add salt pork, parsley, garlic and crushed
pepper seeds. Add rabbit; brown well on all sides. Add
salt, pepper, sugar and vinegar; mix well. Pour ½ cup of
the wine over the rabbit. Cover tightly; simmer 10 minutes.
Blend tomato paste with warm water; add to pan. Lower
heat; add pine nuts and raisins. Cover tightly; simmer 20
to 30 minutes, or until rabbit is tender. Add remaining ½
cup wine; boil rapidly for 1 minute. Serve immediately.
Serves 4 to 6.

Fish & Seafood

"Fish without wine is like an egg without salt."

—Auguste Escoffier

The art of fish cookery is best approached with boldness and imagination. It's easy with California wine as your culinary ally, and with one paramount rule in mind: do not overcook. Enhance the delicate flavor of any fish simply, with wine and butter; or prepare your dish with a creamy wine-and-mushroom sauce. Either way, wine blends and perfects the flavors, eliminating the sometimes "fishy" taste, and rewarding you with exquisite dining pleasure.

HALIBUT PORTUGUESA

Mrs. Walter H. Sullivan Jr., Beaulieu Vineyard, Rutherford

1 to 1½ lbs. halibut steak
Salt
Lemon juice
2 small ripe tomatoes (or 1 large), chopped
1 medium-sized onion, finely minced
2 cloves garlic, crushed
¼ cup olive oil
1 tsp. sugar
¼ cup chopped fresh parsley
3 Tbs. tomato paste
¾ cup California Sherry
½ cup water
3 slices lemon
3 Tbs. butter

Place halibut in an oiled shallow baking dish. Sprinkle with salt and a few drops lemon juice. Simmer tomatoes, onion and garlic in olive oil until soft and golden. Add salt to taste (about 1 teaspoon), sugar, parsley, tomato paste and Sherry (which has previously been brought to a boil twice); simmer until well blended. Add water, stirring to blend. Pour sauce over the fish; top with lemon slices. Cover dish completely with aluminum foil, wrapping foil around bottom of dish. Bake in moderately-hot oven (375 degrees) for 1 hour. Serve with fluffy boiled rice. Serves 3 to 4.

FISHERMAN'S STEW

Paul H. Huber, E. & J. Gallo Winery, Fresno

1 lb. salmon, cut in 2-inch squares
1 lb. rock cod, cut in 2-inch squares
Salt and pepper
Allspice
½ cup diced, parboiled salt pork
2 Tbs. butter
2 cloves garlic, crushed
2 Tbs. chopped parsley
2 tsp. minced fresh thyme
Flour
2 cups California white table wine
1 cup water
1 bay leaf
½ tsp. crushed peppercorns
2 cooked crabs (use large legs, claws and body, quartered)

Rub squares of salmon and rock cod with salt, pepper and allspice; chill. Brown salt pork in butter along with garlic, parsley and thyme. Dust fish with flour; sauté lightly in seasoned butter. Add wine, water, bay leaf and crushed peppercorns. Simmer 20 minutes; remove bay leaf. Add crab; cook 10 minutes longer. Thicken liquid, if desired. Serve over toasted garlic French bread. (If more gravy is desired, more wine may be added during cooking.) Serves 4 to 6.

LING COD MARGUERY

Mrs. Anthony Cribari, Cribari Winery, San Jose

While in Atlantic City, I ordered fillet of sole marguery in casserole, and asked the waiter how it was cooked. This recipe is my own interpretation, using California ling cod. The dish can be made the day before and kept in the refrigerator until you want to heat and serve it.

> *1 (2-lb.) piece ling cod*
> *2 cups California white table wine*
> *1 cup water*
> *1 small onion, sliced*
> *½ tsp. oregano*
> *2 (10-oz.) packages frozen chopped*
> * spinach*
> *2 Tbs. butter*
> *2 Tbs. flour*
> *⅓ tsp. salt*
> *Few grains white pepper*
> *1 small can evaporated milk*
> *3 Tbs. California Dry Sherry*
> *½ cup grated Swiss cheese*
> *½ lb. cooked small shrimp*
> *Buttered bread crumbs*

Boil ling cod slowly in white wine and water along with onion and oregano until tender, about 7 to 10 minutes. Do not overcook. Cool fish; remove skin and bone. Strain cooking liquid and reserve for later use. Cook frozen spinach in double boiler, seasoned as desired; drain well. Butter a 12 x 8 x 3-inch baking pan. Spread spinach on bottom of pan; place boned cod on top to cover spinach. Melt butter in saucepan; stir in flour, salt and white pepper until smooth. Gradually add evaporated milk and enough reserved cooking liquid to make 1½ cups. Cook in double boiler stirring, until sauce is thickened and creamy. Add Sherry, grated cheese and shrimp. Pour over fish and spinach. Sprinkle with buttered bread crumbs. Bake in moderate oven (350 degrees) for 20 minutes, or until heated through. Good with baked potato and mixed green salad. Serves 6 to 8.

BAKED TROUT ST. HELENA

Mrs. Robert Mondavi, Robert Mondavi Winery, Oakville

> *3 to 5 lbs. fresh whole trout*
> *Salt and pepper*
> *1 (No. 2½) can solid-pack tomatoes*
> *2 Tbs. olive oil*
> *2 Tbs. chopped parsley*
> *1 small clove garlic, minced*
> *½ cup California Sauterne or other*
> * white table wine*

Clean trout well; salt and pepper inside and out. Place in baking dish. Cover with tomatoes, olive oil, parsley and garlic. Bake in a hot oven (400 degrees) for 30 to 40 minutes, or until fish flakes easily. Baste during baking with wine. Serves 3 to 5.

SEAFOOD GELATIN

Prepare Lemon-Flavored gelatin using a California white table wine for half the liquid. Add crab or shrimp along with plenty of chopped celery and chopped tart apple. Spoon into green pepper shells. When firm, cut into slices and serve on greens with a seafood cocktail dressing.

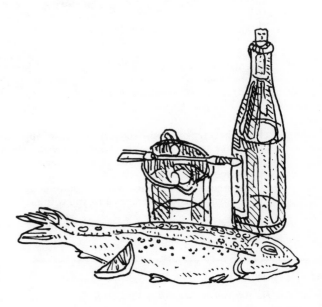

PISTACHIO SALMON IN CREAM

Shirley Sarvis, Food & Wine Consultant, San Francisco

Do not combine cream and wine until just before baking. Garnish with watercress. Pass black pepper if you wish.

> *4 pieces salmon fillet, each*
> * about ½ lb.*
> *Salt*
> *1¼ cups heavy (whipping) cream*
> *2 Tbs. minced green onions*
> * (white part only)*
> *3 Tbs. dry white table wine*
> *3 Tbs. very finely chopped,*
> * very lightly toasted pistachios*

Wipe fillets dry. Sprinkle lightly with salt. Arrange in a single layer, well apart, in a buttered shallow baking dish. Mix together cream, onions, ½ teaspoon salt, and wine; pour over fish. Bake, uncovered, in a 400 degree oven just until flesh barely separates when tested with a dinner knife, about 15 minutes. Lift each fillet to a warm plate, spoon cream sauce over, and sprinkle nuts down center. Serves 4.

LA DARNE DE SAUMON DE GASPÉ, FRONTENAC

Mrs. John D. Bartlett, Charles Krug Winery, St. Helena

½ lb. mushrooms, finely chopped
1 medium-sized white onion, finely
   chopped
1 sprig parsley, finely chopped
3 Tbs. butter
2 cups Hollandaise sauce
6 salmon steaks
3 cups California white table wine

Sauté mushrooms, onion and parsley in butter until golden. Blend mixture into Hollandaise sauce; whip gently until well mixed. Chill sauce until firm. In large skillet, place salmon steaks and cover with wine. Cover and poach gently until fish is bright pink and wine has been reduced to below the salmon level. Remove salmon; place in baking dish. Cover each piece of salmon with a generous spread of firmed sauce. Broil under moderate heat for 5 minutes, until sauce becomes glazed and golden brown. Serve on hot platter or dish with poaching wine poured around fish. Serves 4 to 6.

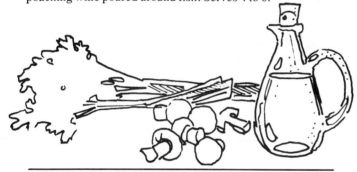

SARATOGA SOLE

Mrs. Jack Farrior Jr., Paul Masson Vineyards, Saratoga

8 fillets of sole, about 2 to 2½ lbs.
¼ cup butter
¼ tsp. pepper
1 lb. small shrimp (fresh,
   if possible)
1½ (10½-oz.) cans mushroom soup,
   undiluted
¾ cup California Dry Sherry
Juice of 1 lemon
¼ to ½ cup grated Parmesan cheese
¼ tsp. paprika

Wipe sole with damp cloth. Place 1 teaspoon butter on each fillet; sprinkle each with pepper. Place ¼ cup shrimp on each fillet; roll up. Put rolls in large clam shells or in a baking dish. Heat soup, wine and lemon juice, stirring to blend. Pour mixture over rolls. Sprinkle with Parmesan cheese, then paprika. Bake in moderate oven (350 degrees) for 30 minutes. Menu might include: butter lettuce salad with piquant dressing; rice; peas with onions; spiced crabapple; fresh fruit. Serves 3 to 4.

QUICK FRIDAY SPECIAL

Mrs. Joseph Concannon Jr., Concannon Vineyard, Livermore

We call this meal our Fisherman's Wharf Special. Joe is often in San Francisco on Fridays for meetings, so he picks up fresh fish and French bread on the way home. Dinner can be on the table 30 minutes after his arrival.

Butter
1 fish fillet or thin fish steak per
   person (sole, red snapper, etc.)
Flour
¼ cup minced onion
Salt and pepper
¼ cup butter, melted
Juice of ½ lemon
½ cup California white table wine
Chopped parsley
Lemon wedges

Heat oven to 450 degrees. Line shallow baking pan with foil (makes cleaning a cinch); place in hot oven. When hot, brush pan well with butter; arrange fish in pan. Dot each piece with butter; sprinkle lightly with flour, onion, salt and pepper. Combine ¼ cup melted butter, lemon juice and wine. Bake fish in hot oven (450 degrees) about 10 to 15 minutes, basting frequently with butter-wine mixture. Serve with chopped parsley and lemon wedges. Since this is a quick meal, we usually have this dish with French fried potatoes, a crisp green salad and French bread. Serves 4 to 6.

JAPANESE CHARCOAL-BROILED FISH

Mrs. Jim Tanaka, Louis M. Martini, St. Helena

2 Tbs. California Sherry
2 Tbs. lemon juice or
   California wine vinegar
½ cup soy sauce
½ tsp. sugar
6 fish steaks (salmon is excellent)
1 piece ginger, grated very fine
Cayenne

Combine Sherry, lemon juice or wine vinegar, soy sauce and sugar. Broil fish over charcoal. Put fish in shallow dish; cover with sauce and let stand about ½ hour. This dish need not be hot when eaten, but if you prefer it that way, put fish into hot oven for a few minutes before serving. Sprinkle with cayenne and garnish with grated ginger. Or, to prepare fish another way, rub fish with salt; place on skewers. Broil over charcoal until brown. Dip into sauce and broil again. Repeat this process 3 times. This is a good method to use with a hibachi. Serves 4 to 6.

FILLET OF SOLE SAN JOAQUIN

Mrs. Leon S. Peters, Fresno

This one I created myself by combining parts of several recipes.

> *1 onion, chopped*
> *¼ cup butter or margarine*
> *½ cup chopped parsley*
> *½ cup cooked rice, seasoned with*
> *   butter and salt*
> *½ tsp. salt*
> *⅛ tsp. pepper*
> *2 eggs*
> *¾ cup milk*
> *8 fillets of sole*
> *Fine dry bread crumbs*
> *1 (10½-oz.) can mushroom soup*
> *1 cup California Dry Sherry or*
> *   white table wine*
> *Parmesan cheese*

Sauté onion in butter; add parsley and cook until onion is soft and translucent. Add cooked rice; season with salt and pepper. Beat eggs with milk; season lightly with a little additional salt. Spread rice mixture evenly over fillets; roll up and secure. Dip each fish roll in the egg mixture, then in bread crumbs. Let the coating set for half an hour or longer in the refrigerator. Brown rolls lightly on all sides in melted butter, about 10 minutes. Remove rolls to a flameproof platter. Heat mushroom soup with wine; simmer about 15 minutes, stirring frequently. Pour the sauce around the fish rolls; sprinkle with Parmesan cheese. Brown under the broiler. Serve with buttered zucchini and a lime and pear molded salad. Serves 6 to 8.

BAKED FISH AU CHABLIS

Attilio Boffa, San Antonio Winery, Inc., Los Angeles

> *2 lbs. halibut, salmon or bass*
> *   (slices or fillets)*
> *Salt and pepper*
> *1 large onion, sliced*
> *1 cup California Chablis*
> *3 Tbs. butter*
> *2 sliced tomatoes, or 1 (8-oz.)*
> *   can tomato sauce*
> *½ green pepper, sliced*
> *2 Tbs. Worcestershire sauce*

Sprinkle fish with salt and pepper; cover with onion slices. Pour wine over; marinate 1 hour. Melt butter in large shallow baking pan. Remove fish and onion sliced to baking pan; cover with tomatoes or tomato sauce, green pepper slices and sprinkling of salt. Bake in moderately-hot oven (375 degrees) about 35 minutes, or until fish is tender. Mix remaining wine in which fish was marinated with Worcestershire sauce; use to baste fish frequently during baking. Serves 4 to 5.

SALMON A LA MARSALA

Mrs. Ralo D. Bandiera, Bandiera Wines, Cloverdale

> *2 Italian sausages, sliced*
> *10 lb. salmon, whole*
> *6 carrots, sliced*
> *6 whole white onions*
> *½ cup diced celery*
> *1 tsp. oregano*
> *½ tsp. rosemary*
> *3 tsp. salt*
> *¼ tsp. pepper*
> *2 cups California Marsala*

In a very large Dutch oven, fry sausage until partially brown. Add whole salmon and brown. Cover and simmer 30 minutes. Add remaining ingredients; cook over low heat until tender, about 1 to 1½ hours. Menu to serve with this dish might include: tossed salad with olive oil and wine vinegar dressing; Italian garlic bread; and pineapple sherbet topped with green crème de menthe. Serves 10 to 12.

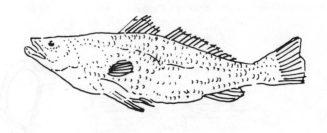

WINERY LAKE BAKED SALMON

Veronica di Rosa, Winery Lake Vineyards, Napa

> *1 lb. fresh salmon (the piece*
> *   next to the tail is best)*
> *3 Tbs. fresh herbs (any two of*
> *   the following: basil, savory,*
> *   parsley, or marjoram)*
> *2 Tbs. fresh chives*
> *2 Tbs. butter*
> *1 cup whole wheat croutons*
> *   or stale bread*
> *2 rashes thick bacon*
> *Fresh ground pepper*
> *½ cup dry white wine or French*
> *   Vermouth (approximately)*

Preheat oven to 350 degrees. Butter an oval baking dish. Fillet and wash the fish, save the bones for stock. Place the salmon in the baker flesh side up. Pour in enough wine to cove the bottom of the dish. Grind the herbs in a Cuisinart. Add croutons and grind until the mixture is coarse. Add bits of butter; do not overblend. Pepper to taste. Heap lightly on each fillet. Cut the bacon in half and place it over the stuffing. Pop it in the oven and bake for 35 minutes. Serve with lemon wedges, sliced tomatoes, and fresh greens.

FISH IN WINE SAUCE

Rudolf Weibel, Weibel Champagne Vineyards,
Mission San Jose

1½ lbs. fish fillets
1 cup California white table wine
    such as Chablis or Grey Riesling
1½ Tbs. lemon juice
12 large mushrooms, sliced
1 Tbs. butter
2 egg yolks
1 cup heavy cream
3 Tbs. butter
1 Tbs. chopped parsley
¾ tsp. salt
⅛ tsp. pepper

Poach fish fillets in wine and lemon juice until tender. Remove fish to hot platter, and keep warm while making sauce. Sauté mushrooms in 1 Tbs. butter. Heat wine in which fish was cooked to boiling and continue cooking 10 minutes. Beat egg yolks, add cream. Pour hot wine over egg-cream mixture, stirring constantly. Add 3 tablespoons butter, mushrooms, parsley, salt and pepper. Pour over fillets. Serve immediately. Serves 6.

BAKED WHOLE SALMON
PAUL REDINGER

Jan Sherrill, Sherrill Cellars, Woodside

This is good with any whole fish.

1 whole salmon, cleaned
2 cups diced carrots
1½ cup diced onion
1 cup chopped parsley
2 Tbs. each butter and olive oil
1 to 2 cups Sherrill
    Monterey Chardonnay
Salt and pepper to taste

Sauté onion in butter and oil on medium heat for 4 to 5 minutes. Add carrots, celery and parsley, continue to saute for 6 to 8 minutes. Add 1 cup wine, sauté 15 to 20 minutes until vegetables are crisp/done. Season with salt and pepper to taste. Fill center cavity of fish and put remaining vegetables on top. Baste with wine. Bake at 350 degrees for approximately 10 minutes per inch of thickness of fish. This is usually around 25 to 30 minutes for the 3 to 4 pound fish. Baste with wine once or twice during cooking. Serve with vegetables, french bread and more wine. Serves 4 to 5.

BAKED FISH SALAD

Karl Wente, Wente Bros., Livermore

⅔ cup mayonnaise
⅓ cup California Dry Sherry
1 cup finely crushed potato chips
2 cups flaked, cooked or canned fish
    (halibut, salmon, tuna, etc.)
2 hard-cooked eggs, coarsely chopped
½ cup chopped celery
2 Tbs. capers
2 Tbs. chopped parsley
1 Tbs. minced onion
Salt and pepper to taste

Stir mayonnaise and Sherry together until blended. Add ¾ cup of the potato chips and all remaining ingredients. Turn mixture into greased baking shells or individual casseroles. Sprinkle remaining ¼ cup potato chips over the top. Bake in a moderate oven (350 degrees) for 30 minutes. Serves 4.

QUICK SEAFOOD MARYLAND

Quick Seafood Maryland is the dish to prepare when Friday night is movie or visiting night. Mrs. Dale C. Perry, Department of Viticulture & Enology, University of California, Davis, prepares her version right off the pantry shelf. Take a can of condensed cream of chicken soup, add 1 tablespoon instant minced onion, a can of tuna or crab and a can of shrimp. Combine with 2 hard-cooked chopped eggs; heat thoroughly. Just before serving add ¼ cup California Dry Sherry and serve over rice. Serves 5 to 6.

BAKED SOLE PAPRIKA

Dino Barengo, Barengo Winery, Acampo

1½ lbs. fillets of sole or
    other white fish
1 small onion, thinly sliced
1 cup dairy sour cream
1 Tbs. flour
⅓ cup California Sauterne or
    other white table wine
1 tsp. anchovy paste
½ tsp. paprika
Salt and pepper

Arrange fish in greased shallow baking dish. Cover with onion slices. Mix all other ingredients and pour over fish. Bake in moderately-hot oven (375 degrees) about 25 minutes, or until fish is tender. Serves 4.

TUNA-LIKE-BEEF CASSEROLE

Mrs. George D. Beitzel, Gibson Wine Company, Elk Grove

2 (6 or 7-oz.) cans tuna
1 (6-oz.) can broiled mushrooms
1 clove garlic
1 bay leaf
½ tsp. salt
¼ tsp. dried basil
½ tsp. Tabasco sauce
1 (15-oz.) can tomato sauce
¼ cup California red table wine
1 (8-oz.) pkg. noodles or spaghetti,
    cooked and drained
2 (10-oz.) pkgs. frozen chopped
    spinach, cooked and drained
½ cup grated Parmesan cheese

Drain oil from tuna into a skillet; set tuna aside. Drain mushrooms, reserving liquid. Add mushrooms, garlic, bay leaf, salt, basil and Tabasco to oil in skillet; sauté about 10 minutes. Add tuna, mushroom liquid, tomato sauce and wine; continue cooking 5 minutes longer. In a 3-quart casserole or baking pan, place layers of cooked noodles, cooked spinach and the tuna mixture. Sprinkle with Parmesan cheese. Bake in a moderately-hot oven (400 degrees) for 20 minutes, or until heated through. Serve with hot bread and tossed salad with tart dressing. Serves 8 to 10.

BROILED TROUT SANTA ROSA

Mrs. E. Jeff Barnette, Martini & Prati Wines, Inc.,
*   Santa Rosa*

This recipe is original, created in my own kitchen. It requires only a few minutes to prepare and is delicious.

4 fresh or frozen trout
Salt and pepper
2 Tbs. melted butter or
    margarine
⅔ cup California white table wine
3 slices bacon, fried crisp, drained
    and crumbled
2 Tbs. slivered almonds
3 Tbs. grated Parmesan
    cheese

Wash and dry trout. Season with salt and pepper; arrange in broiler pan. Brush trout with part of melted butter; broil, basting 2 or 3 times with wine. When done on one side, turn and brush with remaining butter. Return to broiler until second side is done, basting again with wine. Just before done, sprinkle trout with bacon, almonds and cheese. Return to broiler to melt cheese. Spoon pan juices over trout before serving. With this include baked potatoes with sour cream and chives, broccoli or asparagus spears, garlic bread and tossed green salad. For dessert, a lemon meringue pie. Serves 2 to 4.

SCALLOPS A LA PIERRE

Mrs. Leon S. Peters, Fresno

1 lb. scallops
¼ cup butter
2 Tbs. chopped chives or
    green onions
1 Tbs. finely chopped parsley
¼ cup California white table wine
Salt and pepper

Wash scallops thoroughly. Heat butter in medium-sized heavy skillet. Add scallops, chives, parsley, wine, salt and pepper. Cover and cook about 10 minutes, until liquid is reduced to an almost syrupy consistency. Serve with rice pilaf and a green salad with tomatoes and cucumbers. Serves 2.

POACHED SCALLOPS A LA PORTUGAISE

Perla Meyers of Perla Meyers Cooking School at Trefethen
*   Vineyards, Napa*

1½ lbs. bay scallops
1 cup fish stock
1 cup Trefethen Eschol
    White Wine or Riesling
1 small sliced onion
1 bouquet
2 cloves of peeled crushed garlic
4 to 5 peppercorns
3 fresh ripe tomatoes peeled and chopped
2 Tbs. finely minced shallots
2 Tbs. butter
Salt and freshly ground pepper
4 egg yolks
¼ cup creme fraiche or heavy cream
1½ sticks of butter or more

Make a bouillon with the stock, wine and herbs. Cook the bouillon for 20 minutes and strain. Combine the bouillon together with the scallops in a saucepan and bring to a simmer and poach until scallops turn opaque. Strain scallops leaving a little liquid to cover them and keep them from drying. Reduce the bouillon to ⅓ cups and set aside.

In a small skillet make a tomato fondue out of the butter, shallots and tomatoes. Season with salt and pepper and reserve. In a heavy saucepan combine the reduced fish stock, egg yolks and crème fraiche. Whisk the mixture until it just starts to thicken. This is best done in the container of a double boiler or by setting the saucepan in a larger skillet with hot water. Whisk in the cold butter and whisk the sauce until it is thick and smooth. Add the tomato mixture and season with salt and pepper. Add the well drained scallops and serve on individual serving plates garnished with sprigs of parsley and triangles of bread sautéed in butter.

SHRIMP AND ASPARAGUS CASSEROLE

Mrs. Leonard Maullin, Paul Masson Vineyards, Saratoga

This recipe was given to me by my sister several years ago, and is a family favorite. We also like it for entertaining, since it combines the hot vegetables and seafood. It also serves excellently as a luncheon entrée. It can be made ahead of time, and refrigerated. Just bring to room temperature before baking. If you wish to double the recipe for a large buffet, add only ½ pound more shrimp. It will then serve about 12 to 14.

> *2 (10-oz.) packages frozen asparagus*
> *spears*
> *¼ cup butter*
> *¼ cup flour*
> *1 cup milk*
> *½ cup cream*
> *½ cup California white table wine*
> *1 tsp. salt*
> *⅛ tsp. pepper*
> *1 lb. cooked shrimp, diced*
> *1 egg yolk*
> *½ cup grated Parmesan cheese*
> *Buttered bread crumbs*

Cook asparagus following package directions until almost done; drain. Meanwhile, melt butter in saucepan; stir in flour. Gradually blend in milk, cream and wine; cook, stirring constantly, until thickened. Season with salt and pepper. Stir into sauce the shrimp, egg yolk and cheese. In buttered 2 to 3 quart casserole, arrange asparagus and shrimp sauce in layers, ending with sauce. Top with buttered bread crumbs. Bake in moderate oven (350 degrees) for 30 minutes. Serve with hot buttered noodles dusted with toasted sesame seeds, tossed salad, assorted relishes, hot crusty rolls and dessert. Serves 6 to 8.

VALLEY LOBSTER TAILS

Mrs. Michael J. Bo, Almaden Vineyards, Los Gatos

> *4 small lobster tails*
> *2 (10½-oz.) cans condensed cream*
> *of mushroom soup*
> *4 Tbs. chopped green onions,*
> *including some tops*
> *2 tsp. dry mustard*
> *⅔ cup California Dry Sherry*
> *Parmesan cheese*

Cook lobster tails in boiling salted water for 10 minutes. Shell lobster and dice the meat. Heat the undiluted mushroom soup, stir in onions, mustard, Sherry and diced lobster. Spoon into individual baking dishes and sprinkle with grated Parmesan cheese. Brown under broiler. Serve with broiled tomato halves topped with salt, pepper and Italian dried herbs, carrots cooked in consommé and white wine and baked potato. Serves 4.

SARATOGA SHRIMP

Saratoga shrimp of Mrs. Otto Meyer, Paul Masson Vineyards Saratoga, is based on raw shrimp sautéed in garlic-flavored oil. When shrimp are browned-Sherry, chili sauce and Worcestershire sauce are added and mixture simmered about 30 minutes until thickened. Shredded cheddar cheese is then added, allowed to melt, with salt and pepper to taste. Serve immediately on brown or white rice.

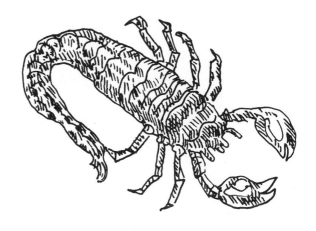

SHRIMP AMANDINE

Mrs. Norbert C. Mirassou, Mirassou Vineyards, San Jose

> *¾ cup raw rice (2¼ cups cooked)*
> *¼ cup chopped green pepper*
> *¼ cup chopped onion*
> *2 Tbs. butter*
> *½ tsp. salt*
> *⅛ tsp. pepper*
> *⅛ tsp. mace*
> *1 (10-oz.) can tomato soup,*
> *undiluted*
> *1 cup light cream*
> *1 cup California Dry Sherry*
> *1½ lbs. small fresh shrimp, or*
> *2 lbs. fresh prawns*
> *½ lb. fresh crab meat*
> *½ cup sliced blanched almonds*

Cook rice in salted water until tender. Drain if necessary. Sauté green pepper, onion in butter for about 5 minutes. Add seasonings. Blend soup and cream together and add Sherry. Stir in rice, fish, almonds and sautéed vegetables. Toss together and bake in a 2½ quart casserole in moderate oven (350 degrees) until heated through and all liquid is absorbed. This casserole is even better upon reheating. Moisten with a few extra tablespoons of Sherry, if necessary. This is a good dish for meatless days. Serve with asparagus spears, squash, mixed green salad and hot rolls. For dessert-baked apricots with cookies. Serves 8 to 10.

FROG LEGS PINOT BLANC
Norbert C. Mirassou, Mirassou Vineyards, San Jose

As far as we know, this is an original recipe.

> ¼ cup butter
> 1 tsp. minced garlic
> 4 pairs frozen frog legs (large)
> ½ cup chopped parsley
> 1 cup California Pinot Blanc or
>   other white table wine

Preheat electric skillet to 320 degrees; add butter and garlic. When butter is melted, add frog legs. Cover and cook at 320 degrees with vent open for 10 minutes. Sprinkle parsley over frog legs; add wine. Recover pan, with vent closed, and lower heat to 280 degrees; cook until tender, about 15 to 20 minutes. Place frog legs in serving dish and pour over remaining pan juices. Serve with rice, squash cooked with mushrooms and tomatoes, and heart of lettuce salad.

SHRIMP CASSEROLE HARPIN
Mrs. Bruno T. Bisceglia, Bisceglia Bros. Wine Co., Madera

This recipe is especially good for luncheon or buffet.

> 1 lb. cooked shrimp
> 1 Tbs. lemon juice
> 3 Tbs. oil
> ¾ cup uncooked rice
> ¼ cup finely chopped green pepper
> ¼ cup finely chopped onion
> ¼ cup butter or margarine
> 1 tsp. salt
> ⅛ tsp. pepper
> ⅛ tsp. mace
> Dash of cayenne
> 1 (10½-oz.) can condensed
>   tomato soup
> ¼ cup water
> 1 cup heavy cream
> ¼ cup California Sherry
> ½ cup slivered blanched almonds
> 2 cups cornflake crumbs

If shrimp are large, cut in half lengthwise. Place in 2-quart casserole; sprinkle with lemon juice and oil. Reserve about 8 halves for garnish. Cook rice following package directions; drain. Sauté green pepper and onions in 2 tablespoons of the butter for about 5 minutes. Add along with cooked rice, seasonings, undiluted soup, water, cream, Sherry and ¼ cup of the almonds to shrimp in casserole. Mix lightly. Bake in moderate oven (350 degrees) about 20 minutes. Meanwhile, combine remaining 2 tablespoons butter with crumbs, remaining almonds and reserved shrimp. Top casserole with crumb mixture; bake 15 minutes longer, or until mixture is bubbly and crumbs lightly browned. Serves 6 to 8.

FROG LEGS IN WINE
Mrs. Alvin Ehrhardt, United Vintners'
Community Wineries, Lodi

> 12 pairs frog legs (small)
> 2 Tbs. butter
> 2 Tbs. flour
> ½ cup California white table wine
> 2 Tbs. minced watercress
> 2 Tbs. minced scallions
> Salt
> Freshly ground pepper
> 1 egg yolk
> 1 Tbs. cold water
> Cayenne

Soak frog legs in cold water for 3 hours; drain on cloth. Melt butter in top pan of chafing dish over medium flame. Add frog legs; saute 3 minutes on each side. Sprinkle with flour, mixing constantly. Add wine, watercress and scallions; season with salt and pepper. Simmer 15 minutes. Remove frog legs to a warm platter. Whip egg yolk with cold water. Spoon a bit of wine mixture into egg and beat well. Remove wine mixture from heat; add egg mixture and stir well. Return pan over flame. Stir sauce constantly until thickened to desired consistency. Pour over frog legs and sprinkle with cayenne. Serves 4.

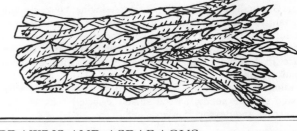

PRAWNS AND ASPARAGUS
Mrs. Tom Leong, Paul Masson Vineyards, Saratoga

> 1 lb. medium-size prawns,
>   cleaned and shelled
> 2 Tbs. oil
> ½ tsp. salt
> 1 lb. fresh asparagus, sliced in
>   1-inch lengths, using only
>   tender parts
> 1 tsp. minced fresh ginger
> 2 to 3 Tbs. soy sauce
> 1 Tbs. monosodium glutamate
> 1 Tbs. cornstarch dissolved in
>   ¾ cup cold water
> ¼ cup California Dry Sherry

Sauté prawns in hot oil, stirring constantly, until pink. Season with ¼ teaspoon salt. Remove from pan; set aside. Add all remaining ingredients, except Sherry, to same pan; bring to boil. Cover and cook only until asparagus is tender-crisp. Add Sherry when asparagus is almost tender. Stir in prawns; serve immediately. Serves 2 to 4.

SEAFOOD THE VINTNER'S WAY
Mrs. Louis A. Petri, United Vintners, Inc., San Francisco

> 1 Tbs. butter
> 1½ cups cooked shrimp, crawfish,
>   lobster or crab
> ¾ cup California Sherry
> 3 egg yolks
> 1 cup light cream
> 1 tsp. salt
> Few drops Tabasco
> Buttered toast

In top of double boiler, over simmering water, melt butter; add shellfish and cook 5 minutes. Add Sherry and heat 3 minutes more. Beat egg yolks slightly and stir in cream. Add to fish in double boiler, stirring constantly until thick. Do not boil. Serve at once on buttered toast. Serves 2.

CRAB CURRY CREPES
Mrs. Dan Turrentine, Wine Advisory Board, San Francisco

This recipe was found in a newspaper long ago. This is marvelous when your husband brings a guest home unexpectedly at lunch time, because all the ingredients can come from your emergency shelf.

> 3 eggs
> 1 cup milk
> 1½ tsp. salt
> ⅔ cup flour
> Butter
> Curried Crab Filling (see below)
> Hollandaise Topping (see below)
> Sliced almonds

Make crêpes by combining eggs, milk, salt and flour in bowl and beating with rotary-beater until smooth. Heat a 6- or 7-inch frying pan, butter lightly, and pour in 2 tablespoons batter. Rotate pan to let batter spread, and cook until just golden brown on bottom and set on top. Lift out and repeat, adding butter to pan for each crêpe. When all are cooked, spoon scant ¼ cup crab filling onto each crêpe, fold over and arrange in buttered baking dish, seam side down. Spoon hot topping over crepes and sprinkle with almonds. Bake in hot oven (425 degrees) until heated through. Good with tossed salad, rolls and chocolate cake for dessert. Serves 3 to 4.

CURRIED CRAB FILLING: Heat 1 (10½-oz.) can white sauce with ¼ cup California Sherry, ¼ teaspoon grated lemon rind, ¼ teaspoon nutmeg and ½ teaspoon curry powder. Season with salt and pepper. When sauce is hot and blended, add 1½ cups cooked crab meat and 2 tablespoons chopped parsley and heat.
HOLLANDAISE TOPPING: Blend 1 (6-oz.) can Hollandaise sauce with ½ cup sour cream and heat through.

OYSTERS IN CHAMPAGNE
Marjorie Riley, The Christian Brothers, Napa

For a Sunday night supper your guests will long remember, first go for an early Sunday drive to the Tomales Bay area, and stop at one of the several oyster beds for a big burlap bag of fresh oysters. They are surprisingly inexpensive. Then hurry home, scrub the shells well, pry them open and remove the oysters.

> 3 dozen oysters, cleaned and
>   shucked
> ½ cup butter
> ½ cup toasted bread crumbs
> 1 Tbs. minced parsley
> Salt and pepper
> 2 cups California Champagne
>   or a white table wine

Place oysters in large shallow baking pan in which butter has been melted. Baste oysters well with melted butter. Sprinkle with bread crumbs, parsley, salt and pepper. Pour in Champagne. Heat slowly in oven until the oysters become plump and the edges fluted and crinkly. Be sure you don't let it boil. Serve at once on slices of toasted, buttered French bread with a green salad and the rest of that bottle of Champagne. On second thought, it's better not to invite any guests; two of you can finish everything. Serves 4 to 6.

BUFFET PICKLED FISH

Buffet pickled fish uses a whole striped bass, salmon or halibut. Mrs. Frank Garbini of Wente Bros., Livermore, prepares this dish the way her mother did, in an original recipe. Brush fish with olive oil; bake in moderate oven (350 degrees) until it flakes easily. Skin fish, if desired. Place fish in enamel or glass container. Make enough marinade to cover fish completely in the proportion of ¼ cup California red table wine, ¾ cup California wine vinegar. To flavor marinade add chopped carrots, celery, onion, garlic, parsley, salt, pepper and any desired herbs. Simmer marinade 15 minutes. Strain out vegetables and pour hot marinade over fish. Turn fish occasionally. This will keep for several weeks in the refrigerator. Serve chilled with a California red table wine. (For more elegance, Mrs. Garbini suggests using a gelatin glaze over the fish.)

SHRIMP RICHERT

Mrs. Nina Concannon Radisch, Concannon Vineyard, Livermore

5 lbs. raw shrimp
1½ cups butter or margarine, melted
½ cup lemon juice
¾ cup chopped chives or green
   onion tops
¼ tsp. salt
⅛ tsp. pepper
½ cup soft French bread crumbs
½ cup California Sherry
¼ cup toasted, slivered blanched
   almonds

Shell and devein shrimp. Arrange shrimp close together in single layer in shallow baking dish. Combine butter, lemon juice, chives, salt and pepper; pour over shrimp. Top with bread crumbs; sprinkle with Sherry. Bake in a hot oven (400 degrees) for 20 minutes. Sprinkle almonds over shrimp the last 5 minutes of baking. Nice with rice and salad. Serves 10 to 12.

CALAMARI ZINFANDEL

Dante Bagnani, American Industries, San Francisco

3 lbs. squid (calamari) fresh or frozen
4 Tbs. olive oil
2 cloves garlic
2 Tbs. fresh parsley
2 tsp. salt
½ tsp. pepper
1 cup Zinfandel
3 cups peeled plum tomatoes
3 cups peas (fresh or frozen—optional)

Clean squid and cut into rings. Heat olive oil and add garlic. Cook until golden, then discard. Add squid, parsley, salt and pepper. Cook three or four minutes, add wine, and continue cooking until wine evaporates. Add tomatoes. Simmer mixture 15 to 20 minutes. Add peas. Continue cooking about ten minutes.

SHERRY-CRAB SOUFFLE

Mrs. Michael J. Bo, Almaden Vineyards, Los Gatos

2 Tbs. butter
2 Tbs. flour
1½ cups hot milk
Salt, pepper, Tabasco
1 cup sliced mushrooms
   canned or fresh
½ cup California Sherry
4 eggs, separated
2 cups crab meat

Make a white sauce by melting butter in upper part of double boiler and blending in flour. Add milk, stirring briskly to avoid lumping. Season with salt, pepper and Tabasco. Remove from heat. Stir in mushrooms and Sherry. Add beaten egg yolks and blend well. Fold in crab meat. Beat egg whites until stiff and fold in gently. Pour into a 1½-quart casserole, place in a pan half filled with water, and bake in a preheated moderate oven (350 degrees) for about 30 minutes or until golden brown. Serve with cold tomato soup and steamed artichokes. Serves 4.

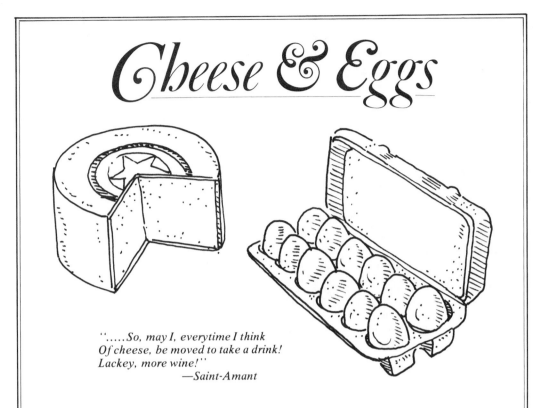

Cheese & Eggs

*".....So, may I, everytime I think
Of cheese, be moved to take a drink!
Lackey, more wine!"*
—Saint-Amant

From earliest times wine and cheese have been a memorable marriage, almost an indispensable blend in the cuisines of many countries. What other taste companions combine so delicately with eggs, or so robustly with pastas and rice? The contemporary cook finds a similar culinary joy pairing California wine with these same straightforward foods for the ultimate in goodness.

BROWN RISOTTO WITH WINE
Mrs. Louis P. Martini, Louis M. Martini, St. Helena

1 (10½-oz.) can beef bouillon
1 (10½-oz.) can water
⅓ cup soy sauce
⅔ cup California red table wine
1 lb. lean round or chuck steak,
   treated with meat tenderizer
⅓ cup butter
½ cup thinly sliced onion
1 large clove garlic, chopped
1½ cups white long-grain rice,
   uncooked

Combine beef bouillon, water, soy sauce and wine. Heat to boiling; simmer. Meanwhile, cut beef into very small pieces. Heat butter in large frying pan. Sauté beef, onion and garlic until meat is browned. Add rice; continue cooking until rice is slightly browned. Add hot bouillon mixture. Lower heat; cover and cook slowly, about 25 minutes, or until rice is light and fluffy. Serves 4 to 6.

MUSHROOM-WILD RICE CASSEROLE
Mrs. C. Dudley Warner, Cresta Blanca Wine Company, Livermore

1 cup wild rice, uncooked
½ green pepper, diced
½ lb. fresh button mushrooms
   (or 1 (4½-oz.) jar sliced mushrooms)
¼ cup butter or margarine, melted
2 Tbs. flour
½ tsp. salt
⅛ tsp. pepper
½ cup chicken bouillon
½ cup California white table wine

Cook rice following package directions. In a skillet, sauté green pepper and mushrooms in butter until mushrooms are lightly browned. Add flour, salt and pepper. Gradually stir in bouillon and wine. Cook over low heat, stirring constantly, until slightly thickened. Add rice. Place in greased 1-quart casserole; bake in moderately-slow oven (325 degrees) about 30 minutes. Serves 4 to 6.

WINEY CHEESE BAKE

Mrs. Norbert C. Mirassou, Mirassou Vineyards, San Jose

6 slices day-old bread
Butter
1½ cups ground ham
1 tsp. prepared mustard
1 green pepper, finely chopped
 (optional)
2 eggs, slightly beaten
1 cup milk
½ cup California Dry Sherry
¼ tsp. salt
⅛ tsp. pepper
2½ cups sliced or diced processed
 American cheese

Remove crusts from bread; spread with butter. Arrange 3 slices in greased baking dish. Mix ham with mustard and green pepper, if desired. Spread over bread slices in baking dish; cover with remaining 3 slices of bread, buttered side up. Cut each diagonally in two. Combine eggs, milk, Sherry, salt and pepper; pour over bread. Top with sliced or diced cheese. Chill at least 4 hours in refrigerator. Bake in moderately-slow oven (325 degrees) for 1 hour, or until a rich golden brown. Serve with molded fruit salad for a luncheon. Serves 4 to 6.

SPAGHETTI RÉCHAUFFÉ

Spaghetti réchauffé is an original invention for reheating left-over spaghetti and sauce. Frank Muller, Di Giorgio Wine Company, Di Giorgio, California, says: I learned this on evenings my wife was out, but had left enough spaghetti with rather vague instructions on heating it. Add a little California red table wine (a dry white is acceptable and won't alter color of the spaghetti), enough to moisten it well, stir gently and heat. Use covered skillet over low heat, stirring occasionally, or heat in covered casserole in slow oven (300 degrees). Break up the cold meat balls and toss them in, too. Serve with a green salad, garlic bread, fruit for dessert, and a California dry red table wine.

MUSHROOM PILAF

John Daniel Jr., Inglenook Vineyard Co.. Rutherford

½ lb. fresh mushrooms
½ cup chopped green onion
1 clove garlic, finely chopped
⅓ cup butter or margarine
1 tsp. salt
1 cup processed cracked wheat
1 cup California Rosé
¾ cup Jack or Cheddar cheese cubes

Remove stems, peel and slice mushrooms. Cook mushrooms with green onion and garlic in butter until soft but not browned. Add salt and cracked wheat. Stir in wine. Cover tightly and cook over low heat until tender, about 25 minutes. Remove cover and poke cubes of cheese into surface of hot pilaf. Serves 4.

BREAD CUSTARD CHABLIS

Mrs. Fred Perelli-Minetti, A. Perelli-Minetti & Sons, Delano

I first enjoyed this dish at my grandmother's luncheons in Duluth, Minnesota.

8 slices bread, crusts removed
4 slices American cheese
2 cups cream
1 tsp. dry mustard
1½ tsp. salt
4 eggs, beaten
¼ cup butter
¼ cup flour
1 cup milk
Dash of pepper
Dash of paprika
½ cup California Chablis or
 other white table wine
1 cup cooked mushrooms, crabmeat,
 or chicken

Arrange 4 slices of bread in bottom of 8-inch square glass baking dish. Top with cheese slices and remaining bread slices. Combine cream, mustard, 1 tsp. salt and beaten eggs. Pour over sandwiches; let stand 4 hours. Bake in moderately-hot oven (375 degrees) for 45 minutes or until brown. Meanwhile, melt butter in saucepan; stir in flour. Gradually add milk, stirring constantly until thickened and smooth. Add remaining ½ teaspoon salt, pepper and paprika. Just before serving, add wine and cooked mushrooms, crabmeat or chicken. When sandwiches are done, cut diagonally into halves. Place on warm plates and cover with sauce. Serve immediately with spiced peach or pear on each plate. Serves 3 to 4.

SPAGHETTI IN WINE
Mrs. Jack Pandol, Delano Growers Co-op Winery, Delano

⅓ cup California Sherry
⅓ cup butter
⅓ cup olive oil
½ tsp. oregano
1 clove garlic, crushed
1 (8-oz.) pkg. spaghetti
cooked and drained
Chopped parsley

Combine Sherry, butter, olive oil, oregano and garlic in a small saucepan; bring to boiling. Toss with hot spaghetti and parsley. Use as side dish with meat or poultry. Serves 4 to 6.

BURGUNDY LASAGNE
Mrs. Leon S. Peters, Fresno

A friend gave me this recipe. We have served it at buffet parties in our home and it has been very popular.

2 (1½-oz.) packages spaghetti
sauce mix
1 tsp. oregano
2 tsp. lemon juice
1 large onion, chopped
1 Tbs. oil
2 lbs. ground lean beef
2 cups mushrooms
½ cup chopped parsley
Garlic, if desired
2 tsp. salt
Pepper
1 cup California Burgundy or
other red table wine
15 wide lasagne noodles
Jack or Mozzarella cheese,
sliced ¼-inch thick
1 lb. cottage cheese or ricotta
cheese
Grated Parmesan cheese

Prepare spaghetti sauce mix following package directions; add oregano and lemon juice. In large, heavy skillet brown onion in heated oil. Add meat and brown. Add mushrooms, parsley, garlic (if desired), salt, pepper and wine. Simmer slowly. Cook lasagne noodles according to package directions. To assemble dish, spoon some of the spaghetti sauce in the bottom of a (13x9-inch) baking dish; top with layer of noodles. Layer in the following order; half of the meat and mushrooms, a layer of noodles, sliced Jack or Mozzarella cheese, layer of noodles, cottage cheese or ricotta, layer of noodles, remaining half of meat and mushrooms, remaining spaghetti sauce and top with Parmesan cheese. Bake in moderately-slow oven (325 degrees) about 40 minutes, or until heated through. Since this is a hearty dish, I like to serve it with a light fruit salad. Serves 6 to 8.

MOCK RAVIOLI
Mrs. Mildred Parriott, Beringer Bros., Inc., St. Helena

¾ cup oil
2 medium onions, finely chopped
1 clove garlic, finely chopped
1 lb. ground lean beef
2 tsp. salt
¼ tsp. pepper
1 tsp. Italian herbs
1 (6-oz.) can tomato paste
1 (8-oz.) can tomato sauce
1 cup California Burgundy or
other red table wine
1 cup water
1 (½-oz.) package dried
chopped mushrooms
1 (No. 2) can spinach, drained or
2 lbs. fresh spinach, finely
chopped
⅓ cup bread crumbs (dried French
bread is preferred)
¾ cup grated Parmesan cheese
1 tsp. ground sage
2 cloves garlic, mashed
4 eggs, well beaten
1 lb. butterfly or bow-tie
macaroni

Heat ¼ cup of the oil in a large, heavy skillet. Add onions and 1 clove chopped garlic; sauté until golden brown. Add beef and brown. Add 2 teaspoons salt, pepper, Italian herbs, tomato paste and sauce, wine, water and dried mushrooms. Simmer slowly for 1 hour. Meanwhile, combine spinach, bread crumbs, remaining ½ cup oil, ½ cup Parmesan cheese, sage, 2 cloves garlic (mashed) and beaten eggs; mix well. Cook macaroni according to package directions in boiling, salted water. Oil well a large casserole. Alternate layers of macaroni, spinach filling and meat sauce; repeat until all ingredients are used. Sprinkle top with remaining ¼ cup Parmesan cheese. If ingredients are warm, bake in moderate oven (350 degrees) for 30 minutes. If ingredients are cold, bake for 1 hour. If preferred, lasagne paste may be used instead of the macaroni. Also, this dish can be frozen. A tossed green salad, a bottle of California Burgundy or other red table wine, and dinner is served. Serves 8 to 12.

SHERRY RAREBIT
Mrs. E. F. Handel, East-Side Winery, Lodi

1 lb. sharp American cheese,
cut in cubes
⅔ cup (1(6-oz.) can) evaporated milk
⅓ cup California Dry Sherry
Hot toasted crackers or Melba toast

Heat cheese and milk in chafing dish or top of double boiler until cheese is melted. Add Sherry slowly, stirring constantly. Serve over toasted crackers or Melba toast. Serves 3 to 4.

SCRAMBLED EGGS WITH LOX
Mrs. Bertram Silk, Italian Swiss Colony, Asti

We usually serve this for late breakfasts.

> 6 eggs
> 1 small strip smoked salmon (lox),
>   cut into small pieces (2 to 3 Tbs.)
> ½ small onion, chopped
> 1 Tbs. chopped green pepper
> ¼ cup California white table wine
> ½ tsp. salt
> ⅛ tsp. pepper

Combine all ingredients; mix well. Cook in frying pan, mixing constantly until eggs are done. Serves 3 to 4.

WINE-CHERRY PANCAKES
Rita Darlow, Paul Masson Vineyards, Saratoga

These cherry pancakes are from the German cuisine (Kirschpfannkuchen).

> 4 medium-sized dinner rolls (preferably
>   French type)
> Water
> 2 eggs
> ¼ cup sifted all-purpose flour
> 2 tsp. sugar
> ½ tsp. salt
> ½ cup milk
> ½ cup California Gamay Beaujolais
>   or other red table wine
> 1 (1-lb.) can tart pitted red cherries,
>   drained
> Butter (about 5 Tbs.)
> Cinnamon-Sugar (½ cup sugar mixed
>   with 1 tsp. ground cinnamon

Soak rolls in water to cover. In a mixing bowl, beat eggs lightly; beat in flour, sugar, salt, milk and wine until smooth. Squeeze rolls dry; crumble into batter. Fold in drained cherries. Heat a small amount of butter in frying pan over medium heat until butter begins to bubble. Drop batter from end of tablespoon into frying pan in mounds, about 1½ inches in diameter. Sauté until crisp and golden on one side. Turn very carefully with a wide spatula; brown on second side. Serve hot, buttered and sprinkled lightly with cinnamon-sugar. Makes about 3 dozen little pancakes. Serve these at a "pancake supper" with crisp bacon and coffee. Serves 4 to 6.

EGGS POACHED IN WHITE WINE
Rudolf Weibel, Weibel Champagne Vineyards,
Mission San Jose

> 1 Tbs. butter
> ½ cup California Sauterne, Chablis
> or other white table wine
> 4 eggs
> Salt and pepper
> Few grains of cayenne
> 2 Tbs. crumbled blue cheese
> Hot buttered toast

Melt butter in skillet; add wine. Slip in eggs, one at a time. Season with salt, pepper and cayenne. Poach until whites are nearly firm. Sprinkle with cheese; heat until melted. Serve on hot buttered toast. Serves 3 to 4.

EGGS WITH CREAM CHEESE
Mrs. Harold Berg, University of California, Davis

This is an annual, traditional breakfast during the holiday season. For 12 guests I use at least three dozen eggs, and serve Champagne instead of orange juice before the meal.

> ½ cup cream
> 2 Tbs. butter
> 1 (3-oz.) package cream cheese,
>   softened
> 6 eggs
> 1 tsp. salt
> ¼ tsp. white pepper
> 3 Tbs. California Sherry

Heat cream over low heat in a skillet or chafing dish along with butter and cream cheese. Stir with a fork until a smooth, creamy paste. Beat eggs just until blended; add to cream mixture. Season with salt and pepper. Cook and stir over low heat until egg mixture is softly scrambled. Just before serving, stir in Sherry. Serve with buckwheat hotcakes, bacon or sausage. Serves 3 to 4.

PARMESAN EGGS
Mrs. J.W. Fleming, Lockeford Winery, Lodi

This recipe was given to me by a friend, but I'm not sure that it is original. It makes a wonderful company dish, served with hot biscuits.

> 2 Tbs. butter
> 2 Tbs. California Dry Sherry
> 2 eggs
> Salt and pepper
> 2 Tbs. Parmesan cheese

Brown butter in skillet; add Sherry. Bring to boiling; break eggs into mixture. Season with salt and pepper. When egg whites begin to set, remove skillet from heat. Sprinkle with cheese. Place skillet under broiler and brown cheese. (Cheese browns quickly, so watch closely.) Serves 2.

PASTA WITH CLAM SAUCE
Mrs. Fred Perelli-Minetti, A. Perelli-Minetti & Sons,
Delano

Our version of pasta enjoyed at Positano on Amalfi Drive in Italy—must admit that their fresh clams were the hit.

> ½ cup butter
> 2 Tbs. flour
> 2 cups bouillon
> ½ cup California Dry Vermouth
> 2 (7½-oz.) cans minced clams,
>   undrained
> 3 small cloves garlic, crushed
> 1 lb. spaghetti or macaroni

In a saucepan, melt butter; stir in flour. Add bouillon; cook, stirring until mixture thickens. Add Vermouth, undrained clams and garlic. Simmer 15 to 20 minutes. Meanwhile, cook spaghetti or macaroni following package directions. Drain and combine with sauce. A tossed green salad after this pasta is soothing and satisfying. Serves 4 to 6.

SHERRIED FRENCH TOAST
L. N. Bianchini, Italian Swiss Colony, Asti

> ½ cup milk
> ¼ cup California Sherry
> ¼ cup sugar
> Dash of salt
> Grated rind of 1 lemon
> 8 slices stale bread
> 3 eggs well beaten
> 2 Tbs. butter or margarine
> Powdered sugar
> Cinnamon

Mix the milk, Sherry, sugar, salt and lemon rind. Soak slices of bread in this mixture for several minutes, then drain them and dip them in the beaten eggs. Sauté in butter until golden brown, turning to brown both sides. (add a little more butter, if necessary, during cooking.) Sprinkle with powdered sugar and cinnamon. Serve at once. Delicious for breakfast with sausages or bacon. Powdered sugar and cinnamon may be omitted, if desired, and honey or maple syrup may be served with Sherried French Toast. Serves 4.

RISOTTO WITH CHICKEN LIVERS
Robert Setrakian, California Growers Wineries, Cutler

> ⅓ cup butter or margarine
> 1 medium-sized onion, minced
> ½ lb. chicken livers, cut in small
>   pieces.
> 1½ cups raw rice
> ⅛ tsp. powdered saffron (optional)
> ½ cup California Sauterne or
>   other white table wine
> 3 cups boiling chicken broth
> Salt and pepper
> ½ cup grated Parmesan cheese

Melt butter in a large, heavy skillet. Add onion and chicken livers; sauté gently, stirring frequently, for 5 minutes. Add rice; sauté very gently, stirring frequently, for 10 minutes. Dissolve saffron in a little of the wine; add to rice with remaining wine, chicken broth, salt and pepper; stir well. Cover and simmer gently for about 25 minutes, or until rice is tender and all liquid is absorbed. Stir in cheese just before serving. Serves 6.

Salads

"Successful diplomacy and making a salad present the same problems —namely, knowing how much oil to mix with one's vinegar."
—Oscar Wilde

A salad can be a simple arrangement of crisp greens, tastefully supported by oil and wine vinegar...an ideal companion for a heavy meal. It can be a free improvisation of ingredients—cheese, fish, vegetables, colorful gelatins in molded forms, made doubly flavorful with the fresh subtle tang of pure California wine vinegar—and often the addition of wine as well. Make a cool summer meal of a hearty salad. Serve soup and salad for a light Sunday supper. Toasted French bread and California wine for sipping will complete the menu.

TART BURGUNDY GELATIN SALAD

Mrs. William V. Cruess, University of California, Department of Food Science and Technology, Berkeley

> 1 (No. 1) can shredded beets
> ½ cup California Burgundy, Claret
>   or other red table wine
> 1 (3-oz.) package lemon flavored
>   gelatin
> 1 cup grapefruit juice
> 1 clove garlic, crushed
> 1 tsp. horseradish
> ¼ tsp. salt

Drain beets, reserving ½ cup liquid. Combine beet liquid and wine; heat to boiling. Add gelatin; stir until dissolved. Add grapefruit juice, garlic, horseradish and salt. Chill until slightly set; fold in beets. Chill until set. Serves 6 to 8.
WINE DRESSING: Combine 1 cup bottled mayonnaise dressing with ½ cup California Burgundy or Claret. Makes about 1½ cups.

WINE-MARINATED ARTICHOKE HEARTS

Mrs. John B. Ellena, Regina Grape Products Co., Etiwanda

Artichoke hearts lend a touch of delicacy to any meal.

> 2 pkgs. frozen artichoke hearts
> 1 cup salad oil
> ½ cup California white wine vinegar
> ¼ cup California white table wine
> ¼ cup chopped red onion
> 1 Tbs. chopped parsley
> 1 tsp. finely chopped garlic
> ½ tsp. salt
> ½ tsp. seasoned pepper

Cook artichoke hearts according to package directions, being careful not to over-cook. Cool. Combine all other ingredients and mix well. Pour over artichoke hearts and let stand at least three hours before serving. This dressing may be used on other vegetables also. Very good on fresh string beans that have been cooked just until tender. This is nice with a roast prime ribs of beef. Serves 4 to 6.

ROSÉ-STRAWBERRY SALAD MOLD
*Mrs. C. Dudley Warner Jr., Cresta Blanca Wine Company,
Livermore*

2 (3-oz.) packages strawberry-
    flavored gelatin
1½ cups boiling water
1½ cups California Rosé
2 (10-oz.) packages frozen straw-
    berries, thawed
1 (8½-oz) can crushed pineapple,
    undrained
1 cup dairy sour cream

Dissolve gelatin in boiling water. Stir in Rosé, strawberries
and undrained pineapple. Pour half of mixture into
a large (8-cup) mold; refrigerate until set. Spread sour cream
over top. Spoon or carefully pour remaining gelatin mixture
over top; refrigerate until set. Unmold on salad greens.
Especially nice when served with chicken or turkey. Serves
10 to 12.

SHERRIED TOMATO-SHRIMP ASPIC
Mrs. Louis W. Pellegrini Sr., Italian Swiss Colony, Asti

2 envelopes unflavored gelatin
½ cup cold water
2 cups tomato juice
1 tsp. salt
1 stalk celery, chopped
1 small onion, chopped
4 sprigs parsley
½ cup California Dry Sherry
¼ cup finely chopped celery
½ cup small shrimp

Soften gelatin in cold water. Combine tomato juice, salt,
1 stalk celery, onion, parsley and wine in saucepan; cover
and simmer 15 minutes. Strain mixture. Add softened
gelatin, stirring until dissolved; cool. Stir in ¼ cup celery
and shrimp. Pour into oiled individual molds. Chill until
firm, about 2 hours. Unmold on salad greens and serve
with a dab of mayonnaise. This is good with any meat,
poultry or fish menu. Serves 4 to 6.

AVOCADO-LIME MOUSSE
Mrs. Karl Kaska, The Christian Brothers, Napa

Nothing could be much lovelier for a bridge luncheon
than this.

1 (3-oz.) package lime-flavored gelatin
½ cup hot water
½ cup California Muscat
¼ cup mayonnaise
½ cup heavy cream, whipped
1 Tbs. lime juice
½ tsp. onion juice
½ tsp. salt
1 cup finely diced avocado
½ cup finely diced celery
1 Tbs. grated green pepper
Salad greens
Orange or grapefruit sections

Dissolve gelatin in hot water; add wine. Chill until
slightly thickened. Beat until frothy. Blend in mayonnaise,
whipped cream, lime juice, onion juice and salt. Fold
in avocado, celery and green pepper. Pour into lightly oiled
1-quart ring mold; chill until firm. Unmold on salad greens
and garnish with citrus fruit sections. Serve with crisp
fried chicken drumsticks, hot rolls. Serves 4 to 6.

CHERRY-PINEAPPLE SALAD MOLD
*Mrs. John M. Filice, San Martin Vineyards Company,
San Martin*

I serve this salad on a chop plate on a bed of lettuce,
filling the center of the mold with mayonnaise. It is as
pretty to look at as it is good to eat.

1 (1 lb. 14-oz.) can sweet cherries
1 (3-oz.) package cherry-flavored
    gelatin
½ cup California Port
Salt
1 (3-oz.) package lime-flavored
    gelatin
1 cup hot water
1 (No. 2) can crushed pineapple
1 cup dairy sour cream

Drain cherries, reserving juice. Measure juice and add
enough water to make 1½ cups. Bring to boiling. Add cherry-
flavored gelatin, stirring until dissolved. Cool to lukewarm;
add Port and dash of salt. Chill until slightly thickened.
Coarsely chop cherries; fold into slightly thickened gelatin.
Pour into a 2-quart mold; chill until set. Meanwhile, dissolve
lime-flavored gelatin in hot water. Drain pineapple, reserving
juice. Measure ½ cup juice; add lime-flavored gelatin
along with a dash of salt. Chill until slightly thickened.
Beat in sour cream until mixture is light and fluffy. Fold in
crushed pineapple. Pour on cherry layer. Chill. Serve with
chicken at buffet lunch or supper. Serves 8 to 10.

APPLE-RAISIN SLAW

Mrs. Joe Roullard, Petri Wineries, Escalon

>1 cup seedless raisins
>¼ cup California Rosé
>3 apples, diced without paring
>1 Tbs. lemon juice
>4 cups raw cabbage, shredded
>1 cup mayonnaise

Combine raisins with wine; cover and let stand several hours or overnight. Sprinkle coarsely diced apples with lemon juice and stir well. Mix with raisins and liquid and the shredded cabbage. Add mayonnaise; season to taste. Toss and serve at once. This goes well with ham, roast pork or turkey. Serves 6 to 8.

LUNCHEON SALAD WITH WINE-CHEESE DRESSING

Mrs. Frank G. Cadenasso, Cadenasso Winery, Fairfield

>1 head lettuce or other salad greens
>3 tomatoes, peeled
>12 stalks cooked broccoli
>12 anchovy fillets
>12 deviled egg halves
>6 canned artichoke hearts, halved
>Wine-Cheese Dressing (see below)

To assemble salad, line salad plates with crisp greens. Place ½ of a tomato, cut side up, in center of each plate; top tomato with broccoli stalks; lay anchovy fillets crisscross over broccoli. Arrange deviled egg halves and artichoke hearts around tomato. Pass Wine-Cheese Dressing.
WINE-CHEESE DRESSING:Combine in a mixing bowl, 1 cup salad oil, ½ cup California Sauterne or other white table wine, ¼ cup California wine vinegar, ½ cup grated Parmesan cheese, 2 raw eggs, 1 teaspoon salt, ½ teaspoon *each* salt, garlic salt, coarsely ground black pepper and paprika, ¼ teaspoon Worcestershire sauce. Beat until well blended. (If dressing is not to be used immediately, store in covered container in refrigerator and beat well just before serving.) Makes about 2 cups dressing. Serves 4 to 6.

POTATO SALAD, WARM OR COLD

Mrs. John B. Ellena, Regina Grape Products Co.,
Etiwanda

>6 potatoes
>¼ cup California Sauterne
>2 cups dairy sour cream
>⅓ cup California white wine vinegar
>1 Tbs. sugar
>1 tsp. salt
>¼ tsp. pepper
>Dash of paprika

Boil potatoes until tender; peel and slice. Add wine and toss; cover and cool slightly. Combine sour cream with remaining ingredients. Pour over potatoes and toss. (If to be served cold, add dressing after potatoes have completely cooled in wine.) This potato salad warm, goes well with steak. As a cold dish it is good with cold baked ham and fried chicken. Serves 4 to 6.

FRUIT SALAD AU NATURE

Mrs. Mildred Parriott, Beringer Bros., Inc., St. Helena

>1 fresh pineapple, cut in
>   bite-size pieces
>12 mandarin oranges, separated
>   into sections
>2 bunches white table grapes
>3 or 4 apples, peeled and diced
>½ cup slivered almonds
>Papaya slices (optional)
>Sherry Cheese Dressing

Combine fruit and chill. At serving time, sprinkle on almonds, and garnish with slices of papaya, if desired. Pass dressing separately. Serves 4 to 6.

SHERRY CHEESE DRESSING: Soften 1 (3-oz.) package cream cheese with a fork. Gradually blend in 1 tablespoon lime or lemon juice, 1 tablespoon sugar, ¼ cup California Sherry and few grains salt. Makes about ⅔ cup dressing.

HOP KILN'S HOUSE FRENCH DRESSING
Marty Griffin, Hop Kiln Winery, Healdsburg

½ tsp. garlic (1 clove diced)
1 tsp. paprika
¾ tsp. basil
¼ tsp. pepper
Pinch of bay powder, parsley and
    peppermint leaves, to individual
    taste
2 Tbs. honey
⅓ cup red wine vinegar
½ cup oil (olive or other)
1 cup catsup

BLUE CHEESE SALAD DRESSING
Mrs. J.W. Fleming, Lockeford Winery, Lodi

I got this recipe originally from Mrs. E.J. Wallof, my neighbor and dear friend.

1 clove garlic, minced
1 Tbs. savory salt
¼ lb. blue cheese
1 cup salad oil
½ cup California wine vinegar
1 cup dairy sour cream
Coarse black pepper

Combine garlic, savory salt, blue cheese and ¼ cup of the oil; beat until smooth. Beat in ¼ cup of wine vinegar, a litle at a time. Add sour cream, remaining ¼ cup wine vinegar and ¾ cup salad oil, and coarse black pepper. Beat well and chill. Serve with any chilled greens. Makes about 2¾ cups.

RED WINE SALAD DRESSING
Mrs. Roy Taylor, formerly Wine Institute, San Francisco

This is a Roy original.

4 cloves garlic
1 cup salad oil
⅓ cup California red wine vinegar
⅓ cup California red table wine
Dash of Worcestershire sauce
1 tsp. salt
1½ tsp. tarragon

Peel garlic; cut in half and put in oil. In separate container, combine vinegar, wine, Worcestershire sauce, salt and tarragon. Let stand overnight. Remove garlic from oil. Pour oil into salad dressing bottle; strain vinegar mixture into bottle. Shake well before using. Makes 1⅔ cups.

HANNA FROMM'S OWN SALAD DRESSING
Mrs. Alfred Fromm, The Christian Brothers, Napa

⅓ cup California Burgundy or other
    red table wine
⅔ cup olive oil
⅓ cup California red wine vinegar
1 tsp. salt
Dash of freshly ground pepper
½ cup chopped watercress
½ cup chopped onion

In an ice-cold bowl, mix Burgundy, olive oil, wine vinegar, salt and pepper; stir to mix thoroughly. Add chopped watercress and onion. Pour over salad greens and toss well. Makes about 1 pint.

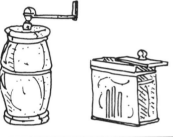

TOSS-WITH-A-FLOURISH RED WINE SALAD

Toss-with-a-flourish red wine salad can be done right at the table for real serving flair. Mrs. E. F. Handel, East-Side Winery, Lodi, suggests that you rub the salad bowl with garlic if desired. Tear a head of lettuce into pieces and drop into bowl. Pour 4 tablespoons olive oil over lettuce, sprinkle with ½ teaspoon salt, add black pepper to taste and toss until lettuce is well-coated with oil and seasoning. Pour 1 tablespoon lemon juice over all, toss again and serve at once. For variety Mrs. Handel advises any or all of the following: thinly sliced green onions; radishes; cucumber slices; avocado cubes; tomato quarters; chopped hard-cooked eggs. You can prepare this salad, serving 4 to 6, in the kitchen if table-tossing is not one of your talents.

COSMOPOLITAN SALAD DRESSING
Mrs. Herman Archinal, The Christian Brothers, Reedley

1 (5-oz.) jar blue cheese spread
1 (3-oz.) package cream cheese
1 cup dairy sour cream
¼ cup California Dry Sherry
1 Tbs. grated onion
Garlic powder (optional)
½ tsp. paprika
Salt

Combine all ingredients, beating until smooth. Cover and chill several hours to blend flavors. Good on any mixture of crisp greens, fresh tomato salad and aspics—any salad served with a meat meal. Makes about 1 pint.

Vegetables

"Let first the onion flourish there; Rose among roots, the maiden fair, wine-scented . . ."
—*Robert Louis Stevenson*

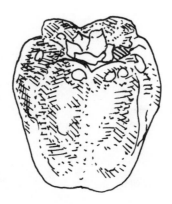

Snowy cauliflower, golden carrots, bright garden-green vegetables! Serve them because they're colorful and crisp, rather than just "good for you," cooking for looks as well as flavor. Try California wine for simmering, or season butter sauces with wine for new and exciting vegetable taste. You'll realize that extending wine cookery to vegetables is a whole new dimension, that adds a truly adventurous spirit to the meal. And vegetables so cooked blend even more subtly with the main dish, and with the California table wine accompanying.

PEAS CONTINENTAL

Mrs. Bruno T. Bisceglia, Bisceglia Bros. Wine Co., Madera

Vegetables need a pick-up now and then, and this is a good one.

> 1 cup sliced fresh or canned
>   mushrooms
> ¼ cup minced onion
> 2 Tbs. butter or margarine
> ¼ tsp. salt
> Dash of pepper
> ¼ tsp. nutmeg
> ¼ tsp. dried marjoram
> ¼ cup California Sherry
> 2 cups hot, cooked peas, fresh,
>   frozen or canned

Sauté mushrooms and onion in butter until barely tender, about 5 minutes. Add seasonings and Sherry; simmer 5 minutes. Add hot peas. Serves 4 to 6.

CHILI BEANS BURGUNDY

Louis A. Petri, United Vintners, Inc., San Francisco

> 4 lbs. pinto beans
> 4 Tbs. chili powder
> 1 clove garlic
> 2 lbs. salt pork, cut in
>   ¼-inch cubes
> Salt to taste (depending on
>   saltiness of pork)
> 3 cups California Burgundy or
>   other red table wine

Wash beans. Cover with water and soak overnight. In large kettle, cover beans with several inches of water; bring to boiling. Reduce heat and simmer for 1 hour, adding more water as needed. Add 1 tablespoon chili powder; simmer 1 hour longer. Add garlic, 1 tablespoon chili powder and salt pork; continue simmering another hour. Add remaining 2 tablespoons chili powder; taste and add salt if necessary. Continue simmering to blend chili. Add wine; simmer until beans are soft. Serve at a barbecue, with green salad and French bread. Serves 18 to 24.

HOLIDAY CABBAGE WITH RED WINE
Mrs. Adolf L. Heck, Korbel Champagne Cellars,
Guerneville

This dish has been a "traditional must" with our Thanksgiving and Christmas turkeys, ever since the kids were little. I also serve it on other occasions and it is especially good with roast pork, baked ham or roast beef.

> *1 medium-sized head red cabbage*
> *(about 1½ lbs.)*
> *¼ cup olive or other oil*
> *Salt and white pepper*
> *⅓ cup brown sugar*
> *¾ cup California Burgundy, Claret*
> *or other red table wine*
> *⅓ cup California red wine vinegar*
> *2 to 3 Tbs. cornstarch*

Remove core and finely shred cabbage. Heat oil in deep heavy skillet or Dutch oven. Sauté cabbage over medium high heat for about 10 minutes, stirring often. Remove from heat. Sprinkle with salt, pepper, and brown sugar. Return to heat; cook, stirring, until sugar dissolves. Combine wine, wine vinegar and cornstarch; add to cabbage, mixing well. Simmer about 30 minutes. (More sugar or vinegar may be added, according to taste.) A good holiday menu including this dish might be: turkey with mushroom stuffing; parsley-buttered potatoes; asparagus Hollandaise; cranberry marmalade; hot rolls; pumpkin chiffon pie. Serves 6 to 8.

CAULIFLOWER IN WINE
Mrs. Helen L. Denton, Louis M. Martini, St. Helena

> *2 Tbs. butter*
> *4 cups thinly sliced cauliflower*
> *1 cup thinly sliced celery*
> *1 Tbs. minced onion*
> *1 chicken bouillon cube*
> *½ cup California white table wine*
> *½ tsp. salt*
> *⅛ tsp. pepper*
> *1 tsp. monosodium glutamate*

Melt butter in large, heavy frying pan. Add cauliflower, celery and onion. Combine bouillon cube with wine, salt, pepper and monosodium glutamate; pour over vegetables. Cook quickly over high heat, turning constantly. Cook until vegetables are barely tender and still crisp, about 7 to 8 minutes. Serve at once. Serves 4 to 6.

ARTICHOKES IN WHITE WINE
Mrs. Howard E. Williams, E. & J. Gallo Winery, Modesto

I like this way of cooking artichokes so well that I hardly ever cook them any other way.

> *4 artichokes*
> *¼ cup olive oil*
> *¾ cup California white table wine*
> *Juice of ½ lemon*
> *¼ cup finely chopped onion*
> *½ tsp. salt*
> *¼ tsp. freshly ground pepper*
> *¼ tsp. oregano*

Cut off tip and spiny point of each leaf about ¾ inch down; also cut off stem so it will set evenly. Spread to open; remove inner small leaves and choke, using large end of a melon ball tool. Place upright in kettle small enough to keep artichokes in position while cooking. Combine all remaining ingredients; pour into open top of the artichokes. Boil about 45 minutes, or until tender, adding more wine, if necessary. Serve in small shallow bowl; use sauce for dipping each leaf. This is excellent with any lamb dish such as leg of lamb roast, shish kabob, chops. Serve with eggplant casserole, and for dessert—fresh fruit. Serves 3 to 4.

ARTICHOKES GOURMET

Artichokes Gourmet is an elegant way to prepare a canned vegetable, says Doris Paulsen of Wine Institute, San Francisco. Place in a saucepan 16 to 20 canned artichoke bottoms which have been rinsed in cold water. Add enough California white table wine to cover bottom of pan. Heat thoroughly. Remove artichokes. Place on baking sheet. Fill each cavity with ½ teaspoon liver paté; top with dab of butter; sprinkle with fine herbs. Pour into each cavity some of wine left in the pan. Broil until butter is melted and paté is slightly browned, about 5 minutes. Serve with steak or roast.

MUSHROOMS DELICIOUS
Mrs. Irving H. Marcus, Berkeley

> *2 lbs. small black mushrooms*
> *¼ cup California Light Muscat*
> *¼ tsp. salt*
> *¼ tsp. minced onion*

Combine all ingredients in a saucepan. Cover tightly; simmer very briefly over very low heat. Add a little more wine, if necessary. These are delicious hot as a main course, or chilled and drained as hors d'oeuvre. Serves 5 to 6.

ZUCCHINI, MONTEVIDEAN STYLE
Walter E. Kite, Guild Wine Co., Lodi

Cooks in our family consider this a pleasant one-dish meal, frequently served on Fridays as such, omitting the ground beef and adding 2 to 3 more eggs.

> 6 small zucchini
> 4 Tbs. olive oil
> 4 Tbs. butter
> 1 lb. lean ground beef
> 1 medium red onion, sliced
> 1 (No. 303) can whole tomatoes
> ½ cup California white table wine
> 1¼ tsp. salt
> ⅛ tsp. pepper
> 3 eggs, slightly beaten

Slice zucchini thinly, pat dry with paper towel. Heat 2 tablespoons olive oil and butter in heavy skillet. Add zucchini and cook until lightly browned, turning frequently. Meanwhile, brown meat in separate pan in remaining 2 tablespoons olive oil. Add onion. Combine meat mixture with zucchini, and stir in tomatoes, wine and seasonings. Cover skillet and bake in moderate oven (350 degrees) 30 to 40 minutes. Remove from oven and add slightly beaten eggs, cutting lightly through mixture. Return to oven and bake a few minutes longer until egg is well cooked. Most of the moisture should be taken up in the baking process. Serve with celery and carrot sticks, sour dough rolls, apple pie and cheese for dessert. Serves 4 to 6.

CHESTNUTS AND BEANS SEMIONE
Paul U. Frei, Italian Swiss Colony, Asti

This was served to us with the risotto at a small ristorante in Semione, Switzerland.

> 8 oz. frozen chestnuts, slightly
>   thawed (see below)
> 8 oz. frozen Italian green beans
> ½ small onion, chopped
> 6 slices cooked bacon, drained
>   and crumbled
> ½ cup California white table wine

Put all ingredients into saucepan with a tight-fitting lid. Cover and bring to boil; cook 4 to 6 minutes, or until beans are done and chestnuts heated through. Serve with pat of butter and season with salt and pepper.

TO FREEZE CHESTNUTS: When chestnuts are available, score them across the round surface and roast slightly until shells and skins can be removed easily. Sort nuts. Boil good nuts until almost done, but still firm. Put in plastic bags in 8-ounce portions. Remove air, close, freeze. Serves 3 to 4.

MUSHROOM STROGANOFF
Marty Griffin, Hop Kiln Winery, Healdsburg

> 1 lb. fresh mushrooms
> ½ lb. flat noodles
> 1 Tbs. butter
> 1 tsp. Tamari or soy sauce
> 1 cup sour cream
> ½ cup yoghurt
> 1 clove garlic, crushed
> 1 small onion, finely chopped
> 2 Tbs. fresh parsley, chopped
> ¼ cup Gewurtztraminer,
>   (Recommended: Hop Kiln's
>   "A Thousand Flowers")

Begin cooking noodles in conventional manner. Cut the mushrooms in half and sauté with the butter, wine, Tamari sauce, finely chopped onion and crushed garlic. Remove from heat, add chopped parsley and stir in the sour cream and yoghurt. Serve immediately over the hot noodles and salt and pepper to taste. Serve with a mixed green salad and you have a very tasty meatless meal.

QUICK GREEN BEANS SAUTERNE

Quick Green Beans Sauterne, using frozen French-cut green beans, comes from Mrs. Guy N. Baldwin Jr., Mont La Salle Vineyards, Napa. Place package of frozen beans in ½ cup boiling water and bring to second boil. Add a vegetable bouillon cube, 3 tablespoons California Sauterne, ½ teaspoon salt and 2-ounce can drained mushrooms. Cook till tender and serve. Mrs. Baldwin likes this dish with baked ham, with a chilled California Rosé on the side.

GREEN BEANS WITH A FLOURISH
Mrs. Emanuel B. Jaffe, E. & J. Gallo Winery, Modesto

> 2 Tbs. minced onion
> 3 Tbs. butter
> 1 lb. cut green beans,
>   fresh or frozen
> ¼ cup boiling water
> ¼ cup California Sherry
> ¼ tsp. salt
> ¼ tsp. monosodium glutamate
> ¼ cup chopped cashews

Brown onion in butter. Add beans; toss until all beans are coated with butter. Add boiling water and Sherry. Season with salt and monosodium glutamate. Cook in covered saucepan until tender, adding small amounts of water and Sherry, as needed. Toss with cashews just before serving. Serves 4 to 6.

GREEN BEAN FRITATTA
Mrs. Kerby Anderson, Guild Wine Co., Lodi

> *1 green pepper, chopped*
> *1 small onion, chopped*
> *Olive oil*
> *3 (1-lb.) cans green beans, drained*
> *½ cup grated Parmesan cheese*
> *3 cloves garlic, pressed*
> *¾ cup bread crumbs*
> *3 eggs, beaten*
> *¼ tsp. salt*
> *⅛ tsp. pepper*
> *Dash of sage and oregano*
> *¼ cup olive oil*
> *¼ cup California Sherry*

Sauté green pepper and onion in a little heated olive oil until soft, but not brown. Combine with green beans and all remaining ingredients. Pour into buttered (2-quart) oblong baking dish. Sprinkle with additional grated Parmesan cheese and paprika. Bake in moderately-slow oven (325 degrees) for 40 minutes. Serve cold, cut in squares as an hors d'oeuvre, or serve hot with an Italian dinner of ravioli, etc. Serves 10 to 12.

EASY GOURMET GREEN BEANS
Mrs. James Concannon, Concannon Vineyard, Livermore

This bean dish goes as well at a picnic as with a roast.

> *1 (10½-oz.) can condensed cream*
> *of celery soup*
> *¼ cup California Sauterne or Chablis*
> *1 (5-oz.) can water chestnuts*
> *2 (16-oz.) cans green beans, drained*
> *¼ cup shredded Cheddar cheese*
> *Paprika*

Blend soup with wine. Drain and dice water chestnuts. Stir into soup mixture. In a well-greased, one-quart casserole, spoon alternate layers of soup mixture and beans, beginning and ending with soup mixture. Sprinkle with cheese and dust lightly with paprika. Bake in moderate oven (350 degrees) about 25 minutes. Serves 4 to 6.

LODI CARDONI
Mrs. Peter A. Amodei, Woodbridge Vineyard Association, Lodi

> *1 medium-large head cardoni*
> *2 cloves garlic*
> *4 eggs, well beaten*
> *1 cup bread crumbs*
> *1 cup grated Parmesan or*
> *   Romano cheese*
> *3 Tbs. olive oil*
> *½ cup California Sauterne or other*
> *   white table wine*
> *1 tsp. salt*
> *1 tsp. rosemary*
> *½ tsp. basil*
> *1 tsp. monosodium glutamate*
> *(optional)*

Clean cardoni and discard outer brown leaves. Scrape, removing strings; cut into 1-inch pieces. Parboil 5 minutes in salted water with 1 clove garlic; drain well, 2 hours or even overnight. Combine cardoni with beaten eggs, remaining clove garlic (pressed) and all other ingredients; mix well. Put in a well-oiled 10-inch pan or equivalent flat casserole. Bake in moderate oven (325 to 350 degrees) for 1 hour, or until firm and browned. (Excellent, too, as an entree with a good macaroni gravy.) Serves 6 to 8.

SHERRIED GREEN BEANS
Mrs. Don Rudolph, Cresta Blanca Wine Company, Livermore

> *2 quarts prepared, fresh green beans*
> *Ice water*
> *½ cup diced bacon*
> *1 large onion, chopped*
> *1 (4-oz.) can sliced mushrooms*
> *2 cloves garlic, crushed*
> *1 Tbs. sugar*
> *1 tsp. salt*
> *Pepper*
> *4 or 5 dashes Tabasco sauce*
> *¼ cup California Sherry*
> *½ cup blanched almonds*

Crisp prepared beans in ice water for 12 to 24 hours. Pour off one-half the water. Fry bacon; sauté onion in drippings. Add bacon and onion to beans along with mushrooms, garlic, sugar, salt, pepper and Tabasco sauce. Cook 30 minutes. Add Sherry; cook 10 minutes longer. Just before serving, add almonds. Serves 10 to 12.

PORT MAILLOT VEGETABLES

Mrs. Mario Lanza, Wooden Valley Winery, Suisun City

> *½ cup carrots*
> *¼ cup onion*
> *½ clove garlic*
> *¼ cup celery*
> *½ cup cauliflower*
> *2 leaves lettuce*
> *¼ cup fat*
> *½ cup dried lima beans, cooked*
> *¾ cup California white table wine*

Cut carrots, onion, garlic, celery, cauliflower and lettuce in long narrow shred, julienne style. Sauté in heated fat, but do not brown, about 20 to 30 minutes. Add cooked lima beans and wine. Cook 1 minute longer. Serve around hot baked ham, veal, pork or lamb. Serves 3 to 4.

BACLAZANA

Edward Polverino, Louis M. Martini, St. Helena

> *1 large onion*
> *1 large eggplant*
> *2 large green peppers*
> *3 large fresh tomatoes*
> *½ cup oil*
> *½ cup California white table wine*
> *1 tsp. sugar*
> *1 tsp. Worcestershire sauce*
> *Salt and pepper*

Chop onion, eggplant, green peppers and tomatoes coarsely. Heat oil in skillet; add vegetables. Cook slowly, stirring constantly, for 30 minutes. Add remaining ingredients; continue cooking 30 minutes longer. Serve hot as a side dish or cold as a spread. Serves about 6.

EGGPLANT TOKAY

Eggplant tokay is one of those marvelous vegetable dishes that can be easily prepared a day ahead, refrigerated, then baked when wanted. Pare an eggplant and cut into cubes. Sauté cubes in 2 to 3 tablespoons of hot fat until transparent. Arrange eggplant in baking dish about 6x8x½ inches. Sprinkle with ¼ teaspoon salt, ⅛ teaspoon pepper. Combine 2 tablespoons California Tokay with one 15½-ounce can spaghetti sauce with mushrooms, and spread mixture over eggplant. Sprinkle with 2 tablespoons bread crumbs; top with 1 tablespoon melted butter. Bake in a moderate (350 degrees) oven for 25 to 30 minutes.

VINTNER'S SURPRISE

Mrs. Edmund A. Rossi Jr., Italian Swiss Colony, Asti

This is my own concoction. Special garnishes such as tiny bits of crisp bacon, finely grated hard-boiled eggs or a bit of Parmesan cheese also could be used.

> *6 large fresh artichokes*
> *¾ cup California white table wine*
> *3 (10-oz.) packages frozen chopped*
> *   spinach*
> *2 (6-oz.) cans white sauce (or 1⅓*
> *   cups basic white sauce)*
> *⅛ tsp. nutmeg*
> *¼ tsp. salt*
> *Freshly ground black pepper*
> *Bread crumbs*
> *Butter*

Cook artichokes in boiling salted water until tender, about 25 minutes. Remove all leaves; discard choke. Place artichoke bottoms in flat dish. Pour over wine; marinate overnight or at least 6 to 8 hours. Cook spinach according to package directions; drain well. Add white sauce, nutmeg, salt and pepper to spinach. Heat artichoke bottoms in wine until liquid is reduced to ¼ cup; add wine to spinach mixture. Place artichoke bottoms in individual ramekins or in shallow baking pan. Completely cover each artichoke bottom with generous scoop of spinach mixture. Sprinkle with bread crumbs and top with pat of butter. Bake in moderate oven (350 degrees) for about 30 minutes, or until spinach is bubbly and crumbs browned. Not only good as a dinner vegetable, this can also be served as luncheon. Serves 4 to 6.

CELERY ROOT RING MOLD

Doris Paulsen, Wine Institute, San Francisco

> *1 to 2 celery roots*
> *1 Tbs. scraped onion*
> *1 Tbs. chopped parsley*
> *Dash each: pepper, paprika,*
> *   garlic salt*
> *½ tsp. salt*
> *½ cup cracker crumbs*
> *2 Tbs. California white*
> *   table wine or sherry*
> *1 cup whipping cream*
> *4 eggs, separated*

Cover celery root with water; cook whole until tender, about 30 minutes. Peel. Force pulp through a sieve or blender (or mash finely); measure 1 cup of puree. Mix puree with onion, parsley, seasonings, crumbs, wine and unwhipped cream. Beat egg yolks slightly; stir into puree mixture. Beat egg whites until stiff; fold in carefully. Pour into a well-greased 5-cup ring mold; set in a pan of hot water. Bake in a moderate oven (350 degrees) for 30 minutes or until set. Let stand a few minutes, then unmold. Fill center with creamed fish, turkey or chicken. Center can also be filled with cooked peas. Serves 6 to 8.

BARTLETT SPUDS
Mrs. John D. Bartlett, Charles Krug Winery, St. Helena

> 6 medium-size potatoes, thinly
>   sliced
> 1½ tsp. salt
> ⅛ tsp. pepper
> 6 oz. Gruyere cheese
> 3 tsp. prepared mustard
> 1 medium-size onion, thinly sliced
> 1¼ cups California white table wine
> ¼ cup bread crumbs
> ¼ cup grated Parmesan cheese

In a buttered, 2-quart casserole, arrange layer of thinly sliced potatoes, salt and pepper. Cover with thin layer of Gruyere cheese; dot with mustard. Top with thinly sliced onions, salt and pepper. Repeat layers until dish is filled (about 3 layers), ending with potatoes. Pour over wine. Sprinkle with bread crumbs and Parmesan cheese. Cover and bake in moderate oven (350 degrees) for 1 to 1½ hours, or until tender. Serves 8 to 12.

SHERRY SWEET POTATOES
Mrs. Lewis A. Stern, E. & J. Gallo Winery, Modesto

Probably one of the newest adventures in cooking is the use of wine in cooking vegetables. This Sherry sweet potato recipe is a delightful discovery, we think!

> 3 lbs. sweet potatoes
> ½ cup butter, melted
> ½ cup California Dry Sherry
> ¼ tsp. nutmeg
> ¼ tsp. cinnamon
> ½ tsp. grated orange rind
> Salt and pepper
> Cream (optional)
> Brown sugar

Boil sweet potatoes in their jackets for 20 to 30 minutes, or until tender. Drain; peel; mash well. Add butter, Sherry, nutmeg, cinnamon, orange rind, salt and pepper; whip until fluffy. Add a little cream if mixture seems too dry. Pile in a greased shallow baking dish; sprinkle lightly with brown sugar and cinnamon. Bake in a hot over (400 degrees) until top is lightly browned. This is a delicious accompaniment to ham or turkey. A good menu would be: baked ham with pineapple glaze; green beans; cole slaw salad; dinner rolls. Makes 6 to 8 servings.

SURPRISE SWEET POTATOES
Mrs. Alvin Ehrhardt, United Vintners'
Community Wineries, Lodi

> 6 medium-size sweet potatoes
> 1 (No. 2) can sliced pineapple
> ¾ cup butter
> 1½ cups brown sugar (packed)
> ½ cup California Sherry
> ⅛ tsp. salt
> ½ tsp. nutmeg
> ½ to ¾ cup raisins
> ½ cup chopped pecans

Boil potatoes until tender; peel and slice into ½-inch pieces. Place layer of sweet potatoes in buttered casserole; top with layer of pineapple. Repeat layers to top of dish. Gently heat butter, sugar, Sherry, salt and nutmeg, stirring until sugar is dissolved. Pour over sweet potatoes and pineapple; sprinkle with raisins and pecans. Bake in a moderate oven (350 degrees) for 1 hour. Serve with ham or pork roast. Serves 4 to 6.

FRIED SHERRY-CHEESE ONIONS

Fried Sherry-Cheese Onions are a really special vegetable which Mrs. E. Jeff Barnette, Martini & Prati Wines, Inc., Santa Rosa, serves at Christmas or Thanksgiving dinner. For about 6 servings, slice 6 onions and separate into rings. Season with ½ teaspoon each monosodium glutamate, salt, pepper and sugar. Saute onions in 5 tablespoons butter until limp, stirring occasionally. Add ½ cup California Sherry; cook rapidly 2 or 3 minutes. Sprinkle with Parmesan cheese and serve. This would go along beautifully with broiled steak or hamburger.

POTATOES MAGNIFIQUE
Richard Norton, Fresno State College, Dept. of
Viticulture and Enology

> 4 strips bacon, chopped
> ¼ cup butter
> 2 Tbs. chopped onion
> 4 large potatoes
> ½ tsp. salt
> ⅛ tsp. freshly ground pepper
> 1½ cups California Sauterne or
>   Chablis or other white table wine.

In a large, heavy saucepan, sauté bacon until golden. Add butter and onion; continue cooking until onion is golden. Pare potatoes; cut into pieces about the size of a small egg. Add potatoes to saucepan; sprinkle with salt and pepper. Add wine to barely cover potatoes. Cover pan and simmer until potatoes start to crumble (about 1 to 1¼ hours). Add more wine, if necessary, to keep potatoes from becoming dry. This side dish goes well with chicken, pork or fish. Serves 6 to 8.

SQUASH SOUFFLÉ

Mrs. David Ficklin, Ficklin Vineyards, Madera

We have used yellow crookneck squash for this recipe, too, in which event I add chopped parsley for more color.

4 or 5 medium-size zucchini
¾ cup California white table wine
¼ lb. Cheddar cheese,
   grated (about 1¾ cups)
⅓ cup bread crumbs
Salt and pepper
Dash of garlic salt (optional)
2 eggs, lightly beaten with fork

Cook squash in wine until soft; drain. Mash squash; mix in cheese, bread crumbs and seasonings. Add eggs, mixing well. Turn into a greased casserole (or straight-sided soufflé dish). Bake in moderate oven (325 to 350 degrees) about 40 minutes. (The soufflé will rise a bit, but will not come above the top of the dish as a cheese soufflé will do.) This works equally well with a winter oven meal or summer barbecue. Hard to beat with chicken done over charcoal and a summer combination salad. Serves 4 to 6.

EGGPLANT-MEAT CASSEROLE, CREOLE

Mrs. Emanuel B. Jaffe, E. & J. Gallo Winery, Modesto

This is one of the nicest ways to glamorize a needlessly neglected vegetable. This distinctively-flavored casserole can be used either as a main course or tasty side-dish.

1 large eggplant
1 onion, finely chopped
1 green pepper, chopped
1 lb. ground beef
¼ cup fat
1 cup tomato purée
½ cup California Sherry
2½ cups soft bread crumbs
1 cup grated Parmesan cheese
1½ tsp. salt
⅛ tsp. pepper
1 tsp. sugar
½ tsp. monosodium glutamate

Pare and dice eggplant. Cover with boiling salted water; let stand 5 minutes. Brown onion, green pepper and meat in fat until onion is soft and yellow, about 5 minutes. Add tomato purée and Sherry; heat thoroughly. Add drained eggplant and all remaining ingredients. Transfer to buttered 3-quart casserole. Cover and bake in moderate oven (350 degrees) for 30 minutes. Remove cover; increase heat to 400 degrees. Bake 15 minutes, or until golden brown on top. (Small portions of this casserole can easily be reheated in a covered saucepan with a few tablespoons of water, over low heat.) Serves 8 to 10.

SQUASH WITH MUSHROOMS

Norbert C. Mirassou, Mirassou Vineyards, San Jose

6 summer, crookneck or zucchini
   squash
½ tsp. salt
⅛ tsp. pepper
1 Tbs. butter or margarine
1 large onion, chopped
½ cup California Zinfandel or
   other red table wine
1 (8-oz.) can tomato sauce
1 (4-oz.) can mushrooms, drained

Wash squash; cut into cubes. In large saucepan, combine squash with all remaining ingredients. Simmer slowly until squash is tender, about 10 minutes. This is a hearty dish, and is a good accompaniment to either white fish or beef. Serves 3 to 4.

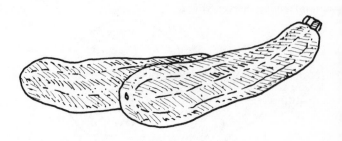

EGGPLANT-ZUCCHINI CASSEROLE

Mrs. Kerby Anderson, Guild wine Co., Lodi

When the man of the house refuses to eat eggplant or zucchini—this dish will keep him guessing. But, watch him clean his plate and ask for more.

1 medium-size eggplant
6 zucchini
2 slices bacon, diced
1 onion, chopped
1 clove garlic, chopped
½ tsp. salt
⅛ tsp. pepper
½ cup California Sherry or Rosé
⅓ cup bread crumbs
⅓ cup grated Parmesan cheese
¼ tsp. paprika

Cube unpared eggplant; cut zucchini in small pieces. Cook in boiling salted water about 10 minutes, or until tender; drain. Fry bacon until lightly browned. Add onion and garlic; sauté over low heat. Add bacon and onion to cooked vegetables. Turn into buttered 3-quart casserole. Add all remaining ingredients. Bake in moderately-slow oven (325 degrees) 30 to 40 minutes. Serves 10 to 12.

AVOCADO CLUB SANDWICH

Philo Biane, Brookside Vineyard Company, Guasti

> *8 slices white bread*
> *Mayonnaise*
> *8 to 12 slices crisp cooked bacon*
> *8 thin tomato slices*
> *12 avocado slices*
> *Salt and pepper*
> *Wine Cheese Sauce (see below)*

Toast bread and spread one side of each slice lightly with mayonnaise. Put two slices together, sandwich fashion, with 2 or 3 slices bacon, 2 slices tomato and 3 slices avocado, seasoning with salt and pepper. Serve at once with hot Wine Cheese Sauce spooned over.

WINE CHEESE SAUCE

> *2 cups grated Cheddar cheese*
> *¼ cup California Chablis or*
>   *other white table wine*
> *¼ cup cream*
> *¼ tsp. salt*
> *⅛ tsp. dry mustard*
> *1 tsp. Worcestershire sauce*

Melt cheese in top of double boiler over hot (not boiling) water. Stir in remaining ingredients and keep warm until ready to use. Serves 4.

SAUERKRAUT À LA VERMOUTH

Sauerkraut à la vermouth uses all those lovely herbs and spices already in the Vermouth bottle. Mrs. Charles H. van Kriedt of California Wineletter, combines 1 part California Dry Vermouth with 2 parts chicken bouillon, adding chopped onion, unpeeled tart apple, chopped, and caraway seeds. Heat mixture; add rinsed sauerkraut and simmer at least 2 hours. For richer flavor, sausage or spareribs are added during last hour of cooking. Serve with a California white table wine.

SAUERKRAUT IN WINE

Sauerkraut in wine blends California Sauterne with sauerkraut, minced garlic and black pepper. Mrs. Alexis Farafontoff, Scott Laboratories, Inc., Richmond, combines these ingredients in a covered pan to simmer for ½ to ¾ hour, adding more wine if necesary. She serves this with roast lamb, hot Italian sausage or frankfurters, along with California Pinot Noir.

Desserts

"Sweet is the vintage, when the showering grapes In Bacchanal reel to earth Purple and gushing."
—Lord Byron

Americans love sweets, and many cooks will plan their menus around the crowning touch of dinner—dessert. If a spreading waistline has called a halt to creamy-rich and calory-high confections, remember that a most sophisticated and satisfying finale to a meal can be fruit, cheese and wine attractively served. Have the cheese on a cheeseboard, warmed to room temperature, the fruit chilled, and your choice of dessert wine for after dinner sipping—California Port, Sherry, Muscatel, Tokay.

SUMMER PEACHES SABAYON

Mrs. Frank Franzia, Franzia Brothers Winery, Ripon

> 6 firm, ripe, fresh peaches
> ½ cup sugar
> 1 cup water
> ¼ tsp. almond extract
> 4 large egg yolks
> ¼ cup light brown sugar
> ⅓ cup California Cream Sherry
> ⅓ cup heavy cream, whipped

Quickly dip peaches in boiling water, and then in cold water; slip off skins with a sharp knife. Cut peaches in half; remove pits. Mix sugar and water in a 1-quart saucepan. Bring to boiling point; boil 2 to 3 minutes. Add almond extract and peach halves. Cover and cook until peaches are tender but hold their shape, about 6 to 8 minutes. In the top of a double boiler, beat egg yolks until thick and lemon-colored. Add brown sugar; gradually beat in Sherry. Stir and cook over hot (not boiling) water until mixture is very thick. Remove from hot water; cool. Refrigerate until cold, about 15 minutes. (Or, place pan in ice water to chill.) Fold in whipped cream. Place two peach halves in each serving dish; top with the Sabayon Sauce in the center of each peach half. Serves 6.

SHERRIED WATERMELON

Mrs. Frank Muller, Di Giorgio Wine Company, Di Giorgio

I have some rather ornate plates with a wide border of pink and gold, so I like watermelon with grape leaves to complete the color scheme. However, with a mixture of fruits, it could be used in sherbet glasses for either fruit cocktail or dessert.

> 1 watermelon
> ½ cup sugar
> ½ cup California Sherry
> 1 Tbs. lemon juice
> Few grains of salt
> 1 sprig of mint, bruised (optional)

Cut the deep pink heart of the watermelon into ¾-inch cubes or balls. Combine sugar, Sherry, lemon juice and salt; let stand until sugar is dissolved. Place watermelon cubes in a large jar; pour over Sherry mixture. Add sprig of mint, if desired. Refrigerate several hours, turning jar back and forth several times to expose all watermelon to marinade. Serve in sherbet glasses as a fruit cocktail. Or, serve on romaine lettuce or grape leaves (well-washed, dried and chilled). Other melons or fruit can be substituted, if desired. This is nice for a luncheon, with crab salad in aspic or hot casserole, and hot rolls. Serves 6 to 8.

BAKED APRICOTS PAYSANNE

Mrs. Norbert C. Mirassou, Mirassou Vineyards, San Jose

This is a light dessert which goes well after a filling dinner. It is also a good fruit dish for brunch.

>　1 (12-oz.) package dried apricots,
>　　or mixed dried fruits
>　1 cup seeded raisins
>　2½ cups water
>　½ cup California Sherry
>　¼ cup sugar
>　Juice of 1 lemon
>　1 orange, unpeeled and thinly
>　　sliced

Wash dried fruit and raisins. Place dried fruit, raisins and water in a 1½ quart casserole. Bake in a moderately-slow oven (325 degrees) for 1 hour. Add Sherry, sugar and lemon juice, stirring until sugar is dissolved. Add orange slices. Chill. Serves about 6.

PEARS SABAYON

Mrs. Michael J. Bo, Almaden Vineyards, Los Gatos

>　4 egg yolks
>　1 cup sifted powdered sugar
>　Dash of salt
>　¼ cup California Dry Sherry
>　¾ cup whipping cream
>　12 canned pear halves,
>　　drained and chilled (see below)

Beat egg yolks with sugar and salt in top of double boiler until smooth; add Sherry. Cook over hot (not boiling) water for about 8 to 10 minutes, stirring constantly. Remove from heat and cool. Whip cream until it holds peaks, and when sauce is completely cold, fold in whipped cream. Serve over chilled, drained pears. NOTE: Pears can be chilled with either ¼ cup of Sherry or Port added to ½ cup of the syrup. Use syrup later as baste for pork, chicken or ham, with a couple of tablespoons of wine vinegar added. Serves 6.

PESCHE BOURDALONE

*Mrs. Rosalind Consiglieri, L. Foppiano Wine Co.,
　Healdsburg*

>　⅓ cup sugar
>　2½ Tbs. flour
>　⅛ tsp. salt
>　⅓ cup California Sherry
>　2 cups milk
>　2 egg yolks
>　¾ cup crushed macaroons
>　½ tsp. vanilla
>　6 peach halves, fresh or canned
>　Caramel sauce (see below)
>　Sugar

Combine ⅓ cup sugar with flour and salt; stir in Sherry. Scald milk; add gradually to beaten egg yolks. Add sugar mixture slowly. Cook, stirring constantly, in top of double boiler until custard thickens. Add crushed macaroons. Cool. Stir in vanilla. In individual dessert glasses, pour a layer of custard. Top with peach half, then more custard. Carefully pour on hot Caramel Sauce so that sauce remains on top. Sprinkle lightly with about ¼ teaspoon sugar. Chill.
CARAMEL SAUCE: Melt ¾ cup sugar in heavy skillet, stirring constantly. When golden brown, add ¾ cup boiling water. Cook, stirring, until thick. Serves about 6.

EPICUREAN PEACH COBBLER

*Mrs. Vincent L. Vandevert, United Vintners, Inc.,
　San Francisco*

I always double this recipe because it disappears so fast!

>　1 cup sifted all-purpose flour
>　1 tsp. baking powder
>　½ tsp. salt
>　2 eggs
>　1½ cups sugar
>　2 Tbs. butter or margarine
>　2 Tbs. milk
>　½ cup California Sherry
>　3 cups sliced peaches (fresh or
>　　canned)

Sift together flour, baking powder and salt. Beat together eggs, 1 cup of sugar, add butter and milk. Add flour mixture; mix well. Pour into greased 9-inch square pan. Simmer Sherry and remaining ½ cup of sugar together for 3 to 4 minutes; add peaches. Pour hot peach mixture over batter in pan. Bake in moderately-hot oven (375 degrees) for 30 minutes. Serve warm with a dollop of whipped cream or vanilla ice cream. Also good served cold. Serves 6 to 8.

VINTNER'S DATE PUDDING

Mrs. Vernon Singleton, University of California
Department of Viticulture & Enology, Davis

My mother always made a date pudding similar to this. Since I didn't have her recipe, I did a little experimenting. and I think the addition of Sherry is very good. I believe women favor this recipe more than men. This is a very quick, easy and successful dessert to serve at a card party.

> 1 cup brown sugar (packed)
> ½ cup California Sherry
> 1½ cups hot water
> 2 Tbs. butter
> 1 cup granulated sugar
> 1 cup sifted all-purpose flour
> 2 tsp. baking powder
> ⅓ cup butter
> 1 cup pitted dates, thinly sliced
> ½ cup chopped nuts
> ½ cup milk

Combine brown sugar, Sherry, hot water and 2 tablespoons butter in saucepan. Bring to boil; lower heat and simmer for 3 minutes. Sift granulated sugar, flour and baking powder together. Cut in ⅓ cup butter. Mix in dates and nuts. Add milk and mix well. Spread evenly in a greased 9-inch square pan. Pour hot Sherry mixture over the top. Bake in moderately-hot oven (375 degrees) for 50 minutes. Serve warm or cold, with topping of whipped cream, if desired. Serves 9 to 10.

FLAMBÉED APPLES

Flambéed apples top off dinner dramatically. Peel and core apples as for baking. Put in saucepan with ¼ cup sugar, ½ cup water and ½ cup California Burgundy or Port. Cover; simmer until fork-tender but not soft. (About ½ hour, but this depends on type of apple, so test.) Arrange on heat-proof platter; fill centers with currant jelly. Pour over apples a sweet simple syrup. (Use ready-made syrup, or make your own by boiling 2 parts sugar and 1 part water for 5 minutes.) Set aside, but do not refrigerate. Immediately before serving, warm some California Brandy, ignite, pour over apples and serve while flaming.

STUFFED APPLES

Stuff apples for baking with fruit cake, crumbled and lightly moistened with California Port. During baking, baste apples with equal parts Port and cider for rich flavor.

STUFFED PEARS MILANESE

Mrs. Opal Armstrong, Paul Masson Vineyards, Saratoga

This simple and delicious dessert is one of many which I learned from Mr. Jorge Kniegge, San Francisco chef and teacher extraordinary.

> 4 firm fresh pears
> 3 Tbs. sugar
> 4 maraschino cherries, chopped
> 24 toasted, blanched almonds,
>   chopped
> 4 drops almond extract
> ½ cup California Sherry

Peel and cut pears in half lengthwise. Remove cores and fill each pear half with a mixture made by combining sugar, cherries, almonds and almond extract. Place pears in a shallow baking dish; pour 1 tablespoon Sherry over each pear half. Bake in moderately-slow oven (325 degrees) for 15 minutes, or until tender but not soft. Although a Dry Sherry is equally as good in making this dessert, I prefer to use a Cream Sherry. Serves 4.

HONEY APPLE CRISP

Mrs. Frank Indelicato, Delicato Winery, Manteca

> 4 cups sliced cooking apples
> ¼ cup granulated sugar
> 1 Tbs. lemon juice
> ¼ cup California Sauterne
> ½ cup honey
> 1 cup sifted all-purpose flour
> ½ cup brown sugar (packed)
> 1 tsp. salt
> ½ cup butter

Spread apples in a half-quart baking dish. Sprinkle with granulated sugar, lemon juice and wine; pour honey over top. Mix flour, brown sugar and salt; work in butter until crumbly. Spread crumb mixture over apples. Bake in moderately-hot oven (375 degrees) about 40 minutes, or until apples are tender and crust is crisply browned. Menu preceding this dessert could include pork chops, candied sweet potatoes, tossed green salad and a platter of olives, green onions, carrot sticks and garbanzo beans. Serves 6.

GRAPE TART
Mrs. John B. Cella II, Cella Wineries, Fresno

> *1 (9-inch) tart shell of slightly*
> * sweet pastry*
> *3 cups seedless grapes, washed*
> * and stemmed*
> *½ cup sugar*
> *¾ cup California sweet white wine*
> * such as Malvasia Bianca or*
> * Sweet Sauterne*
> *2 Tbs. California Brandy*
> * or kirsch*
> *2 Tbs. cornstarch*
> *2 Tbs. sugar*

Prepare slightly sweet pastry by adding 1 tablespoon sugar to flour of standard pastry recipe. Roll to ⅛ inch thickness and line pie plate as usual. Toss grapes with ½ cup sugar and fill tart shell. Bake in moderate oven (350 degrees) 20 minutes or until crust is golden. Meanwhile, combine wine and Brandy in sauce pan. Mix cornstarch and sugar; blend with wine. Cook over boiling water, stirring constantly, until thick and clear. Cool sauce slightly and pour over grapes in shell. Chill well before serving. Serves 6.

PINK PEARS ROSÉ
Mrs. Stanley Strud, California Wine Association, Lodi

> *6 Bartlett pears*
> *6 whole cloves*
> *1 cup sugar*
> *½ cup water*
> *½ to ¾ cup California Rosé*
> *4 to 6 drops red food coloring*

Peel pears, leaving stem attached. Stick a clove into each pear; place in deep, small kettle. Add sugar, water, wine and enough red food coloring to give desired color. Poach gently until pears are clear and syrup has thickened; baste now and then, or very carefullly turn pears. Chill. Serve very cold as either salad or dessert. A menu to go along with this dish might include a pork roast, steamed rice, sweet and sour red cabbage, and cookies with the pears. Serves 6.

OLYMPIAN ORANGES
Mrs. Paul U. Frei, Italian Swiss Colony, Asti

> *3 or 4 tart oranges*
> *1 (12-oz.) package macaroons or*
> * amaretti (almond or coconut)*
> *2 (11-oz.) cans mandarin orange*
> * segments, drained*
> *⅔ to 1 cup California Marsala or*
> * Tokay*

Peel oranges; slice thinly crosswise; remove seeds. In a deep dish, place macaroons, mandarin orange segments and orange slices in alternate layers; pack rather tightly. Pour wine evenly over top. Chill about 2 hours before serving. Serve with whipped cream. Serves 6 to 8.

HOT FRUIT COMPOTE
Mrs. Leonard Maullin, Paul Masson Vineyards, Saratoga

> *3 (1-lb. 13-oz.) cans of fruit, drained*
> *2 medium ripe bananas*
> *Coconut, brown sugar*
> *1 (15-oz.) can or jar of applesauce*
> *½ cup California Sherry or Brandy*

Thoroughly butter a shallow glass container or casserole, 1 to 1½ quart size. Arrange drained fruits in it. (I prefer to assort them, such as pears, peaches and plums. However, just one kind may be used.) Arrange thin fingers of banana on top of fruit. Sprinkle lightly with coconut. Then, sprinkle well with brown sugar. Spread with applesauce. Pour Brandy or Sherry over. Bake in moderate oven (350 degrees) about 30 minutes. Serve hot. Serves 6 to 8.

CALIFORNIA ORANGE SOUFFLÉ

*Mrs. Catherine Menth, California Wine Association,
San Francisco*

4 large oranges
2 Tbs. butter or margarine
2 Tbs. flour
¼ cup milk
¼ cup California Sherry
1 Tbs. grated orange peel
3 egg yolks
3 egg whites
¼ tsp. salt
6 Tbs. sugar
½ cup stale cake cubes
Sugar

Cut oranges in half. With grapefruit cutter remove pulp, being careful not to cut through shell because it's going to hold soufflé. Set shells in custard cups in shallow baking pan. Cut enough orange pulp into sections to make ½ cup. (Use remainder for breakfast.)

Prepare soufflé as follows: Melt butter and blend in flour. Add milk; then Sherry. Cook until thick and smooth, stirring constantly. Add orange peel and egg yolks. Cook a minute or so longer, stirring. Remove from heat. Beat egg whites with salt until frothy. Add sugar, a tablespoon at a time, and continue beating until stiff peaks form. Gently fold in egg yolk mixture. Spoon a heaping tablespoon into each prepared orange shell. Arrange 2 or 3 cake cubes over it and on them place orange sections. Spoon in remainder of soufflé mixture, filling only ¾ full. (If there is soufflé left over, bake in individual baking dishes rather than filling orange shells to much—soufflé needs room to puff up.) Sprinke each with a teaspoon of sugar. Bake in moderately-hot oven (375 degrees) about 25 minutes. Serves 8.

STRAWBERRY WINE FLUFF

Mrs. Jake Rheingans, Sanger Winery Association, Sanger

1 (3-oz.) package strawberry-flavored
   gelatin
1 cup hot water
½ cup California Port
1 pint vanilla ice cream
Strawberry Port Sauce (see below)

Dissolve gelatin in the hot water; add Port; chill. When mixture is slightly thickened, add the ice cream and beat with a rotary or electric beater until smooth. Pour into a serving dish; chill until firm. Serve with Strawberry Port Sauce below.

STRAWBERRY PORT SAUCE: combine 1½ cups crushed strawberries with 3 tablespoons California Port and sugar to taste. Chill thoroughly before serving. Serves 6.

ORANGE SHERRY CREAM

Mrs. August Sebastiani, Sebastiani Vineyards, Sonoma

½ cup sugar
1 envelope plain gelatin
¼ tsp. salt
2 tsp. grated orange rind
⅔ cup orange juice
3 eggs, separated
1 Tbs. fresh lemon juice
½ cup California Sherry
1 cup whipping cream
1 (3-oz.) package lady fingers
1 (10-oz.) package frozen raspberries,
   thawed

Combine sugar, gelatin, salt and orange rind in top of double boiler. Stir in orange juice and lightly beaten egg yolks. Place over hot water; cook, stirring frequently, until mixture thickens, about 10 to 15 minutes. Remove from heat; stir in lemon juice and Sherry. Cool until slightly thickened. Beat egg whites until stiff; whip cream. Fold egg whites and cream into gelatin mixture. Line an 8 or 9-inch spring form pan with lady fingers with tips cut off. Carefully pour gelatin mixture into pan. Chill until firm. Cut into wedges and serve with thawed raspberries. Serves 8 to 10.

CRÈME AU VIN

Mrs. Lewis A. Stern, E. & J. Gallo Winery, Modesto

This is a mouth-watering taste idea to stir the imagination. It is well worth the extra few minutes it takes the hostess for last-minute combining and serving.

1 cup sugar
1½ cups California Sauterne or
   other white table wine
Juice and grated rind of 1 orange
Juice and grated rind of 1 lemon
1 Tbs. cornstarch
6 egg yolks, beaten
2 egg whites, stiffly beaten

Combine sugar, 1 cup of wine, and juice and grated rind of orange and lemon; bring to boil. Dissolve cornstarch in remaining ½ cup of wine; add to hot wine mixture. Cook for 1 minute, stirring constantly. Stir a little of hot mixture into beaten egg yolks. Return to pan; cook over low heat, stirring constantly, until mixture just reaches the boiling point. Strain into chilled bowl; cool, then chill. At serving time, fold in stiffly beaten egg whites. Pile high into sherbet glasses and serve with light wafer-type cookies. Serves 5 to 6.

BONET

Mrs. Frederick Rolandi, Jr., Martini & Prati Wines, Inc.,
Santa Rosa

12 large macaroons
½ cup California Sherry
1 quart milk
Grated rind of ½ lemon and
½ orange
8 coffee beans
1¼ cups sugar
8 eggs
1 tsp. vanilla

Place macaroons in bowl and pour over Sherry. Set aside. Mix milk, grated rinds and coffee beans. Scald, then set aside to cool. Melt ½ cup of the sugar over low heat. When bubbly and the color of caramel (DO NOT BURN) pour into 2½-quart heat-proof glass bowl. Line bowl with marinated macaroons. Beat eggs with remaining ¾ cup sugar. Strain cooled milk slowly into beaten eggs and stir to blend. Add vanilla. Pour over macaroons in bowl. Set bowl in larger pan of water and bake in moderately-hot oven (400 degrees) 45 minutes to 1 hour until custard is done and testing straw comes out smooth. Cool, then refrigerate until serving time. Invert bowl on platter so dessert is "bottom side up, like an upside down cake". Serve in wedges on dessert plates or spoon into sherbet dishes. Serves 8 to 10.

SPANISH WINE CREAM

Mrs. Leonard Maullin, Paul Masson Vineyards, Saratoga

This is an authentic Spanish recipe, very typical of Continental Europe. It is a light dessert, not too sweet, and very elegant. I serve it after any type of company dinner.

1 (4/5-qt.) bottle California Riesling
or other white table wine
¾ cup plus 1 Tbs. sugar
6 eggs
4 egg yolks (additional)
Juice of 2 large, juicy lemons
1 tsp. cornstarch mixed with
small amount of cold water
4 egg whites, stiffly beaten

Combine all ingredients, except beaten egg whites, in very large saucepan. Beat continuously with rotary or electric beater over medium heat. Just before mixture reaches boiling point, remove from heat. Blend stiffly beaten egg whites into hot mixture; continue beating for several minutes. Pour into serving glasses and refrigerate 6 to 8 hours. Garnish with small bits of glacé fruit and serve with small decorated cookies.

SHERRY-MALLOW, SAN MARTIN

Mrs. John M. Filice, San Martin Vineyards Co., San Martin

I find this dessert is best served in individual sherbet glasses. We like it served plain or garnished with fresh, whole sugared strawberries, or sliced fresh peaches.

1 (1-lb.) package miniature
marshmallows
2 cups California Cream Sherry
1 cup whipping cream, or 2
(2-oz.) packages whipped
dessert topping mix

Place marshmallows in mixing bowl; pour over Sherry. Let stand for several hours, stirring frequently, until soft, soggy and transparent looking. Whip cream (or prepare whipped dessert topping mix according to package directions, omitting vanilla flavoring). Lift marshmallows out of Sherry with a slotted spatula or spoon, shaking off as much Sherry as possible. Fold marshmallows into whipped cream or dessert topping. Place in sherbet glasses; refrigerate overnight or at least 8 hours before serving. I usually serve this dessert when there are guests. It is light and pleasant after a heavy meal, and especially good after chicken, turkey or roast beef. Serves 8.

SHERRY CUSTARD

A custard favorite from South of the Border comes from Mrs. George Al Berry, of Roma Wine Company, Fresno. Combine 6 egg yolks, 6 tablespoons granulated sugar and dash of salt in top of cold double boiler; beat with rotary beater until thick and lemon-colored. Gradually beat in 6 tablespoons California Sherry. Place over hot (not boiling) water; beat until thick and fluffy, about 4 to 6 minutes. Remove from heat and serve immediately in sherbet glasses.

BISCUIT TORTONI

Mrs. Joseph S. Vercelli, Souverain Winery, Geyserville

>   *1 cup whipping cream*
>   *¼ cup sifted powdered sugar*
>   *1 egg white, stiffly beaten*
>   *½ cup finely crumbled macaroons*
>   *2 Tbs. California Sherry*

Whip cream; gradually fold in sugar and egg white alternately with the crumbled cookies. Add Sherry. Chill at least 2 hours. Serve in dessert dishes. Top with ½ teaspoon apricot jam or sprinkle with macaroon crumbs, if desired. Serves 5 to 6.

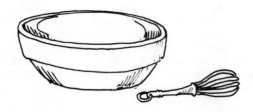

DANISH STRAWBERRY MOUSSE

Doris Paulsen, Wine Institute, San Francisco

This is an old Danish recipe served to us in Denmark.

>   *1 quart strawberries, washed*
>   *and hulled*
>   *½ cup sugar*
>   *½ cup California white table wine*
>   *2 envelopes unflavored gelatin*
>   *½ cup cold water*
>   *½ cup boiling water*
>   *2 cups heavy cream, whipped*

Reserve several whole strawberries for garnish; press remaining berries through a sieve. Add sugar and wine; stir well. Chill. Soften gelatin in cold water; add boiling water, stirring to dissolve. Cool. Combine gelatin with chilled strawberry mixture. Beat with a rotary beater until fluffy and slightly thiickened. Fold in whipped cream. Turn into 2-quart oiled mold. Chill 3 hours or longer. Unmold onto a chilled platter; garnish with reserved strawberries. This is excellent served as an afternoon dish, with tea, Sherry or other wine and cookies. If served as a dinner-time dessert, a good preceding menu might include veal birds stuffed with wild rice; buttered green beans with chives, and tomatoes sliced with cucumbers in sour cream. Serves 6 to 8.

CUSTARD'S LAST STAND

Mrs. Frank Lico, San Martin Vineyards Co., San Martin

This recipe was give to me by my mother, and I hope that when my three children marry they will try it on their loved ones. This dessert is good after any meat dish because it is so light. It is rich enough to serve the girls at bridge, and simple enough to serve to your family.

>   *⅓ cup sugar*
>   *1 quart milk*
>   *6 eggs*
>   *¼ to ½ cup sugar*
>   *¼ cup California Brandy*
>   *12 to 14 shortbread cookies*

In 8-inch custard pan, put ⅓ cup sugar. Melt sugar over high heat, tipping pan to coat bottom and sides well. When sugar is golden brown, set aside while preparing custard. Combine milk and eggs in a large bowl; beat well. Add ¼ to ½ cup sugar, or to taste. Blend in Brandy. Crumble cookies over the milk mixture; stir well. Pour Custard mixture over burnt sugar in custard pan. Place pan in larger pan containing 1 inch water. Bake in moderate oven (350 degrees) for one hour. Test doneness by inserting knife in middle of custard before removing from oven. Cool custard at room temperature. When cool, slip knife around sides of pan. Invert pan on a platter with a rim so that the syrup from the sugar will not be lost. Chill 3 to 4 hours. Makes 8 to 10 servings.

STRAWBERRY RED WINE PARFAIT

Mrs. Lewis A. Stern, E. & J. Gallo Winery, Modesto

>   *1 (12-oz.) package frozen*
>   *strawberries*
>   *1 (3-oz.) package strawberry-*
>   *flavored gelatin*
>   *1 tablespoon sugar*
>   *½ cup California Burgundy or*
>   *other red table wine*
>   *½ cup whipping cream, stiffly*
>   *beaten*

Thaw berries; drain juice into measuring cup. Add enough water to juice to measure 1 cup. Heat liquid to boiling. Add gelatin and sugar; stir to dissolve. Add wine; cool until mixture is syrupy. Beat until foamy. Fold in stiffly beaten cream and strawberries. Heap into parfait glasses; chill until firm. Serve with thin vanilla wafers. (If a parfait pie is desired, line a buttered glass pie plate with 1½ cups vanilla wafer crumbs to make a delicate crust. Fill with parfait mixture; chill.) Serves 6 to 8.

ENGLISH TRIFLE LIVERMORE
Mrs. James Concannon, Concannon Vineyard, Livermore

One of the many versions of the Trifle, this is an attractive and easily prepared finale to complement any menu.

1 (8-inch) round sponge cake
½ cup raspberry jam (or 1 quart fresh raspberries, sweetened to taste)
½ to ¾ cup California Sherry
1 (3-oz.) package instant vanilla pudding mix, prepared according to package directions
6 almond macaroons, crumbled
2 Tbs. blanched and shredded or slivered almonds
1 cup whipping cream
Glacé cherries (or fresh whole raspberries)

Slice sponge cake across into 5 or 6 (¼ to ½-inch thick) rounds. Spread 2 or 3 slices with jam (or fresh raspberries). in a deep crystal bowl (about 9 inches wide), alternate layers of cake, sprinklings of Sherry, prepared pudding, crumbled macaroons and almonds, ending with pudding. Chill for 1 to 2 hours, or until set. Whip cream; pile on top of trifle. Decorate with cherries (or fresh raspberries). Serves 6 to 8.

MUSCATEL PUDDING

Mrs. Ralo D. Bandiera, Bandiera Wines, Cloverdale

1 (3-oz.) package ladyfingers
1 cup California Muscatel
2 (3-oz.) packages vanilla pudding mix

Line each of 8 sherbet glasses with 3 split ladyfingers. Soak each piece of ladyfinger with 1 teaspoon Muscatel. Prepare pudding mix according to package directions. Pour over wine-soaked ladyfingers. Chill ½ hour and serve. Makes 7 to 8 servings.

SHERRY TRIFLE ANGLAIS
Dr. James F. Guymon, University of California, Department of Viticulture and Enology, Davis

1 sponge cake, 2 or 3 days old
⅔ cup California Cream Sherry
2 cups fresh strawberries, sweetened to taste
1 Tbs. cornstarch
2 cups milk
½ cup sugar
Pinch of salt
3 egg yolks
1 Tbs. Jamaican rum
½ tsp. vanilla
Slivered almonds
1 cup heavy cream, whipped
2 Tbs. California Brandy

Bake or buy sponge cake to fit serving dish. Let the cake stand uncovered to dry out for a few days. Line the bottom of the serving dish with the dried or stale cake. Slowly pour Sherry over cake. Set aside. Save a few berries to slice for garnish. Crush remainder of berries and sweeten to taste. Chill in refrigerator. Blend cornstarch with small amount of milk to make a paste, then stir it into rest of milk and cook in upper part of double boiler until slightly thickened. Add sugar and salt. Beat egg yolks; add small amount of hot milk mixture to them, then stir yolks into balance of hot milk mixture and cook, stirring continuously, over hot water for few minutes until mixture coats spoon. Remove from heat; cool. Add rum and vanilla. To assemble dessert, spread chilled strawberries over cake and pour on custard. Chill thoroughly. Sprinkle with slivered almonds and decorate with reserved, sliced strawberries. Top with whipped cream flavored with Brandy. Serves 6 to 10.

EASY EGG SURPRISE
Mrs. William Bonetti, Charles Krug Winery, St. Helena

4 (¾-inch) slices pound cake
1 Tbs. sugar
1 Tbs. orange juice
½ cup California Port
1 cup whipped cream
4 canned apricot halves

Place each cake slice in serving dish. Combine sugar, orange juice and Port. Spoon over cake. Cover each serving with whipped cream. Set an apricot half in center of each, and surprise—it looks like an egg, sunny-side up. Serves 4.

ZUPPA INGLESE

Mrs. Robert D. Rossi Jr., United Vintners, Inc.,
San Francisco

6 egg yolks
6 Tbs. sugar
1 Tbs. orange juice
1 tsp. vanilla
½ tsp. lemon extract
½ cup California Cream Sherry
1 angel food cake (1 day old)

Beat egg yolks and sugar until thick and lemon-colored. Add orange juice, vanilla and lemon extract; slowly beat in Sherry. (Sauce will be thin.) Cut the cake into three layers. Place one layer on a serving platter deep enough to hold sauce; pour over ⅓ of the sauce. Repeat with second and third layers. Refrigerate overnight. To serve, cut into slices. Makes 8 to 10 servings.

ICE BOX WINE CAKE

Mrs. Robert H. Meyer, Allied Grape Growers, Asti

I prefer to use this recipe for a dessert-bridge or some other occasion when only dessert is served. It is very light but rich and filling.

1 (3-oz.) package ladyfingers
2 Tbs. unflavored gelatin
½ cup cold water
½ cup hot water
6 egg yolks, well beaten
1 cup sugar
2 cups heavy cream, whipped
6 egg whites, stiffly beaten
½ cup California Sherry

Line a 3-quart spring form pan with ladyfinger halves. (Snip off lower rounded edge with scissors to keep them upright. Place snippings and extra ladyfingers in bottom of pan.) Soak gelatin in cold water for 5 minutes; dissolve in hot water. Combine beaten egg yolks and sugar; add dissolved gelatin. Fold in whipped cream and beaten egg whites. Add Sherry. Pour into ladyfinger-lined pan; chill until firm. This cake can be made the day before serving. Serves 10 to 12.

LEMON-GLAZED CHEESE PIE

Mrs. Mildred Parriott, Beringer Bros., Inc., St. Helena

1½ cups graham cracker crumbs
⅓ cup butter, melted
12 oz. cream cheese
2 eggs
¾ cup sugar
2 Tbs. California Brandy
¼ tsp. salt
1 cup chopped seedless raisins
Lemon Glaze (see below)

Combine graham cracker crumbs and melted butter. Reserve ¼ cup crumbs; press remainder over bottom and up sides of an 8 or 9-inch pie pan; set aside. Beat cream cheese until soft; beat in eggs, sugar, Brandy and salt until creamy. Stir in raisins. Pour into prepared crust. Bake in moderate oven (350 degrees) for 20 minutes. Cool. Spread cooled Lemon Glaze over pie; sprinkle with reserved graham cracker crumbs. Serves 6 to 8.
LEMON GLAZE: Mix together ¼ cup sugar, 2 tablespoons cornstarch, ⅛ teaspoon salt, ¼ cup California Dry Sherry and ¼ cup water. Cook, stirring, until mixture begins to thicken. Add ¼ cup additional sugar and ¼ cup lemon juice. Cook until thick and clear. Stir in 1 egg, beaten, and 1 tablespoon butter. Cook a bit longer. Cool.

PARFAIT PIE CHABLIS

Mrs. Guy N. Baldwin Jr., Mont La Salle Vineyards,
Reedley

1 (3-oz.) package strawberry-
flavored gelatin
¾ cup boiling water
1 pint vanilla ice cream
½ cup California Chablis or
other white table wine
¼ cup pineapple juice
1½ cups sliced fresh strawberries,
sweetened
1 (9-inch) baked pie shell, cooled
Whipped cream
Sliced strawberries for garnish

Dissolve gelatin in boiling water. Add ice cream by spoonfuls, stirring until melted. Add Chablis and pineapple juice. Chill until thickened but not set, about 15 minutes. Drain strawberries; fold into gelatin mixture. Turn into baked pie shell; chill until firm. Garnish with whipped cream and sliced strawberries. This is a good dessert to follow a baked ham dinner, as well as being a wonderful summer dessert. Serves about 6.

WINE CREAM ANGEL CAKE
Mrs. Dale C. Perry, University of California,
Department of Viticulture & Enology, Davis

1 (9 or 10-inch) round or square
angel food cake
½ cup California Sauterne
2 cups dairy sour cream
1 cup sifted powdered sugar
1 (3-oz.) package cream cheese,
softened

Carefully split cake in half horizontally. Set aside top portion. Sprinkle bottom half of the cake with ¼ cup of the wine; spread with 1 cup sour cream; dust with ½ cup powdered sugar. Replace top; pour over remaining wine. Blend cream cheese with remaining sour cream and powdered sugar; use to frost cake. Chill 5 hours before serving. Serves 8 to 10.

SHERRY CHEESECAKE MODESTO
Mrs. Lewis A. Stern, E. & J. Gallo Winery, Modesto

Anyone can become a wizard in the kitchen with this fascinating cheesecake.

1½ cups zwieback crumbs
½ cup butter (melted)
¼ cup sugar
1 tsp. cinnamon
4 (8-oz.) packages cream cheese,
softened
1 cup plus 2 Tbs. sugar
2 Tbs. flour
3 Tbs. California Cream
Sherry
1 tsp. grated lemon rind
1 tsp. grated orange rind
4 egg yolks, well beaten
Pinch of salt
2 cups sour cream
4 egg whites, stiffly beaten

Make a zwieback crust by combining zwieback crumbs with butter (melted), sugar and cinnamon. Line bottom and sides of well-buttered (10-inch) spring-form pan with 1¼ cups of mixture; reserve remainder for topping. Chill crust while preparing filling. Cream softened cream cheese with sugar. Add flour, 1 tablespoon Sherry, lemon and orange rinds, beaten egg yolks and salt; mix well. Add sour cream; fold in stiffly beaten egg whites. Pour filling into chilled crust. Bake in moderately-hot oven (375 degrees) for 30 minutes. Remove cake from oven; raise heat to 400 degrees. Sprinkle cake with remaining 2 tablespoons Sherry and reserved zwieback crust mixture. Return cake to oven; bake 15 minutes longer or until set. Turn off heat; open oven door; let cheesecake cool in oven. Chill before serving.

HOLIDAY FRUIT CAKE
Mrs. Joseph S. Concannon, Concannon Vineyard,
Livermore

Recipe has been in Concannon family for generations.

½ lb. whole candied cherries
½ lb. candied pineapple, cubed
½ lb. candied citron,
thinly sliced
½ lb. candied orange peel, diced
½ lb. candied lemon peel, diced
1 lb. pitted dates, sliced
3 (15-oz.) packages raisins
2 (11-oz.) packages currants
1 cup California Sherry
5 cups sifted cake flour
1 tsp. each: cinnamon,
cloves and mace
2 tsp. salt
2 cups butter
1 (1-lb.) package brown sugar
12 eggs, well beaten
1 cup strawberry jam
1 cup light molasses

Combine candied fruits and peels, dates, raisins, currants. Pour over Sherry; let stand overnight. Sift flour with spices and salt 3 times. Cream butter; gradually add sugar, beating until light and fluffy. Add eggs slowly, beating well. Add Sherried fruit, jam and molasses, mixing well. Gradually work in flour mixture. Pour into 5 paper-lined (9x5x3-inch) loaf pans. Bake in slow oven (250 degrees) for 3½ to 4 hours. Test cakes for doneness with a wire tester or straw. Remove cakes from pans; cool on wire rack. Wrap cold cakes in cheese cloth dipped in Sherry. Makes 5 loaves, about 2½ lbs. each.

AL'S FAVORITE RHUBARB PIE
Mrs. Alvin Ehrhardt, United Vintners'
Community Wineries, Lodi

3 eggs
1½ to 2 cups sugar
1 (3-oz.) package strawberry-
flavored gelatin
1 (3-oz.) package raspberry-
flavored gelatin
1 quart (2 lbs.) rhubarb, cut in
1-inch pieces
¼ cup California Port
Pastry for (10-inch) 2-crust pie
1½ Tbs. butter
Evaporated milk

Beat eggs until frothy; stir in sugar. Add gelatins, mixing thoroughly. Combine rhubarb with Port; add to gelatin mixture. Pour into pastry-lined pan. Dot with butter. Cover with top crust in which slits have been cut. Brush with evaporated milk and sprinkle with sugar. Bake in a hot oven (425 degrees) for 40 minutes, or until crust is nicely browned and juice begins to bubble through slits.

BACCHÀNALIAN YULE CAKE

Mrs. Mildred Parriott, Beringer Bros., Inc., St. Helena

7½ oz. dates
⅔ cup candied orange peel
½ cup red maraschino cherries
½ cup green maraschino cherries
½ cup seedless raisins
1½ cups Brazil nuts
1½ cups walnut halves or large pieces
3 oz. California Brandy or Sherry
¾ cup sifted flour
½ tsp. baking powder
½ tsp. salt
3 eggs
¾ cup sugar
1 tsp. vanilla

Mix fruit and nuts in bowl; pour over Brandy or Sherry; let stand several hours. Sift dry ingredients together. Beat eggs; beat in sugar and vanilla. Combine with dry ingredients; add fruit and nuts. Pour into buttered 10x5x3-inch loaf pan lined with waxed paper. Bake in slow oven (300 degrees) for 2¼ hours. Makes 1 loaf.

GOLDEN GATE DATE BREAD

Mrs. Dan Turrentine, Wine Advisory Board, San Francisco

I discovered this recipe many years ago, and substituted wine for water called for in the original recipe. I've made it for 20 years, and never fail to have requests for this really superb recipe each time I serve it. I feel like I am giving a gift to share it.

¾ cup California Sherry
1 tsp. baking soda
1 cup pitted dates, cut up
¼ cup shortening
1 cup sugar
2 eggs, beaten
1 tsp. vanilla
2 cups sifted all-purpose flour
1 tsp. double action
   baking powder
½ tsp. salt
½ cup walnuts, chopped

Heat Sherry to just below boiling. Sprinkle soda over dates in a bowl. Pour over hot Sherry; cool. Cream together shortening and sugar. Add cooled Sherry-date mixture, beaten eggs and vanilla; mix well. Sift flour with baking powder and salt; add to creamed mixture, stirring till blended. Stir in nuts. Pour into 2 greased (7½x4x2½-inch) loaf pans or 1 (8½x4½x3-inch) loaf pan. Bake in moderate oven (350 degrees) for 50 to 60 minutes. This dessert will dress up a family meal, as well as a company dinner. It is also delicious toasted for breakfast. Makes 2 small or 1 large loaf.

PERSIMMON FRUIT CAKE

Mrs. Alvin Ehrhardt, United Vintners'
Community Wineries, Lodi

This recipe has never been in print. It is my own recipe for the moist type of fruit cake we like for the holidays. Folks who won't eat fruit cake ask for more of this.

3 cups persimmon pulp
½ cup California Muscatel
3 cups sugar
2 cups seedless dark raisins
1 cup muscat raisins
3 cups walnuts (large pieces)
1 cup candied mixed fruit
1 cup milk
3 cups sifted all-purpose flour
¾ tsp. cinnamon
¾ tsp. cloves
1½ tsp. salt
2 Tbs. baking soda

In large mixing bowl, combine persimmon pulp, wine, sugar, raisins, nuts, mixed fruit and milk. Resift flour with spices, salt and soda. Add to persimmon mixture and mix well. Pour into well-greased 3-quart heavy aluminum pan with glass cover; set in pan of hot water. Bake, covered, in moderate oven (350 degrees) for 1¾ to 2 hours, or until sides shrink away from pan. Remove cover last half hour. Set pan on wire rack until cool. Invert pan on heavy foil wrap; wrap and store in cool dry place or freeze. If desired, the cake can be baked in a 10-inch tube pan, covered with aluminum foil. (I sometimes take one-third the recipe and steam 2 hours in double boiler or until done, and serve as a pudding with lemon sauce. I sometimes use a combination of walnuts, slivered almonds and Brazil nuts in cake or pudding.) Makes 1 cake, about 6 pounds.

BRANDY CANDY COOKIES

Brandy candy cookies are a pleasing party confection, served with California Sherry. Mrs. Anthony Indelicato of Delicato Vineyards, Manteca, combines 2½ cups finely crushed vanilla wafers with ½ cup chopped nuts, ⅓ cup California Brandy, 1 cup powdered sugar, 1 small can chocolate syrup. Blend well and roll into small balls for serving.

WINE FESTIVAL ANGEL FOOD CAKE
Mrs. A.C. Huntsinger, Almaden Vineyards, Los Gatos

> 1 (10-oz.) package angel food
> cake mix
> ¾ tsp. each: vanilla and
> almond extracts
> 1 envelope plain gelatin
> 3 Tbs. cold water
> ⅔ cup California Sherry
> ¼ cup sugar
> Dash of salt
> 1 pint heavy cream, whipped
> 1 cup crushed peanut brittle

Prepare angel food cake mix following package directions, adding vanilla and almond extracts to batter. Bake in 10-inch tube pan. Invert pan until thoroughly cool, then remove cake from pan and cut crosswise into 2 layers. Meanwhile, soften gelatin in cold water for 5 minutes. Heat Sherry to simmering; add softened gelatin, sugar and salt, stirring until dissolved. Cool, then chill. When mixture begins to thicken, fold in whipped cream. Chill again just until thick enough to spread. Spread part of filling over lower half of cake; place second half on top. Spread remaining filling over top and sides of cake. Chill several hours. About 1 hour before serving, sprinkle peanut brittle over top of cake. Serves 8 to 10.

PORT BERRY PIE
Mrs. Alvin Ehrhardt, United Vintners'
Community Wineries, Lodi

Port adds zip to the berries—my own idea to perk up berry pie.

> 2 quarts ripe, juicy berries
> (blueberries, blackberries,
> loganberries, boysenberries,
> raspberries or strawberries)
> ⅓ cup California Port
> Juice of 1 lemon
> 1 cup sugar
> ⅓ to ½ cup sifted all-purpose
> flour (depending on juiciness
> of berries)
> ½ tsp. cinnamon
> Dash of salt
> Pastry for (10-inch) 2-crust pie
> 1½ Tbs. butter

Wash berries and remove stems; drain well. Pour Port and lemon juice over berries. Mix together sugar, flour, cinnamon and salt. Add to berries and mix lightly. Pour berries into pastry-lined pan. Dot with butter. Cover with lattice crust. Bake in hot oven (450 degrees) for 35 to 40 minutes. Serve slightly warm but not hot.

MINCEMEAT TARTS
Mrs. Dennis Alexander, California Cellarmasters, Lodi

These are served as little individual pies, and are especially nice for Thanksgiving.

> Pastry based on 4 cups flour
> 1 apple, chopped
> Water
> 1 (1-lb. 2½-oz.) jar mincemeat
> ½ cup raisins
> 2 to 4 Tbs. California Sherry,
> Muscatel or Tokay
> California Brandy
> Cream (optional)

Prepare pastry; chill. Cook apple in as little water as possible until tender. Combine with mincemeat and raisins and heat to simmering. Add wine and Brandy to taste. Roll out pastry. Cut into rounds with 3¼-inch cutter. In half of rounds, cut a hole in the center with a doughnut cutter. Place a slightly rounded tablespoon of mincemeat in center of each whole round. Moisten edges. Top with doughnut-shaped round. Press edges so they stick together. Brush tops with cream, if desired; this gives a beautiful color when baked. Bake in hot oven (450 degrees) for 10 to 15 minutes. Serve warm. (The tarts may be frozen and baked just before serving, if desired.) Makes about 3 dozen.

SHERRIED RAISIN BARS
Mrs. Klayton Nelson, University of California,
Department of Viticulture & Enology, Davis

> 1 cup raisins, coarsely chopped
> 1 cup granulated sugar
> ½ cup California Sherry
> ¼ cup water
> 1 Tbs. lemon juice
> 1 tsp. lemon rind
> 1 cup chopped nuts
> 1 cup brown sugar
> ¼ tsp. salt
> 1 tsp. baking soda
> 1¾ cups uncooked quick-cooking
> rolled oats
> ½ cup flour
> ½ cup butter or margarine

Combine raisins, sugar, Sherry and water in saucepan. Bring to boil; reduce heat and simmer, stirring frequently, until mixture is quite thick. Remove from heat; add lemon juice, rind and nuts. Cool. Meanwhile, mix dry ingredients. Work in butter to make a crumbly mixture. Spread half of crumbs in greased 8" pan; pat down firmly. Spread cooled raisin mixture evenly over crumbs; top with remaining crumb mixture, patting down firmly. Bake in moderate oven (350 degrees) for 30 minutes. Cool in pan; cut into small squares. Makes about 16 bars.

PORT WINE ZWIEBACK

Port Wine Zwieback is a treat described by Mrs. Ze'ev Halperin of Reedley, who says: Recently, reminiscing on his trip to America some 50 years ago, my father described the "treat" which his mother had prepared for him and his sister to tide them over the long trip in steerage from their small Russian village to "The Promised Land". He said he hadn't tasted it since then, but he could still recall the flavor. Of course, his mother baked the black bread, which is altogether different from that obtainable here, but I found some suitable substitutes. The bread was prepared to last indefinitely, which of course it did, except that by the time they reached New York they had finished it. I experimented and came up with this variation: Place slices of black bread in a shallow glass pan. Sprinkle with sugar. Soak each slice of bread with Port (about 2 tablespoons per slice, depending on the thickness of the bread). Place in low oven and dry slowly (several hours), turning slices occasionally. Bread should be like zwieback when done. These will keep indefinitely and can be used as cookies.

VINEYARD HERMITS

Mrs. Russel Overby, Italian Swiss Colony, Asti

I call these "Vineyard Hermits" because raisins, as well as wine, are used. You might tuck in a few dozen with your gift bottles of Christmas dessert wine—the cookies ship well and keep fresh for weeks.

½ cup California Burgundy
1 cup raisins
1 cup butter or other shortening
1½ cups brown sugar (packed)
3 eggs
1 tsp. vanilla
1 Tbs. grated lemon peel
½ cup wheat germ
2½ cups unsifted flour
1 tsp. cinnamon
¼ tsp. cloves
¼ tsp. allspice
1 tsp. soda
½ tsp. salt
1 cup chopped walnuts and/or
*   pecans*

Heat wine to boiling point. Remove from heat and add raisins. Let stand until cool. Cream shortening and sugar. Beat in eggs thoroughly, one at a time. Add vanilla, lemon peel and wheat germ. Sift flour with spices, soda and salt. Add to creamed mixture alternately with raisin-wine mixture. Stir in nuts, mixing lightly. Drop by teaspoonsful on greased cookie sheets. Bake in moderately-hot oven (375 degrees) about 12 minutes, or until done. (For crispy cookies, bake at least 15 minutes.) Makes 5 to 6 dozen.

ELK GROVE TURNOVERS
Mrs. George D. Beitzel, Gibson Wine Co., Elk Grove

Another easy filling for these turnovers would be blackberry preserves spiced with blackberry wine. My husband likes the blackberry filling best.

4 oz. cream cheese, softened
½ cup butter or margarine, softened
1 cup sifted all-purpose flour
⅛ tsp. salt
¼ cup crushed pineapple
¼ cup sugar
¼ cup California Cream Sherry
¼ cup water
1 cup chopped apricots (fresh
*   or canned)*
1 Tbs. chopped almonds
*   (optional)*
1 egg, beaten

Cut softened cream cheese and butter into flour and salt, using 2 knives or a pastry blender. Blend well; form into ball. Wrap with plastic wrap or waxed paper; refrigerate for 2 hours, or until ready to make turnovers. Meanwhile, combine crushed pineapple, sugar, Sherry, water and apricots in a saucepan. Cook over low heat until fruit is tender and mixture is thick (about 30 minutes, if fresh fruit is used; 10 minutes, if canned is used). Stir often and add more liquid as necessary. Add chopped almonds, if desired. Refrigerate until cool or ready to make turnovers. When ready to assemble turnovers, roll out dough ⅛-inch thick. Cut out with a 2½ or 3-inch round cutter. Place a half teaspoon or so of the pineapple-apricot mixture in the middle of the round; brush edges with beaten egg. Fold over, using a fork to seal the edges. Either freeze for later use, or place on cookie sheet and bake in moderately-hot oven (400 degrees) for 10 to 12 minutes, or just until golden. Serve hot. (For variety, divide dough into 2 halves; roll out and spread one half with preserve, topping with the other half of pastry. Cut into fancy shapes, if desired.) Makes 3 dozen.

PRISSY PECANS
Mrs. Alvin Ehrhardt, United Vintners' Community
*   Wineries, Lodi*

1 lb. shelled pecans
½ cup butter
¼ cup sugar
2 Tbs. California Sherry
1 tsp. freshly grated nutmeg
Dash of salt

Put pecans in shallow baking dish. Roast in moderately-slow oven (325 degrees) for 20 minutes, turning frequently with fork. Melt butter; combine with sugar, Sherry, nutmeg and salt. Pour over pecans; return to oven for a few minutes, again turning often with fork. When nuts have absorbed most of butter mixture, turn out on paper toweling and dry. Makes about 1 quart.

BRANDY COOKIES
Mrs. Louis P. Martini, Louis M. Martini, St. Helena

2 cups sifted all-purpose flour
¼ tsp. salt
⅔ cup butter
⅓ cup cold milk
1 cup California Cream Sherry
1 tsp. cinnamon
½ tsp. cloves
½ tsp. nutmeg
2 tsp. vinegar
3 Tbs. flour
½ cup brown sugar
2 Tbs. butter
⅓ cup California Brandy
1 cup raisins
1 cup walnuts

Resift flour with salt; cut in ⅔ cup butter until it resembles coarse cornmeal. Mix in milk. Shape into ball; chill. Meanwhile, heat Sherry to boiling; add spices and vinegar. Mix 3 tablespoons flour and brown sugar; work in 2 tablespoons butter. Add to Sherry mixture; cook, stirring constantly, until very thick. Remove from heat; stir in Brandy. Add raisins and nuts. Cool to warm. Roll Chilled pastry into 4 oblong rectangles (4x12 inches); cut into strips, 4 inches wide. Place filling in a row down the center of each strip of pastry; turn in edges, overlapping. Place filled strips on slightly greased cookie sheet. Prick with fork so steam can escape. Bake in moderately-hot oven (400 degrees) until crust is done, about 20 minutes. Remove from oven; with sharp knife, cut the strips diagonally every half-inch, making individual cookies. Remove from cookie sheet before any of the syrup that might leak out hardens. Makes about 3 dozen.

RIPON CHERRY DELIGHT
Mrs. Frank Franzia, Franzia Brothers Winery, Ripon

This is a specialty my folks brought from Italy. We keep up the custom of serving this on Christmas, Easter, New Year's, and other special occasions.

2 cups very ripe Royal Anne or
  Bing cherries
2 teaspoons granulated sugar
California Brandy
California Muscatel

Leave 1 inch of stem on cherries. Wash and dry. Pack in a cold sterilized pint jar to 1-inch from the top. Sprinkle sugar on top. Fill jar half full with Brandy and the remaining half with Muscatel. Heat flat lid in boiling water; seal jar tight. Keep 6 months to 1 year before serving. Serve a few cherries and some of the juice as a holiday aperitif. Makes about 1 pint.

UNIVERSITY DATES
Mrs Emil M. Mrak, University of California, Davis

I make these stuffed dates every Christmas and send them to friends, particularly those in the East.

1 (1½-lb.) pkg. dates, preferably
  fresh
½ cup butter, softened
⅛ tsp. salt
1½ cups sifted powdered sugar
½ to 1 tsp. grated orange rind
¾ cup chopped walnuts
2 or 3 tsp. California
  Cream Sherry

Pit the dates. Beat other ingredients together, moistening with Sherry. Stuff dates with mixture. Roll in additional powdered sugar. These dates will keep indefinitely in the refrigerator. (This confection is best made with fresh dates, because they hold their shape better, and are not too sweet. Dates may be soaked overnight in ½ cup Sherry before stuffing.) Makes about 6 dozen.

NAPA CRÊPES SUZETTE
Brother Norbert, The Christian Brothers, Napa

My mother, Mrs. Elise Meuel of Fresno, is a Frenchwoman, inheriting the traditional French flair for preparing and serving fine food. Crêpes Suzette are one of her favorites, and she loves to serve them from a low table in the living room as the final, perfect touch to a family dinner party.

2 eggs
1½ cups milk
1 cup sifted all-purpose flour
¼ tsp. salt
1 Tbs. oil
Sauce (see below)

Beat eggs; add milk. Add flour with salt and beat thoroughly. Add oil. In a small skillet, pour batter to make very thin 6″ pancakes. When pancakes are browned nicely on both sides, arrange in stacks.

SAUCE
½ cup butter
1 cup sifted powdered sugar
2 Tbs. orange juice
2 tsp. lemon juice
2 tsp. grated orange rind
3 Tbs. California Sauterne
  or other white table wine
6 Tbs. California Brandy

Combine all sauce ingredients except Brandy and heat slowly. Roll crêpes that have been sprinkled with powdered sugar. Place crêpes in chafing dish or electric skillet. Pour sauce into pan with crêpes and heat gently. Add Brandy and set alight. Serves 6 to 8.

MINCEMEAT CAKE

Mrs. Otto Beringer Jr., Beringer Bros. Inc., St. Helena

1 (1-lb. 12-oz.) jar mincemeat
2 cups broken nut meats
1 cup raisins or glace fruit
1 tsp. vanilla
¼ cup California Brandy
¼ cup California Malvasia Bianca
    or Sweet Sauterne
½ cup oil
1 cup sugar
2 beaten egg yolks
1 tsp. soda dissolved in
    1 tsp. water
2 cups sifted flour
2 beaten egg whites

Mix ingredients in order listed, folding in egg whites last. Bake in tube pan in moderate oven (350 degrees) for 1½ to 2 hours. Cool cake 2 to 3 hours before removing from pan. Keep in refrigerator 6 to 7 months. Makes 1 cake, 10 inches.

PLUM-PORT SAUCE

Mrs. Edmund Accomazzo, Cucamonga Winery, Cucamonga

Blend 1 cup juice from can of purple plums with a tablespoon cornstarch, ½ cup California Port and brown sugar to taste. Simmer 10 minutes; add plums and chill. Spoon over creamy vanilla ice cream; serve with almond macaroons. Makes about 1½ cups.

BACCHUS APRICOT SAUCE

Mrs. E.F. Handel, East-Side Winery, Lodi

2 cups apricot marmalade or preserves
½ cup sugar
½ cup California Sherry
Few grains salt

Combine all ingredients in saucepan; mix well. Bring to boil; cool. Serve on sponge cake or pudding. Makes 1½ cups.

SHERRY SPICE SAUCE FOR APPLE PIE

Mrs. Vincent Indelicato, Delicato Winery, Manteca

1 Tbs. cornstarch
½ cup sugar
¼ tsp. each: cinnamon and
    nutmeg
Dash of salt
½ cup water
½ cup California Sherry
1 Tbs. lemon juice
1 tsp. each: grated orange rind
    and lemon rind
2 Tbs. butter or margarine

Mix cornstarch, sugar, cinnamon, nutmeg and salt in a saucepan. Gradually add water, Sherry and lemon juice, stirring until smooth. Add orange rind and lemon rind. Stir over medium heat until mixture boils and thickens, then cook a minute or so longer until sauce is clear. Add butter or margarine. Serve warm with apple pie. Makes 1 cup.

RASPBERRY WHITE WINE SAUCE
Mrs. John B. Cella II, Cella Wineries, Fresno

½ cup sugar
½ cup water
1 cup crushed raspberries
½ cup California Sauterne or other
    white table wine
1 tsp. lemon juice
Whole raspberries

Combine sugar and water and simmer 5 minutes. Pour over raspberries. Cool and press through fine sieve. Add wine and lemon juice. Pour into small serving bowl and float a few whole berries on top. Makes 2 cups.

SHERRY BUTTER-NUT SAUCE

Mrs. Louis Foppiano, L. Foppiano Wine Co., Healdsburg

> ¾ cup dark corn syrup
> ¾ cup (firmly packed) brown sugar
> ⅓ cup California Sherry or Muscatel
> 2 Tbs. cream
> 2 Tbs. butter or margarine
> Dash of salt
> ½ cup finely chopped walnuts or
>   pecans

Combine all ingredients except nuts in a saucepan; bring to a boil, then simmer, uncovered, for 10 minutes, stirring frequently. Remove from heat. Add nuts. Cool to room temperature (1 hour or longer) before serving. Stir well to distribute nuts evenly before spooning over ice cream. (Left-over sauce may be stored in the refrigerator; set container in a pan of warm water to bring to proper consistency before serving.) Makes about 1⅔ cups.

BRANDY-MARMALADE TOPPING

A quick yet sophisticated dessert is no problem even when guests drop in. Thin some orange marmalade or apricot or raspberry jam with a little California Brandy—stirred until smooth—as a topping for vanilla ice cream or any plain unfrosted cake. A sweeter topping can be made if desired, by using Cream Sherry or Muscatel to thin the marmalade or apricot jam—or Port for raspberry jam.

PINEAPPLE PORT SAUCE

Mrs. E. F. Handel, East-Side Winery, Lodi

> 1 cup sugar
> 1 cup crushed pineapple
> 1 cup California Port

Combine all ingredients in saucepan. Cook, stirring, to a heavy syrup, 10 to 15 minutes. Cool. Serve over ice cream or pudding. Makes 1½ cups.

SHERRIED CHOCOLATE SAUCE

Brother Norbert, The Christian Brothers, Napa

In a saucepan combine ¾ cup sugar, 2 tablespoons butter or margarine, 2 (1-oz.) squares unsweetened chocolate, ½ cup cream or undiluted evaporated milk and a dash of salt. Bring to a boil, stirring until ingredients are well blended, then turn heat very low and simmer, stirring occasionally, for 6 or 7 minutes. Remove from heat and add ⅓ cup California Sherry. Serve warm over ice cream, pudding, or any dessert that calls for a chocolate sauce. Makes about 1¼ cups.

Sauces

*"...and then lemons
and wine for sauce."*
—*Ben Jonson*

If ever you've quickly improvised a good sauce or gravy, by stirring wine into the rich pan drippings from poultry or meat, you know that memorable results can come from happy accidents—and that often no special recipe at all is needed. Probably no category of cooking offers so gratifying a range for your own ideas. The mingling of flavors in a sauce, gravy, baste or marinade is as personal as mixing colors on a palette. When you have California wines on hand in the kitchen—perhaps a Sherry, a Burgundy and a Sauterne—your culinary mood of the moment can enjoy full play. Start with a recipe for a general guideline, and then experiment. Your inspiration may well be a little masterpiece.

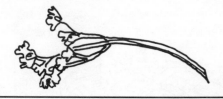

GOLD COAST WINE SAUCE FOR LAMB

*Mrs. William S. Stephens, Paul Masson Vineyards,
Saratoga*

2 Tbs. oil
1 Tbs. chopped onion
1½ Tbs. flour
½ cup chicken stock
½ cup California white table wine
1 Tbs. chopped parsley
Salt

Heat oil; add onion and sauté until light yellow. Stir in flour until smooth, then add stock and wine gradually, stirring until the sauce is smooth and thickened. Add parsley, and salt as needed. Makes 4 to 6 servings.

VINEYARD MUSHROOM SAUCE FOR BROILED STEAK OR FILLET OF BEEF

*Fred Weibel, Weibel Champagne Vineyards, Mission
San Jose*

1 (4-oz.) can sliced mushrooms
2 Tbs. flour
¼ cup butter
¼ cup meat stock
1 Tbs. chopped onion
2½ Tbs. chopped green pepper
3 ripe olives, chopped
Salt and pepper
½ cup California Dry Sherry

Drain mushrooms, reserving ¼ cup mushroom liquid. Brown flour in 2 tablespoons of the butter. Add meat stock and mushroom liquid. Cook, stirring constantly, until thickened. Sauté onion and green pepper in remaining butter; add to sauce. Add olives. Season. Simmer 10 minutes. Remove from heat; stir in Sherry. Makes 1½ cups.

TREFETHEN FAMILY BBQ SAUCE
Janet Trefethen, Trefethen Vineyards, Napa

I have tried numerous **BBQ** sauces but always return to this one. It has been in my family for generations and its aromas bring back may fine memories. It is an excellent marinade for chicken, hamburgers and wild ducks. The ingredients always vary, according to what is in the pantry and my mood, but this is the backbone:

> 20-oz. bottle soy sauce
> 4 Tbs. basil
> 4 Tbs. rosemary
> 4 Tbs. Beau Monde
> 4 Tbs. granulated sugar
> 4 tsp. dry mustard
> 4 cloves garlic, pulverized
> 4 tsp. salt

Place ingredients in small pan and simmer a few minutes. Set aside to cool, add juice and rind of 4 lemons. Use as marinade and basting sauce while cooling.

DOMAINE CHANDON'S BARBECUE SAUCE

> 1 cup Panache (Chandon's
>   aperitif wine)
> ¼ cup each Dijon mustard,
>   brown sugar, vinegar,
>   lemon juice, chili sauce,
>   Worcestershire sauce
> 2 tsp. each onion salt, garlic salt
>   (or one minced clove garlic,
>   one minced small onion, and
>   2 tsp. salt)
> ¼ tsp. each Tabasco sauce,
>   cayenne pepper

For spare ribs,* boil the ribs for three minutes, drain and place in a shallow pan. Puncture with a fork and cover with sauce. Marinate covered for 4 hours or overnight, then barbecue. Baste with sauce every 10-15 minutes during cooking. (May be baked in a 300 degree oven for 1-1½ hours instead.)

*Chicken or pork chops may be substituted; adjust cooking time accordingly.

BURGUNDY WINE SAUCE
Mrs. Ernest Gallo, E. & J. Gallo Winery, Modesto

> 2 Tbs. olive oil
> 2 Tbs. butter
> 2 small green onions or 1 small
>   yellow onion
> 1 Tbs. flour
> 1 tsp. prepared mustard
> 1 tsp. Worcestershire sauce
> ½ cup bouillon or consommé
> ½ cup California Burgundy

Heat oil and butter and sauté onion until soft but not brown; add flour slowly, and stir until well blended. Add mustard, and Worcestershire sauce. When well blended, stir in bouillon and ¼ cup of the wine. Cook, stirring occasionally, in top of double boiler for 30 minutes. Then add remaining wine and cook 15 minutes longer. Serve with wild duck, filet mignon or club roast.

PORT SAUCE FOR WILD DUCK
Mrs. W. Wallace Owen, Calgrape Wineries Inc., Delano

> 1 tsp. salt
> ½ tsp. cayenne
> 1 Tbs. lemon juice
> 1 Tbs. powdered sugar
> 1 Tbs. catsup
> 2 Tbs. meat sauce
> 3 Tbs. California Port

Combine all ingredients, mixing well. Heat and serve over cooked duck. Makes about ½ cup.

VINAIGRETTE SAUCE
Dante Bagnani, American Industries Corp., San Francisco

> 1 cup olive oil
> ½ cup California red wine vinegar
> 2 Tbs. California red table wine
> 2 Tbs. sweet pickle relish
> 2 Tbs. chopped parsley
> 1½ tsp. salt

Combine all ingredients in a covered jar and shake well. Serve on hot or cold cooked vegetables. Good on kidney beans or garbanzos. Makes about 1½ cups.

CALIFORNIA CHUTNEY
Mr. and Mrs. Paul L. Halpern, Italian Swiss Colony, Asti

This recipe was derived from a recipe for mango chutney we used when we lived in the Hawaiian Islands. Since mangoes were not available, we experimented with California fruits and found green fruit a tasty substitute.

> 8 well-packed cups of unripe fruit
> pared and cut in thick chunks
> (use a combination of at least 4
> fruits, such as apples, peaches,
> apricots, pears, nectarines and
> plums)
> 10 cloves garlic, peeled and chopped
> ⅓ cup ginger root, peeled
> and chopped
> 1½ cups nuts, chopped (such as
> walnuts and cashews)
> ⅓ cup seedless raisins, chopped
> 1 cup California wine vinegar
> ½ cup California Rhine or other
> white table wine
> 2 Tbs. California Brandy
> 2 tsp. salt
> 4 cups sugar

Combine all ingredients in heavy saucepan. Using candy thermometer, cook to temperature of 223 degrees. Keep temperature of 223 degrees for 15 to 20 minutes (or until mixture reaches jam consistency), stirring to prevent burning. Pour into hot sterile small jars to within ½ inch of top. Cut through mixture with sterilized knife to release air bubbles. Cool slightly and cover with 1/6 inch melted paraffin. Let stand until paraffin hardens. Put on jar lids or protective coverings. Store in cool, dry place. We serve this chutney with all types of curry—lamb, shrimp, etc. Incidentally, for a much more flavorful curry, we always add Sherry or some other wine to the main curry dish. Makes about 2 quarts.

WINELAND MUSTARD SAUCE
Mrs. John B. Cella II, Cella Wineries, Fresno

> 1½ cups prepared mustard
> ½ cup California white table wine
> 2 Tbs. sugar
> 1 tsp. salt
> 2 Tbs. flour
> ¼ cup water

Combine mustard, wine, sugar and salt in saucepan. Bring to boil over moderate heat, stirring constantly. Mix flour and water; stir into mustard mixture. Reduce heat and simmer for 10 minutes or until thickened, stirring constantly. Serve hot or cold. Makes about 2 cups.

NAPA VALLEY SAUCE PIQUANT
Mrs. Louis P. Martini, Louis M. Martini, St. Helena

> 2 or 3 large fresh tomatoes,
> chopped
> ½ cup very thin red onion slices
> Salt and pepper
> ½ cup California red wine vinegar
> ¼ cup sugar

Combine all ingredients. Chill in refrigerator about 1 hour. Serve over Brown Risotto along with a green tossed salad and hot buttered French bread. Serves 5 to 6.

QUICK RED WINE SAUCE

Quick red wine sauce: Mix condensed onion soup with equal parts California red table wine and water, and add to skillet in which meat has been cooked. Heat to low simmer, stirring to lift up glaze from bottom of pan. Let simmer a few more minutes, stir in some chopped parsley if desired, and pour over meat.

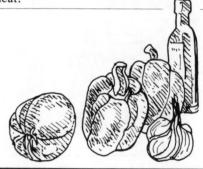

FIESTA FRUIT SAUCE FOR HAM
Mrs. E.R. Oberlander, Woodbridge Vineyard Association, Lodi

This recipe was taken from a magazine several years ago, and I added Sherry as I do to everything.

> 1 (9-oz.) can pineapple tidbits
> 1 (9-oz.) can unpeeled apricot halves
> 1 (3-inch) stick cinnamon
> 12 whole cloves
> 2 Tbs. sugar
> Few grains salt
> 1 Tbs. cornstarch
> ½ cup seedless raisins
> 2 Tbs. California Sherry

Drain fruits, saving juice. Cut apricots in quarters. Combine reserved juice and spices; simmer 5 minutes. Remove spices. Combine sugar, salt, cornstarch and small amount of hot spiced syrup; return to hot syrup. Cook, stirring, until mixture boils and thickens. Add pineapple, apricots and raisins; continue cooking for 5 minutes, stirring occasionally. Add Sherry. Serve warm with baked ham. (Also good using fruit cocktail.) Makes about 1¾ cups.

ALL-PURPOSE SAUCE AMANDINE
Mrs. Russel Overby, United Vintners, Inc., San Francisco

This sauce was invented for an Englishman who said he hated Brussels sprouts. It turned out to be a natural for any vigorous hot vegetable or red-blooded meat. Advice: Cook vegetable or meat just enough to be decent. (P.S.: He STILL hates them.)

> ½ cup butter or margarine
> ⅓ to ½ cup sliced almonds
> 1 small onion, sliced
> 3 large mushrooms, sliced
> 1 tsp. prepared mustard
> Few drops Tabasco sauce
> ⅛ tsp. monosodium glutamate
> ¼ tsp. salt
> ¾ tsp. sugar
> ½ cup California Burgundy
> 1 tsp. arrowroot

Melt butter in heavy skillet. Cook almonds until butter froths pale brown. Add onion, mushrooms and more butter, if needed. Add all remaining ingredients, except arrowroot. Cover and cook over low heat until tender, about 10 minutes. Blend in arrowroot. Continue simmering, stirring constantly, until thickened. Serve with red meat or hot vegetables topped with lemon slices. Makes about 1⅓ cups.

SANTA ROSA VENISON MARINADE
Mrs. Elmo Martini, Martini & Prati Wines, Inc., Santa Rosa

The recipes I submit are Elmo's mothers. She had good recipes, but I find it difficult to put them in writing. Her secret with wild game was garlic, fresh sage and wine.

> Venison steaks
> Meat tenderizer (optional)
> 1 small bunch parsley, finely chopped
> 2 or 3 cloves garlic, finely chopped
> 4 or 5 leaves fresh sage, finely chopped
> ½ cup olive or other oil
> ½ cup California red or white table wine

If steaks are not tender, first treat with meat tenderizer. In a large bowl, arrange steaks; sprinkle with parsley, garlic and sage. Combine oil and wine; pour over steaks. Marinate at least 4 hours, turning several times. Barbecue over hot coals, basting with remaining marinade. (Quartered chicken may also be prepared this way for barbecuing.) Makes about 1 cup.

MINT MARINADE FOR LAMB
Mrs. Louis P. Martini, Louis M. Martini, St. Helena

> ⅔ cup California white table wine
> ⅓ cup creme de menthe
> Lamb, cut in 1-inch squares
> ¼ cup butter, melted
> 1 clove garlic, chopped
> ½ tsp. salt
> ⅛ tsp. pepper

Combine wine and creme de menthe; marinate lamb 3 to 4 hours. Drain on paper towels. Place meat on skewers. Combine melted butter, garlic, salt and pepper. Barbecue or broil meat, brushing with butter mixture. Makes about 1 cup.

SAUCE BÉARNAISE
Mrs. Aldo Fabbrini, Beaulieu Vineyard, Rutherford

A good sauce for steaks, poached salmon and other fish.

> 1 cup California Chablis or other white table wine
> 1 Tbs. California white wine vinegar
> 1½ Tbs. finely chopped shallots or 1½ Tbs. finely chopped scallions with small slice from one clove garlic
> 3 Tbs. chopped parsley
> Large pinch freshly ground black pepper
> 1 Tbs. coarsely scissored fresh tarragon leaves or ¼ tsp. dried tarragon
> 4 egg yolks
> ½ lb. butter
> Dash salt

Combine wine, wine vinegar, shallots, 1 tablespoon parsley, pepper, and tarragon in saucepan and simmer until original amount is reduced by one-third. Cool and strain. Beat egg yolks with salt in top of double boiler. Place over simmering water and beat in strained wine mixture. Mix thoroughly, then add cold butter, cut into approximately 1-inch cubes, one at a time, stirring constantly. The cold butter will help keep temperature low so sauce will not curdle. Watch carefully while stirring, and if necessary lift top pan occasionally for a moment while stirring. Stir until desired thickness is reached; remember that sauce will thicken when cooled. Remove from heat and stir in remaining 2 tablespoons chopped parsley. Makes about 3 cups.

EASY SEAFOOD COCKTAIL SAUCE

Mrs. Jack Pandol, Delano Growers Cooperative Winery, Delano

I got this recipe from Mrs. Steve Pavich of Delano.

> 1 cup catsup
> ½ cup California Sauterne or
>   other white table wine
> Dash or two of Tabasco sauce

Combine all ingredients. Serve over cooked shrimp, raw oysters or cooked crabmeat. Makes about 1½ cups.

RAVIGOTE SAUCE

Joel Newbert, Weibel Champagne Vineyards, Mission San Jose

> ½ cup California white table wine
> ¼ cup California wine vinegar
> 5 Tbs. butter
> 4 Tbs. flour
> 2 cups seasoned veal or chicken
>   broth
> 1 shallot, minced
> 1 tsp. minced chervil or parsley
> 1 tsp. minced tarragon
> 1 tsp. chopped chives
> Salt and pepper

Combine wine and vinegar and simmer down to one half of original amount. Melt 3 tablespoons butter and blend in flour. Add broth and cook until thickened, stirring constantly. Add to wine and simmer 5 minutes. Add herbs and remaining ingredients. Serve hot, on poultry, seafoods or poached eggs. Serves 6 to 8.

CRANBERRY-CLARET JELLY

Mrs. Dennis Alexander, California Cellarmasters, Lodi

This has a beautiful color and is also very good.

> 3½ cups sugar
> 1 cup bottled cranberry juice
> 1 cup California Claret or
>   other red table wine
> ½ (6-oz.) bottle liquid fruit pectin

Put sugar in top of double boiler. Add cranberry juice and wine; mix well. Place over rapidly boiling water; stir until sugar is dissolved, about 2 minutes. Remove from heat; stir in fruit pectin. Skim off foam and pour quickly into glasses. Cover at once with ⅛-inch paraffin. Makes about 6 cups.

SHRIMP COCKTAIL SAUCE DAVIS

Mrs. Harold Berg, University of California, Davis

> 1½ cups shrimp or crabmeat
> ¼ cup tomato catsup
> ¼ cup chili sauce
> ¼ cup lemon juice
> ½ cup California Dry Sherry
> 1 tsp. grated horseradish
> 1 tsp. chopped chives or
>   green onion
> ½ tsp. chopped parsley

Chill shrimp or crabmeat. Combine all remaining ingredients; chill. At serving time, place shrimp in cocktail glass; add sauce. Serves 3 to 4.

CREAMY FISH SAUCE WEST COAST

Mrs. Leon S. Peters, Fresno

> 1 (10½-oz.) can condensed cream
>   of mushroom soup
> ½ tsp. onion salt
> ¼ cup California Dry Sherry
> ½ tsp. curry powder
> Dash of cayenne
> ½ cup mayonnaise

Mix all together. Heat over low heat—do not boil! Serve over broiled fish fillets of poached whole striped bass or fillets. (I like to poach the fish in equal parts of consomme and water, with a pat of butter for extra flavor.)

HUNTER'S WINE SAUCE

Use condensed mushroom soup blended with tomato paste and equal parts California white table wine and water. Mix and cook in skillet where meat has been cooked. Simmer at low heat, stirring meat glaze into the sauce. When sauce is thickened, add tarragon and serve over meat.

Cans, packaged mixes, dried foods and frozen ones have become a basic essential to the American larder, and of the multi-faceted personality of the American housewife as well. With time saved in the kitchen, there is more time to spend with family and friends, and with activities beyond the stove. With a multiplicity of convenience foods on hand, cookery can still be an art, ingeniously combining a variety of ready-to-eat foods to prepare a fine meal, or a "dish-in-a-hurry" when that occasion arises. One simple rule of thumb that will uplift the merely plebian flavor to something really special: when water is called for in the preparation of a convenience food, use some California wine in place of some of the water.

FROZEN SOUPS are a convenient way to enjoy a tureen favorite at a moment's notice. One soup du jour special blends a can of frozen potato soup with ½ soup can of California white table wine and ½ soup can of light cream. Heat slowly, stirring until mixture is smooth. Mix in a 7-ounce can of minced clams. Garnish with chopped green onion.

COOKED SHRIMP OR LOBSTER CHUNKS, canned or frozen, will take on new flavor when marinated for an hour in California Sauterne, with chopped green onion and a little soy sauce. Serve on crisp greens with mayonnaise or dairy sour cream touched with curry powder.

CANNED TOMATO SAUCE enriched with California Burgundy, rosemary and basil is delicious on braised lamb shanks or pork chops. Variation: to the above, add oregano, canned hamburger (chopped) and a can of mushrooms for a rich spaghetti meat sauce—made in minutes.

BRUNCH TREAT: Brown frozen link pork sausage in a skillet. Add some California white table wine; cover and poach until sausage is done.

HAM IN A PASTRY CRUST is real gourmet cookery, but can be done easily, and in a minimum of time using the pantry shelf as a source. Heat a canned ham according to instruction, basting with California Sherry; remove from oven 20 minutes before done. Let cool slightly. While ham is cooling, heat canned cream of mushroom soup, thinning out slightly with Sherry. Using either a prepared biscuit mix or pie crust, roll out pastry to a shape large enough to enclose ham completely. Spread pastry with some of the prepared mushroom mixture; place ham in center. Fold pastry over ham, enclosing it completely on all sides; place in baking dish smooth side up. Make 2 or 3 slits on top to allow steam to escape; brush pastry with a little milk. Bake in moderately-hot (400 degrees) oven 20 minutes or until golden brown. Serve sliced with a sauce made by heating remaining mushroom mixture thinned down further with Sherry.

FLAVOR CHOCOLATE PUDDING MIX with California Sherry and a sprinkling of cinnamon. Serve topped with chopped walnuts or shredded coconut.

JIFFY BEEF STEW can be whipped up when unexpected guests arrive. Fry chopped onion in butter; add California Burgundy and small amount of flour. Cook, stirring until mixture boils and thickens. From the "panic" shelf, add a large can of beef stew, canned button mushrooms, canned pearl onions, and heat thoroughly. Serve with a tossed salad and baked frozen biscuits.

FIVE-MINUTE PILAF takes advantage of some convenience foods. For four servings, combine 1⅓ cups packaged pre-cooked rice, 10½-ounce can condensed onion soup, 2-ounce can sliced mushrooms, undrained, ⅓ cup California Sauterne and 1 tablespoon chopped parsley. Heat to boiling. Remove from heat, cover and let stand five minutes. Serve at once.

WINE AND FOOD COMBINATIONS

These are popular wine and food combinations, those that many people prefer. But there are no rules! The "correct" wine is the one *you* like best.

APPETIZER WINES
AT COCKTAIL TIME

Serve chilled, without food, or with *Hors d'Oeuvre, Nuts, or Cheeses*

CALIFORNIA WINE TYPES

{ *Dry Champagne*
Sherry
Vermouth
Flavored wines }

WHITE TABLE WINES
WITH LIGHTER DISHES

Serve well chilled, with *Chicken, Fish, Shellfish, Omelettes, or any white meats*

Chablis — { *(Similar types)*
White Pinot
Pinot Blanc
Pinot Chardonnay }

Sauterne — { *(Similar types)*
Sauvignon Blanc
Semillon }

Rhine Wine — { *(Similar types)*
Sylvaner
Riesling
Traminer }

RED TABLE WINES
WITH HEARTY DISHES

serve at cool room temperature with *Steaks, Chops, Roasts, Wild Game, Cheese dishes, or Spaghetti*

Claret — { *(Similar types)*
Cabernet
Zinfandel
Merlot }

Burgundy — { *(Similar types)*
Gamay
Pinot St. George
Pinot Noir }

Chianti — { *(Similar types)*
Barbera
Petite Sirah }

DESSERT WINES
AT DESSERT TIME

Serve chilled or at cool room temperature, with *Fruits, Cookies, Nuts, Cheese, Fruit Cake, or Pound Cake*

{ *Muscatel*
Angelica
Cream (sweet) Sherry
Port
Tokay }

SPARKLING WINES
WITH ALL FOODS

All foods
Serve well chilled with any food—
Appetizers, The Main Course, or Desserts
(especially good in festive party punches.)

Champagne — { *Brut (very dry)*
Sec (semi-dry)
Doux (sweet) }

Pink Champagne
Sparkling Burgundy

Wine collecting is undoubtedly one of the most satisfying and useful of all hobbies. No other offers such a happy blend of daily pleasure . . . shared joy with friends . . . the adventure of selecting . . . the fascination of change, as the stored wines age and improve. And your "cellar" can actually be a very small space in your home or apartment, completely above ground, as shown on the next page.

A wine collection of one's own, however modest, offers at least four basic satisfactions. First, convenience. With wine on hand, the drop-in guest presents no problem of frantic last-minute shopping. Second, economy. When you buy wine in quantity to lay away, you save considerably. In most areas, wine is priced 8% to 10% lower when bought by the case. Some merchants will even extend this discount to a mixed case (of several assorted wine types, rather than all of the same wine), where state law permits.

A third satisfaction is gifts. Wine gifts are personal, thoughtful, and blessedly ready at hand when you have your own "library" of wine to draw from. Celebrations—births, betrothals, anniversaries—may be observed in great style, when your cellar of California wine provides the toast. Family traditions often revolve about wine collecting—such as the old English custom of laying down several bottles (or cases) of fine Port upon the birth of a child—to be aged and opened on the child's 21st birthday. An increasing practice in our country, warmly welcomed by any young married couple, is to hold a "cellar starter" shower for a bride. Gifts for such an event, while of course headed by assorted wines of all types, might also include wine accessories—glasses, bottle racks, a good corkscrew, books on wine and wine cookery.

Fourth reason for a cellar, and most important of all to the true wine connoisseur, is that some wines reach their highest peak only after additional aging. Wine is the only beverage that can continue to improve in the bottle. When you select a young wine with this potential (say a California Burgundy or Cabernet Sauvignon) and let it rest under proper storage conditions for several years—opening a bottle every year or two, to determine if flavor and bouquet have at last mellowed to an utter perfection—you explore the excitement of discovery, which is the wine collector's greatest reward. (When the moment of truth occurs, and you feel a wine is in its prime, by all means finish off within a few months all the stored wine of that same bottling. Once finally matured, the quality of a wine—as of a human body—will then start fading subtly.)

How can you tell the aging potential of a wine? One way is to ask a really knowledgeable wine merchant. Another is to remember that different wine types require different time periods to complete their aging. Age alone is *not* a criterion of quality. Most of the world's wines are actually at their best when fresh and young, requiring little if any aging beyond that already done at the winery. Rosés fall into this class. California white table wines are usually aged one or two years before they leave the winemaker, and are normally consumed immediately, like the Rosés—or at most kept only one or two years longer in the private wine cellar. The same can be said of many lighter-bodied reds, such as Clarets, Gamays or Zinfandels, usually already winery-aged and best enjoyed soon—at least within one or two years after purchase. Only with the fuller-bodied reds, such as some of California's Burgundies, Cabernets and Pinot Noirs, does longer home aging—for two, five, or even ten or more years—often pay dividends. Champagnes are like white table wines, best drunk in their pleasurable youth. Sherries and Ports are delightful immediately after purchase, but some take beautifully to laying away for longer years.

The answer, obviously, is not to overstock any home cellar. A good rule of thumb is to lay in about a year's supply of any wine type, except for a larger supply of red table wines that are known to improve. The actual amounts and types to buy will vary, naturally, according to the kind of wine you personally prefer and use most of. Three different cellar starters are suggested here, for $35, $75, and $120 budgets; but since prices also vary throughout the country, even the suggested number of bottles can be only approximate. Where the small "tenth" bottle sizes are available, you may wish to emphasize these rather than the larger "fifths", if yours is a small family or if you don't entertain often. And if you hesitate to invest even $35 in a beginner cellar, you can still acquire a wine collection gradually if, every time you shop for wine, you buy two or more bottles and *lay one away.* This takes will power and patience, but your pride in a growing collection is its own reward.

Where on earth do you find the space to store wines? They're not as space-hungry as you may think. Thanks to the many manufacturers of small wine racks for corked wines and to screw-cap manufacturers for stand-up wines, a mere one-room apartment today can boast its own instant wine cellar...stacked on or in a buffet or a cabinet, hung on the wall or in a closet, tucked under a stairway or even forming a room divider. Racks are widely available, in department stores and shops handling gourmet items. (Your own wine merchant may sell them.) Their styles and materials are many: plastic, walnut, redwood, honeycombed tin, wrought iron, chromed wire, aluminum in smart colors.Most racks hold 12 bottles, but some larger ones can be found. Others are designed for a growing collection, offering individual bottle sleeves or four-bottle tiers that can interlock or stack.

You can, of course, build your own wooden racks or bins if you're handy with a hammer; check Wine Appreciation Guild, San Francisco for any diagrams or literature available on this subject. Even drain-tiles can hold individual bottles, dramatically as well as efficiently. Or, if you buy wine by the case, why not simply store the wine therein? For corked wines—open case, put bottles in upside down so that the wine is in contact with the corks, keeping them swelled and air-tight to protect flavor. Stand screw-cap bottles upright. Keep the case—or any wine rack—in a reasonably cool dark place, away from radiators or stoves. Wine's best friend is a relatively *even* storage temperature, without extreme changes. Between 50 degrees and 60 degrees is considered perfect, but wine can be stored for long periods at as high as 70 degrees, if this temperature varies little. That's all you need to remember, except to avoid bright sunlight, which can affect wine flavor. (For this reason, never buy wine from a sun-bathed store window. And give your business to the merchant who knows enough to store his corked wines so the wine rests on the corks.)

Of all the many rewards of collecting wine, a final pleasure may be mentioned which might seem expendable. Don't dismiss it as trivial: it's a very real help in getting the most out of your wine investment, and it can also lead you to a full-fledged hobby as a wine collector.

This is the keeping of a wine cellar notebook. You should have some sort of record on each wine, if you are going to buy it again or store it long: where and when you purchased it, how much it cost. Some collectors paste in the wine label, soaked off an emptied bottle. To this you may also wish to add each date the particular wine was served, and to whom; and how you and your friends rated it.

You may even go further and list an entire accompanying menu. Your cellar book thus also becomes a safeguard against repeating a dinner dish for the same guests. But, primarily, it remains a memoir of happy occasions: good cheer and fellowship, the congenial sharing of wonderful taste experiences. For that, above all, is the way with wine—and the reason for having your own cellar.

(A variety of Cellar Books are available from The Wine Appreciation Guild—write for catalog.)

$35 WINE CELLAR

No. of Bottles	California Wine Types:

("5th" size indicated here. If smaller "10ths" are more practical for you, increase the number of bottles. You may also try more wine types this way.)

No. of Bottles	California Wine Types:
1	Dry or "Cocktail" Sherry
1	Cream (Sweet) Sherry or Port
1	Dry Vermouth
1	Burgundy (similar types: Pinot Noir, Gamay, Red Pinot)
1	Claret (similar types: Cabernet, Zinfandel, Merlot)
1	Rosé

No. of Bottles	California Wine Types:
1	Rhine (similar types: Riesling, Traminer, Sylvaner)
1	Dry Sauterne (similar types: Dry Semillon, Dry Sauvignon Blanc)
1	Sweet or Haut Sauterne or a Light Muscat type (12%)
1	Champagne (Sec-medium dry; or Brut-very dry)

Plus 1 half-gallon jug of Sherry for cooking or everyday refreshment. (Transfer this immediately to sterilized smaller bottles with screw-caps or with tight-fitting corks. Fill to ¾-inch or 1-inch from top.)

$75 WINE CELLAR

No. of Bottles	California Wine Types:
2	Dry or "Cocktail " Sherry
1	Cream (Sweet) Sherry
1	Port
1	Sweet Vermouth
1	Dry Vermouth
4	Burgundy (similar types: Pinot Noir, Gamay, Red Pinot)
4	Claret (similar types: Cabernet, Zinfandel, Merlot)
2	Rosé
2	Rhine (similar types: Riesling, Grey Riesling, Johannisberg Riesling, Traminer, Sylvaner)

No. of Bottles	California Wine Types:
2	Dry Sauterne (similar types: Dry Semillon, Dry Sauvignon Blanc)
2	Chablis (similar types:Pinot Blanc, Pinot Chardonnay, White Pinot)
1	Sweet or Haut Sautgerne, Sweet Semillon or Light Muscat
2	Champagne (white or pink, "Brut"-very dry, Sec-semi-dry, and Doux-sweet)

Plus 1 half-gallon jug of Sherry (see note under $35 Cellar for economy size purchases in gallons and half-gallons).

$120 WINE CELLAR

No. of Bottles	California Wine Types:
2	Dry or "Cocktail" Sherry
1	Cream (Sweet) Sherry
1	Port
1	Dry Vermouth
1	Sweet Vermouth
6	Burgundy (similar types: Pinot Noir, Gamay, Red Pinot)
6	Claret (similar types: Cabernet, Zinfandel, Merlot)
1	Barbera
2	Rosé
4	Rhine (similar types: Johannisberg Riesling, Grey Riesling, Emerald Riesling, Sylvaner, Traminer)

No. of Bottles	California Wine Types:
2	Chablis (similar types: Pinot Chardonnay, Pinot Blanc, White Pinot)
2	Dry Sauterne (similar types: Dry Semillon, Dry Sauvignon Blanc)
1	Sweet or Haut Sauterne (similar types: Sweet Semillon or slightly sweet white table wine such as some labeled Chenin Blanc, Gewurztraminer)
1	Light Muscat
2	Champagne (white or pink, "Brut-very dry, Sec-semi-dry, and Doux-sweet)
1	Sparkling Burgundy

Plus 1 gallon jug of Sherry (see note under $35 Cellar for economy size purchases in gallons and half-gallons).

*"A feast is made for laughter and
wine maketh merry."*
—*Ecclesiastes 8:15*

Serving wine with meals is only one of the many ways wine can be used for gaiety and refreshment. The marvelous thing about wine is that it "goes" at any kind of function—any time of day. It's easy, correct, and so simple. Wines can be served just poured from the bottle, or blended into a refreshing punch; they may be frosty-cool, or hot, depending on the time of day, the season of the year, or the way you feel. It is that easy. You can make the most casual occasion a gala event—by letting wine speak a warm welcome for you.

AFTERNOON SHERRY:

Holding a board meeting of your PTA? Expecting the girls for bridge? Getting acquainted with the new neighbor? Relax and refresh any afternoon visitor with well-chilled California Cream (Sweet) Sherry, along with bland cookies or crackers and cheese to munch on. Muscatel or Haut Sauterne might be another choice. These same wines are also a popular luncheon aperitif.

PLANNING A SUNDAY BRUNCH?

Champagne is the most elegant way to start the day bubbling. Try it with "Sunday Morning Sausage," page 42, along with scrambled eggs, hot buttered toast or English muffins. Another brunch beverage could be "Orange Blossom Flip", page 15, or perhaps a chilled California Sauterne.

HOLIDAY OPEN HOUSE:

Any day is a holiday when you greet your guests with a festive and traditional glass of Pink Champagne or Sparkling Burgundy . . . with pound cake, cookies, canapes or small sandwiches.

HOT WINE-COLD WEATHER PARTY:

You don't have to go skiing to enjoy this marvelous winter-time refreshment. For a gay and friendly note, just gather guests round your own fireplace, and serve any one of the hot wine drinks from recipes in the "Punch" section of this book. Keep wine hot in a chafing dish if you have one, or in a warming bowl over a candle. Buttered toast "fingers" are a good accompaniment.

HAVING EVENING VISITORS?

As a go-along to quiet conversation, or good TV-watching, set out a tray of crackers, cheese, apples, nuts, and a bottle of California Port, Cream (Sweet) Sherry or Muscatel. For a reviving "late-show" supper snack—heat up canned or dehydrated onion soup, and substitute California Sherry for some of the water.

A PARTY WITH PUNCH!

Whether you plan an informal cocktail party, a backyard or patio gathering, a formal dance or a wedding reception, there's a specific wine punch that is perfect for your function. Try a sparkly Champagne-based punch for weddings or showers, fruit-and-wine punch for summer in the garden, a hot wine punch for winter after-the-game parties. There's a very real trend to punch service for large groups of guests these days, among smart hosts or hostesses. A wine punch is colorful, lively in flavor, reasonable in cost—and, best of all, its advance preparation lets you relax with your guests when they arrive. See the "Punch" section of this book for recipe ideas.

TOASTS AND QUOTES

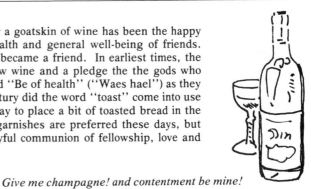

All over the world, a glass ... or a gourd ... or a goatskin of wine has been the happy occasion to drink a pledge to the health, wealth and general well-being of friends. For whoever partook of the shared beverage became a friend. In earliest times, the harvest was celebrated with a sacrifice of new wine and a pledge the the gods who were gracious. The old Anglo-Saxons cheered "Be of health" ("Waes hael") as they lifted their glasses. Not until the late 17th century did the word "toast" come into use in England. It had been the custom of the day to place a bit of toasted bread in the wineglass to add flavor to the wine. Other garnishes are preferred these days, but we still "toast" with wine as a warm and joyful communion of fellowship, love and friendship.

Now then, the songs; but, first, more wine.
The gods be with you, friends of mine!
                                    —*Field*

Here's to mine and here's to thine
  Now's the time to clink it!
Here's a flagon of old wine,
  And here we are to drink it.
                                    —*Richard Hovey*

Never think of leaving perfume or wines to your heir.
Administer these yourself and let him have the money.
                                    —*Martial (40-102 A.D.)*

A house with a great wine stored below lives on in our imagi-
nation as a joyful house, fast and splendidly rooted in the
soil.   —*George Meredith*

Good wine is an aid to digestion and a promoter of good
cheer. I don't think anyone will find a sound argument
against the moderate use of it.   —*George Ade*

I hail with joy—for I am a temperance man and a friend
of temperance—I hail with joy the efforts that are being
made to raise wine in this country. I believe that when
you have everywhere cheap, pure unadulterated wine, you
will no longer have need for either prohibitory or license
laws.
                        —*Louis Agassiz, American Naturalist*

Wine measurably drank, and in season, bringeth gladness
to the heart, and cheerfulness to the mind.
                                    —*Ecclesiasticus 31:28*

Wine that maketh glad to the heart of man.
                                    —*Psalms 104:15*

When you ask one friend to dine,
Give him your best wine!
When you ask two,
The second best will do.
                        —*Henry Wadsworth Longfellow*

Give me champagne! and contentment be mine!
Women, wealth, and ambition—I cast them away.
                                    —*Whyte Melville*

Delicious, effervescent, cold Champagne
Imprisoned sunshine, glorious and bright,
How many virtues in thy charm unite:
Who from thy tempting witchery can abstain.
                                    —*Francis Saltus Saltus*

O Bacchus! let us be
From cares and troubles free;
And thou shalt hear how we
Will chant new hymns to thee.
                                    —*Robert Herrick*

I drink it as the Fates ordain it,
Come, fill it, and have done with rhymes;
Fill up the lonely glass and drain it
In memory of dear old times.
                        —*William Makepeace Thackeray*

Wine, the cheerer of the heart
And lively refresher of the countenance.
                —*Thomas Middleton & William Rowley*

If you drink anything containing alcohol, you can drink
nothing better, as Thomas Jefferson told you long ago, and
every intelligent doctor will tell you today, than a good
light wine, red wine especially, diluted with water, through-
out the meal, with perhaps a small wine glass pure at the
end. The French take that because "it keeps the blood in
the stomach where it is needed for digestion for at least
half an hour after the end of the meal."
                                    —*Arthur Brisbane*

And Noah he often said to his wife when he sat down to
dine, "I don't care where the water goes if it doesn't get
into the wine."   —*Gilert Keith Chesterton*

Wine is the intellectual part of a meal,
Meats are merely the material part.
                                    —*Alexandre Dumas*

Where there is no wine, there is no love.

—Euripides

Wine is one of the most civilized things in the world, and one of the natural things that has been brought to greatest perfection. It offers a greater range for enjoyment and appreciation than possibly any other purely sensory thing that may be purchased. *—Ernest Hemingway*

*I often wonder what the vintners buy
One half so precious as the stuff they sell.*

—Omar Khayyam: (?-1123)

Wine is the most healthful and hygienic of all beverages.

—Louis Pasteur

There are two reasons for drinking wine: one is, when you are thirsty, to cure it; the other, when you are not thirsty, to prevent it....Prevention is always better than cure.

—Thomas Love Peacock

Nothing more excellent or valuable than wine was ever granted by the gods to man. *—Plato*

Never did a great man hate good wine.

—Francois Rabelais

---

*A bottle of good wine, like a good act,
shines ever in the retrospect.*

—Robert Louis Stevenson

---

*Wines that heaven knows when,
Had sucked the fire of some forgotten sun,
And kept it through a hundred years of gloom.*

—Alfred Lord Tennyson

---

*Then sing as Martin Luther sang:
"Who loves not wine, women and song,
He is a fool his whole life long."*
—William Makepeace Thackeray

No poem was ever written by a drinker of water.

—Horace (65-8 B.C.)

You Americans have the loveliest wines in the world, but you don't realize it. You call them 'domestic', and that's enough to start trouble anywhere. *—H. G. Wells*

My manner of living is plain, and I do not mean to be put out of it. A glass of wine and a bit of mutton are always ready, and such as will be content to partake of that are always welcome. Those who expect more will be disappointed. *—George Washington*

---

*If God forbade drinking would He have made
wine so good?*

—Armand Cardinal Richelieu

---

*By wine we are generous made;
    It furnishes fancy with wings;
Without it we ne'er should have had
    Philosophers, poets or kings.*
—Anon.:"Wine and Wisdom", 1710

---

*Wine can clear
The vapors of despair,
And make us light as air.*
*—John Gay:
"The Beggar's Opera"*

Wine rejoices the heart of man, and joy is the mother of all virtue. *—J. W. Goethe*

Wine...cheereth God and man.

—Judges 9:13

When men drink wine they are rich, they are busy, they push lawsuits, they are happy, they help their friends.
—Aristophanes: "The Knights", 424 B.C.

The best wine...goeth down sweetly, causing the lips of those that are asleep to speak. *—Solomon's Song 7:9*

Wine drunken with moderation is the joy of the soul and the heart. *—Ecclesiasticus 31:36*

Who prates of war or want after taking wine?
—Horace: "Carmina", c. 20 B.C.

May our love be like good wine, grow stronger as it grows older. —Old English Toast

May the hinges of friendship never rust, or the wings of love lose a feather. —Old Scottish Toast

May our wine brighten the mind and strengthen the resolution. —Old Saying

I drink to the general joy of the whole table. —William Shakespeare

Good company, good wine, good welcome, make good people. —William Shakespeare

By the bread and salt, by the water and wine, Thou art welcome, friend, at this board of mine. —Old English Toast

The flavor of wines is like delicate poetry. —Louis Pasteur

In water one sees one's own face; but in wine, one beholds the heart of another.... French Proverb

A man cannot make him laugh—but that's no marvel; he drinks no wine. William Shakespeare

A man who was fond of wine was offered some grapes at dessert after dinner. "Much obliged," he said, pushing the plate to one side. "I am not accustomed to taking my wine in pills." Brillat-Savarin

Wine, one sip of this will bathe the drooping spirits in delight beyond the bliss of dreams. Be wise and taste. —John Milton

Don't make the mistake of ordering a good meal and then expect to enjoy it with ice water as a beverage. A rich meal without wine is like an expensive automobile equipped with hard rubber tires. The whole effect is lost for the lack of a suitable accompaniment. Rich and heavy foods which are unpalatable with water can only be appreciated with a suitable wine. Wine warms the stomach and hastens digestion. —Roy Louis Alciatore: Proprietor of Antoine's Restaurant, New Orleans

A book of verses underneath the bough, A jug of wine, a loaf of bread,—and thou. —Omar Khayyam (?—1123)

If food is the body of good living, wine is its soul. —Clifton Fadiman

Wine is a constant proof that God loves us and loves to see us happy. —Benjamin Franklin

The slowly unfolding story of wine and food contains the saga of human culture, good manners and well being. —Crosby Gaige

Wine gives strength to weary men. —Homer, 850 B.C.

Five qualities there are in wine's praise advancing: Strong, beautiful, fragrant, cool, and dancing. —John Harrington: "The Englishman's Doctor", 1608

Wine to the poet is a winged steed; Those who drink water gain but little speed. —Nicaentus, c. 250 B.C.

May friendship, like wine, improve as time advances. —Old English Toast

Give me a bowl of wine; In this I bury all unkindness. —William Shakespeare: "Julius Caesar"

INDEX TO RECIPES

The Wine Advisory Board Cookbooks
"The Classic Series on Cooking With Wine"

This series of eight wine cookbooks is the largest collection of cooking with wine recipes available in the World. There is no duplication of features or recipes in the Wine Advisory Board Cookbooks. Specific wine types are recommended as table beverages for all main dishes. The present series represents over 3,000 different recipes of all types using wine. From wine cocktails, hors d'oeuvres, salads, soups, wild game, fish, eggs, many different main dishes to desserts and jellies; the magnitude of this collection of wine recipes is overwhelming. Who could possibly develop and test such a large number of recipes? These books are the result of the cooperation of over 400 people in the wine industry. In

1961 the Wine Advisory Board began collecting the favorite and best recipes of various winemakers and their families. Most of the recipes are old family favorites, tested with time and then re-tested and proven in Wine Advisory Board test kitchens. We are particularly pleased with the recipes and wine choices from staff members of the Department of Viticulture and Enology and the Department of Food Science and Technology of University of California, Davis and Fresno.

So here is a series of the very best wine recipes; selected and developed by many of the most knowledgeable wine and food lovers of America.

#500 EPICUREAN RECIPES OF CALIFORNIA WINEMAKERS: Did you know that you can buy wild boar, cook it at home with Burgundy and produce a gourmet treat that your guests will rave about for years? Or, that you can make your reputation as an Epicurean cook by preparing and serving Boeuf a la Bourguinonne, according to the recipe of a famous wine authority? This book includes the most elaborate to simple recipes contributed by California Winemakers, their wives and associates; all selected for their unforgettable taste experiences. Another important feature of this book is the comprehensive index of recipes for the entire six cookbook series. 128 pp, 8½'' x 11'', illustrated, 1978 edition. $5.95 @ ISBN 0-932664-00-8.

#501 GOURMET WINE COOKING THE EASY WAY: All new recipes for memorable eating, prepared quickly and simply with wine. Most of the recipes specify convenience foods which can be delightfully flavored with wine, enabling the busy homemaker to set a gourmet table for family and friends with a minimum of time in the kitchen. More than 500 tested and proven recipes; used frequently by the first families of America's wine industry. 128pp, 8½'' x 11'', illustrated, 1980 edition. $5.95 @ ISBN 0-932664-01-6.

#502 NEW ADVENTURES IN WINE COOKERY BY CALIFORNIA WINEMAKERS: New Revised 1981 Edition, includes many new recipes from California's new winemakers. The life work of the winemaker is to guide nature in the development in wine of beauty, aroma, bouquet and subtle flavors. Wine is part of their daily diet, leading to more flavorful dishes, comfortable living, merriment and goodfellowship. These recipes contributed by Winemakers, their families and colleagues represent this spirit of flavorful good living. A best selling cookbook with 500 exciting recipes including barbecue, wine drinks, salads and sauces. 128pp, illustrated, 8½'' x 11'', $5.95 @ ISBN 0-932664-10-5.

#503 FAVORITE RECIPES OF CALIFORNIA WINEMAKERS: The original winemakers' cookbook and a bestseller for fifteen years. Over 200 dedicated winemakers, their wives and colleagues have shared with us their love of cooking. They are the authors of this book, which is dedicated to a simple truth known for thousands of years in countless countries: good food is even better with wine. Over 500 authentic recipes, many used for generations, are included in this "cookbook classic". Revised Edition 1981, 128pp, 8½'' x 11'', illustrated, $5.95 @ ISBN 0-932664-03-2.

#504 WINE COOKBOOK OF DINNER MENUS by Emily Chase and Wine Advisory Board. Over 100 complete dinner menus with recommended complimentary wines. This book will make your dinner planning easy and the results impressive to your family and most sophisticated guests. Emily Chase worked with the winemakers of California a number of years and was also the Home Economics Editor of Sunset Magazine. She tested recipes for six years and is the author of numerous articles and books on cooking. This edition contains 400 different recipes, suggestions for wines to accompany dinners and tips on serving, storing and enjoying wine. 1981 Edition, 128pp, illustrated, 8½'' x 11'', $5.95 @ ISBN 0-932664-04-0.

#505 EASY RECIPES OF CALIFORNIA WINEMAKERS: "I wonder often what vintners buy one-half so precious as the stuff they sell" questioned Omar Khayyam 1100 A.D. We wonder what the vintners could possibly eat one-half so delicious as the food they prepare. This is a collection of "precious" recipes that are easy to prepare and each includes the vintner's favorite beverage. Many are recipes concocted in the vintner's kitchens and some are family favorites proven for their flavor and ease of preparation. No duplication with the other cookbooks. 128 pp, illustrated, 8½'' x 11'', $5.95 @ ISBN 0-932664-05-9.

#527 IN CELEBRATION OF WINE AND LIFE: "The Fascinating Story of Wine and Civilization." by Richard Lamb & Ernest Mittelberger. With art reproductions from The Wine Museum of San Francisco. The origins, customs and traditions of winemaking and wine drinking explored in depth and explained through the art work and lore of wine through the ages. Such important subjects as wine and health and and love are covered as well as the hows and whys of selecting, cellaring and appreciating wine. 35 Full Color plates and many rare prints richly illustrate this intriguing book. Revised 1980 Edition, 248pp, quality paperback, 10'' x 8'', $9.95 @ ISBN 0-932664-13-X.

#554 WINE CELLAR RECORD BOOK: A professionally planned, elegant, leatherette bound cellar book for the serious wine collector. Organized by the wine regions of the World, helpful for keeping perpetual inventories and monitoring the aging of each wine in your cellar. Enough space for over 200 cases of wine and space to record tasting notes and special events. Illustrated, 12'' x 10½'', six ring binder, additional pages available. $29.95 @ ISBN 0-932664-06-7.

#640 THE CHAMPAGNE COOKBOOK: "Add Some Sparkle to Your Cooking and Your Life" by Malcolm R. Hebert. Cooking with Champagne is a glamorous yet easy way to liven up your cuisine. The recipes range from soup, salads, hors d'oeuvres, fish, fowl, red meat, vegetables and of course desserts—all using Champagne. Many new entertaining ideas with Champagne cocktails, drinks and Champagne lore are included along with simple rules on cooking with and serving Sparkling Wines. Recipes are provided by California, New York and European Champagne makers and their families. The author's 30 years of teaching and writing about food and wine makes this an elegant yet practical book. 128pp, illustrated, 8½" x 11" ppb, $5.95 @ ISBN 0-932664-07-5.

#641 THE POCKET ENCYCLOPEDIA OF CALIFORNIA WINE by William I. Kaufman. A convenient and thorough reference book that fits into your vest pocket and gives answers to all of your questions about California Wines. All the wineries, grape varieties, wines, geography and wine terms are covered briefly and authoritatively by one of America's foremost wine experts. Carry with you to restaurants and wine tastings to make you well informed on your choice of California Wines. 128 compact pages, 7¾" x 3½" with vinyl cover. $3.95 @ ISBN 0-932664-09-1, 1981 Edition.

#673 WINE IN EVERYDAY COOKING by Patti Ballard, The newest and freshest in our famous wine cookbook series. Patti is the popular wine consultant from Santa Cruz who has been impressing winery visitors and guests for years with her wine and food magic. Strong Italian heritage is evident in her recipes and the cooking tips from Patti's grandmother. Chapters range from soup and hors d'oeuvres through pasta, fish and desserts—all of course using wine. 128pp, illustrated, 8½" x 11" ppb, $5.95 @ ISBN 0-932664-20-2, June 1981.

#671 CORKSCREWS, AN INTRODUCTION TO THEIR APPRECIATION by Manfred Heckman. The first authoritative book on corkscrews, their history, science, design and enjoyment: for the connoisseur or the novice. Over 500 corkscrew models are covered with a multitude of photos and 10 full color pages. Essential for the collector and fascinating for anyone interested in wine. 124pp, color cover. English edition available June, 1981, $12.95 @ ISBN 0-032664-17-2.

#672 THE CALIFORNIA WINE DRINK BOOK by William I. Kaufman. Cocktails, hot drinks, punches and coolers all made with wine. Over 200 different drink recipes, using various wines along with mixing tips and wine entertaining suggestions. Today's accent on lighter drinks makes this a most useful handbook, and you'll save money too by using wine rather than higher taxed liquors! Pocket size, leatherette cover, 128 pp, $3.95, June 1981, ISBN 0-932664-10-9.

Each book includes its own index; however, **EPICUREAN RECIPES** includes a comprehensive index for the entire cookbook series. These books are available at bookstores, wine shops and wineries. If you have trouble finding them, they may be ordered direct from The Wine Appreciation Guild. Also, most other wine books and wine related items are available.

HOW TO ORDER BY MAIL: Indicate the number of copies and titles you wish on the order from below and include your check, money order, or Mastercard, or VISA card number. California residents include 6% sales tax. There is a $1.00 shipping and handling charge per order, regardless of how many books you order. (If no order form—any paper will do.) Orders shipped promptly via U.S. Mail—U.S. & Canada shipments ONLY.

ORDER FORM
WINE APPRECIATION GUILD
1377 Ninth Avenue
San Francisco, California 94122

SHIP TO:_____

Address_____

City_____ State_____ Zip_____

Please send the following:

_____ Copies #500 EPICUREAN RECIPES OF CALIFORNIA WINEMAKERS	$5.95@	_____
_____ Copies #501 GOURMET WINE COOKING THE EASY WAY	$5.95@	_____
_____ Copies #502 NEW ADVENTURES IN WINE COOKERY	$5.95@	_____
_____ Copies #503 FAVORITE RECIPES OF CALIFORNIA WINEMAKERS	$5.95@	_____
_____ Copies #504 WINE COOKBOOK OF DINNER MENUS	$5.95@	_____
_____ Copies #505 EASY RECIPES OF CALIFORNIA WINEMAKERS	$5.95@	_____
_____ Copies #640 THE CHAMPAGNE COOKBOOK	$5.95@	_____
_____ Copies #527 IN CELEBRATION OF WINE & LIFE	$9.95@	_____
_____ Copies #554 WINE CELLAR RECORD BOOK	$29.95@	_____
_____ Copies #641 POCKET ENCYCLOPEDIA OF CALIFORNIA WINES	$3.95@	_____
_____ Copies #671 CORKSCREWS	$12.95@	_____
_____ Copies #672 CALIFORNIA WINE DRINK BOOK	$3.95@	_____
_____ Copies #673 WINE IN EVERYDAY COOKING	$5.95@	_____

Subtotal_____

California Residents 6% sales tax_____

Plus $1.00 Shipping and handling (per order) $1.00

TOTAL enclosed or charged to credit card_____

Please charge to my Mastercard or Visa card # _____

Expiration Date_____

Signature_____